Progress in Reading Literacy

# Studies in International Comparative and Multicultural Education

edited by

Wilfried Bos, Dortmund
Marianne Krüger-Potratz, Münster
Jürgen Henze, Berlin
Sabine Hornberg, Dortmund
Botho von Kopp, Frankfurt (Main)
Hans-Georg Kotthoff, Freiburg
Knut Schwippert, Münster
Dietmar Waterkamp, Dresden
Peter J. Weber, Halle (Saale)

Volume 7

Waxmann Münster / New York
München / Berlin

Knut Schwippert (Ed.)

# Progress in Reading Literacy

The Impact of PIRLS 2001
in 13 Countries

Waxmann Münster / New York
München / Berlin

**Bibliographic information published by die Deutsche Nationalbibliothek**
Die Deutsche Nationalbibliothek lists this publication in the
Deutsche Nationalbibliografie; detailed bibliographic data
are available in the internet at http://dnb.d-nb.de.

A study under the auspices of

PIRLS 2001

Progress in International
Reading Literacy

International Association for the Evaluation of
Educational Achievement

**Studies in International Comparative
and Multicultural Education, Volume 7**

ISSN 1612-2003
ISBN 978-3-8309-1759-5

© Waxmann Verlag GmbH, 2007
Postfach 8603, D-48046 Münster

www.waxmann.com
info@waxmann.com

Cover Design: Pleßmann Kommunikationsdesign, Ascheberg
Editing and Setting: Martin Goy, Paula Wagemaker
Print: Hubert & Co., Göttingen
Printed on age-resistant paper, acid-free as per ISO 9706

# Contents

# Foreword

In 2001, two years before the United Nations declared the beginning of the "Decade of Literacy" (2003–2012), the International Association for the Evaluation of Educational Achievement (IEA) conducted the Progress in Reading Literacy Study (PIRLS), the first assessment of IEA's new cycle of studies in the area of reading literacy. With a history of comparative research in the field of education dating back almost 50 years, IEA has a well-established interest in the assessment of reading literacy. IEA's ongoing commitment to research in this area reflects the recognition that reading is not only the linchpin of a student's ability to progress in the education system, but also (arguably) a key determinant of an individual's life chances and future beyond school.

As nations transform themselves to address the demands of the 21st century, including those generated by such factors as increased economic globalization and the requirements of knowledge-based economies, a literate citizenship becomes even more significant. Research on the outcomes of the teaching of reading as undertaken by IEA is one of the principal means by which countries can come to understand the efficacy of their educational and instructional practices and the ways in which antecedent background factors (school, teacher, student, home) are implicated in the learning process. IEA, in its design and conduct of studies like PIRLS, attempts to identify, in particular, those policy-related factors that are amenable to intervention at the school, regional, or national level. Furthermore, IEA has, as an explicit focus, a concern to understand the outcomes of schooling after a fixed period of learning, hence its focus on specific grades. Such a design allows for a close examination of the ways in which curriculum, teaching, school-related factors, and the students' own backgrounds interact in the processes of learning to read.

This combination of policy and of research-driven design considerations is predicated on the belief that the development of new policies is likely to be most effective when they are informed by the outcomes of sound empirical research that addresses the key elements of sound educational planning: curriculum, teaching, school resourcing, and student needs.

While the core business of IEA is to conduct research-based comparative large-scale studies that focus on the outcomes of schooling in key subject-matter areas at important educational transition points, it is also fundamentally concerned with ways in which studies like PIRLS impact on policy development, research, and national capacity building. The considerable investment in research made by funding organizations, participating countries, and IEA itself should be justified by the reassurance that such research makes a difference, ultimately in terms of the improvement of education systems and, equally importantly, in the life chances of individuals.

This publication is an attempt to begin to address the question of what impact projects like PIRLS can have within countries. The chapters that follow not only describe in relatively general terms the overall outcome of the Progress in Reading Literacy Study, but also examine more closely the impact that this study has had within some of the participating countries. The countries that participated in this analysis vary considerably in terms of their wealth, culture, language of instruction, and geographical location. Some, like Sweden, which was the highest performing country, as evidenced by average reading scores, saw an immediate impact, primarily in terms of further developments in research. Others, like Iran, reported a significant impact in such areas as curriculum and teacher in-service training.

While not all the countries that participated in PIRLS 2001 were in a position to participate in the impact study, it is clear from the analysis provided that participation in PIRLS has had a major and lasting impact in many areas in the countries that were able to contribute to the impact research. IEA is indebted to the contributing authors of this publication and would especially like to thank the work of Knut Schwippert, under whose leadership this publication was made possible.

*Hans Wagemaker*

*Executive Director*
*International Association for the Evaluation of Educational Achievement (IEA)*

# Chapter 1
# **Introduction**

*Knut Schwippert*

## 1.1   Overview

This book provides in-depth qualitative information on the impact that the Progress in International Reading Literacy Study (PIRLS), conducted in 2001, has had on various aspects of the education systems of 13 of the 35 countries that participated in it. PIRLS was conducted under the auspices of the International Association for the Evaluation of Educational Achievement (IEA), an organization that can look back on almost 50 years of experience in conducting large-scale international assessments (Husén & Postlethwaite, 1996).

This chapter starts out with a description of PIRLS in terms of its purpose, its participants, and its relevance for understanding and enhancing students' literacy achievement. It then presents a brief look at the development of the Impact of PIRLS Project. This section introduces the purposes of this project as well as the participating countries. It also describes the development of and methodology behind the analytical framework used to guide the authors who documented the impact of PIRLS within the participating countries. The chapter concludes with an outline of the structure of this publication.

## 1.2   PIRLS 2001

The main objective of PIRLS 2001 was to collect data on students' reading achievement at Grade 4 that would provide policy-makers, educators, researchers, and practitioners with useful information for educational development. PIRLS 2001 was the first international reading literacy study for students of this age group conducted in the new millennium, and IEA intends it to be the first in a continuing cycle of trend studies in reading literacy designed to monitor progress in reading achievement (Wagemaker, 2001, p. vi). The study also provides comparative data for those countries that participated in IEA's Reading Literacy Study (RLS) conducted in 1991. Thirty-five countries participated in PIRLS 2001. Figure 1.1 lists them.

**Figure 1.1:  Countries participating in PIRLS 2001**

| | | | |
|---|---|---|---|
| Argentina | Belize | Bulgaria | Canada (O, Q)[1] |
| Colombia | Cyprus | Czech Republic | England |
| France | Germany | Greece | Hong Kong, SAR |
| Hungary | Iceland | Iran, Islamic Rep. of | Israel |
| Italy | Kuwait | Latvia | Lithuania |
| Macedonia, Rep. of | Moldova, Rep. of | Morocco | Netherlands |
| New Zealand | Norway | Romania | Russian Federation |
| Scotland | Singapore | Slovak Republic | Slovenia |
| Sweden | Turkey | United States | |

Source:   Adapted from Mullis, Martin, Gonzalez, & Kennedy (2003, p. 18 ff.).

Two people conducted the professional management of this large-scale study. They were Ina V. S. Mullis and Michael O. Martin of the PIRLS International Study Center at Boston College, USA. They coordinated and conducted all meetings of the National Researcher Coordinators (NRCs) (the people who led the organization of the PIRLS study within the participating countries). Guidance and support from expert groups and technical advisory groups also played a major role in making the study a successful one. The study was conducted in spring 2001, after a two-year period of preparation that commenced with the first NRC meeting in 1999. The first

---

1    Canada is represented by the provinces of Ontario and Quebec only. Note that the national country report in this volume is based on Ontario only.

international report of study findings was published in 2003 (Mullis, Martin, Gonzalez, & Kennedy, 2003).

Large-scale assessments like PIRLS provide information for education administrators and serve system monitoring in the participating countries. Such surveys focus on entire education systems, not on single students. Accordingly, the instruments used to collect data from the students, their parents, and the teachers whose classes were sampled for the study were developed to ensure the collection of reliable, valid, and detailed information about the contexts within which students learn to read. The same can be said of the design used to select participating students, teachers, and schools. If the focus had been on the individual participant, the instruments and the sample design would have required considerable modification. In addition to collecting data on students' achievement in reading literacy, PIRLS 2001 collected information relating to the contexts within which students learn to read. Questionnaires were used to collect information on home and school factors known to be associated with the development of reading literacy. These questionnaires were given to the students, their parents, and the teachers and the principals of the schools the students were attending. The PIRLS group also developed an encyclopedia of reading education in the participating countries (Mullis, Martin, Kennedy, & Flaherty, 2002) to provide information on the national contexts in which the students learn to read. Figure 1.2 illustrates the interrelationship between these national, home, and school contexts. Figure 1.3 provides an example of how one of the participating countries (Germany) visualized a complex model of the factors within their national, home, and school contexts that appeared to influence the reading literacy achievement (outcomes) of their students.

**Figure 1.2: Contexts within which students develop reading literacy**

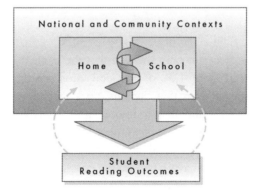

Source:   Campbell, Kelly, Mullis, Martin, & Sainsbury (2001, p. 23).

**Figure 1.3:  Theoretical framework used to depict the two-way relationship between input and process factors and student achievement in Germany as determined through analysis of PIRLS 2001 data**

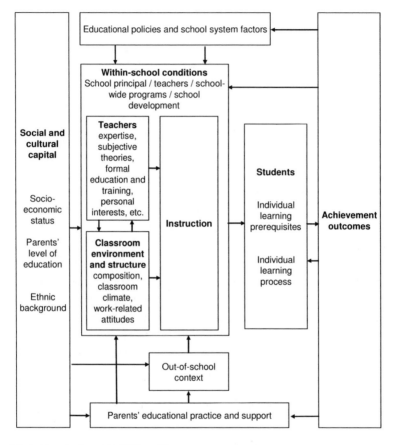

Source:   Adapted from Lankes et al. (2003, p. 16).

The two figures reflect not only the fact that the contexts (Figure 1.2) and the inputs and processes (Figure 1.3) of the education system influence students' achievement outcomes but also that the outcomes themselves feed back into the system. In regard to PIRLS, this insight into what influences students' achievement in reading literacy, and how that achievement influences the system, impacts on practice and policy-making at several levels, ranging from the individual schools (where the results are made available to the teachers) to the national level of educational governance. This volume accordingly documents and describes this impact within the participating countries according to four major areas relating (mainly) to the national and community contexts of the study. These areas are:

1. Public and published opinion
2. Educational policy and administration
3. Teaching and curriculum
4. Educational research.

As this book goes on to show, the degree and type of impact that PIRLS has had in the participating countries varies across them. However, any cross-national exploration of the impact of PIRLS needs to acknowledge that each country was able to modify aspects of the study design to suit particular features of the country and/or to address questions of national interest. Adaptations typically focused on allowing collection of data from sources that would allow comparisons to be drawn between, for example, provinces, federal states, urban and rural areas, and the different tracks (streams) of the education system. However, the PIRLS International Study Center at Boston College stipulated that any modification made at a national level must not compromise the integrity of the study at the international level. This facility to make modifications at national level, the participating countries' diverse historical backgrounds and education systems, and the varying interest shown in the results of the study by administrators, schools, and the public within these countries provide an initial explanation for the diverse impact across countries of the results of PIRLS 2001.

## 1.3    The Impact of PIRLS Project

### 1.3.1    Participating Countries

This project started out with a small interest-group of researchers from the countries that participated in PIRLS. These people wanted to exchange reports on how government agencies, schools, and members of the public received and acted on the PIRLS results in the respective countries. Over time, the group grew in number so that eventually 13 countries provided reports. A number of other countries intended to submit a report but were unable to do so due to lack of personal time or financial resources. The 13 countries that provided reports are:

| | | |
|---|---|---|
| • Canada (Ontario) | • England | • France |
| • Germany | • Hong Kong, SAR | • Hungary |
| • Iran, Islamic Rep. of | • Lithuania | • Macedonia, Rep. of |
| • Romania | • Slovak Republic | • Slovenia |
| • Sweden | | |

Each report forms a chapter of this book and is written from an insider perspective by persons who had a major involvement in PIRLS 2001, generally as NRCs. Each chapter is therefore a product of the authors' backgrounds, experiences, and subjective opinions. The institutional background of the respective authors (see Table 1.1) is particularly important in this regard. Concise biographies of the contributing authors, their research interests, and their involvement in the PIRLS cycle (the next stage of which began in 2006) appear at the end of this book.

**Table 1.1:   Home institutions of the authors of the country reports**

| Country | Authors and institutions | Status of institution |
|---|---|---|
| Canada (Ontario) | Hervé Jodouin<br>Education Quality & Accountability Office | Division in the<br>Ministry of Education |
| England | Liz Twist<br>Department for Research in Assessment and Measurement<br>National Foundation for Educational Research | Independent educational<br>research institute |
| France | Marc Colmant<br>Ministère de l'Éducation Nationale | Division in the<br>Ministry of Education |
| Germany | Knut Schwippert<br>Faculty of Education and Social Science<br>University of Münster | University department |
| Hong Kong, SAR | Shek Kam Tse, Elizabeth Ka Yee Loh<br>Faculty of Education<br>The University of Hong Kong | University department |
| Hungary | Annamária Szabó-Rábai, Péter Vári<br>SULINOVA: Agency for Educational Development and In-service Teacher Training<br>Hungarian Center for Evaluation Studies | Educational research<br>institute |
| Iran,<br>Islamic Rep. of | Abdol'azim Karimi, Parvin Daeipour<br>Ministry of Education | Division in the<br>Ministry of Education |
| Lithuania | Aistė Elijio<br>Ministry of Education and Science | Division in the<br>Ministry of Education |
| Macedonia,<br>Rep. of | Bojana Naceva, Gorica Mickovska<br>Bureau for Development of Education | Division in the<br>Ministry of Education |
| Romania | Gabriela Noveanu, Dragoş Noveanu: Institute for Educational Sciences | Educational research<br>institute |
|  | Nicoleta Litoiu: National Assessment and Examination Service | Independent evaluation<br>agency |
| Slovak Republic | Zuzana Lukačková: SPU–National Institute for Education | Educational research<br>institute |
|  | Ol'ga Zápotočná, Department of Social and Biological Communication | Slovak Academy of<br>Sciences |
| Slovenia | Marjeta Doupona Horvat<br>Center for IEA Studies | Educational research<br>institute |
| Sweden | Monica Rosén, Jan-Eric Gustafsson<br>Göteborg University | University department |

## 1.3.2 Project Objectives

The authors' brief was to provide in-depth qualitative information on the influence that PIRLS has had within their countries on public and published opinion, educational policy, teaching and curriculum development, and educational research. The authors had in common the aim of sharing their experience of the impact of PIRLS so that other countries might gain insight into how respective countries receive and utilize the results of a large-scale international study of educational achievement, and then gain a pool of ideas for the educational opportunities that spring from such a study. These ideas include the following:

- Using the iterative design of a study like PIRLS to complement a country's usual system of monitoring progress across time in a particular area of achievement, such as reading literacy;
- Obtaining guidance on conducting future such studies at both national and international levels;
- Examining national assessment results from an international perspective; and
- Highlighting specific national aspects that might be of international interest.

The across-country perspective is a particularly important feature because it allows participating countries to gain new and expanded understandings of their own national situation in an area of educational achievement.

## 1.3.3 Methodological Considerations

Documenting and analyzing the impact of international large-scale surveys on governance, research, and public opinion is a relatively recent approach. Two studies illustrate the different routes that researchers might take in terms of methodology. The first is documented in *The Impact of TIMSS on the Teaching and Learning of Mathematics and Science* (Robitaille, Beaton, & Plomp, 2000), and the second in *Conditions of School Performance in Seven Countries* (Döbert, Klieme, & Sroka, 2004) and *Features of Successful School Systems* (Döbert & Sroka, 2004).

The impact of TIMSS (Third International Mathematics and Science Study) publication comprises national reports from all participating countries. Written by people highly conversant with TIMSS, the reports set out the following in relation to each country: reason for participation and expectations as to what might be gained from participation; how the study was conducted; reporting and interpretation of the results; and what the more lasting impact of those results might be (Robitaille et al., 2000, p. 15).

The second methodological route centered on conducting in-depth analyses of countries whose students had performed particularly well on PISA (Program for

International Student Assessment) studies. The analysis process involved a two-step design. First, national experts from each of the countries were asked to write an account of their country using a detailed outline developed by the study's working group. This outline required the authors to consider the cultural context of school education, the structure, process, and outcomes of the school system, and the pedagogical underpinnings of both school and classroom practice. These reports, compiled in Döbert et al. (2004), were then analyzed by an independent group of experts charged with identifying and discussing success factors common to the participating countries (Döbert & Sroka, 2004).

This second approach was at first the favored methodological route for documenting the impact of PIRLS 2001. However, a brainstorming session with the PIRLS 2001 NRCs led to the conclusion that the participating countries could afford neither the personnel nor the money to undertake this two-step approach. It also led to the decision to follow the TIMSS approach. Further discussion produced agreement that two modifications should be made to the TIMSS methodology to suit the needs and resources of the Impact of PIRLS Project. The first agreement was to base the impact report from each country on an analytical framework that the authors developed during a series of discussions with one another. The second agreement was to contract an outside expert on comparative education who would analyze the reports and then write a chapter that presented a synthesis of the impact of PIRLS across the countries.

The authors particularly hoped that the first modification would draw out the advantages that participation in an international large-scale survey like PIRLS offers countries. The aim was to make visible the fact that, despite different education systems, each country can readily employ strategies that allow it to gain full benefit from its participation in PIRLS.

One concern in relation to the second modification was that if aspects of the national reports differed markedly, the comparative education expert might be unable to find a common basis for comparison. The analytical framework for this publication endeavored to minimize this potential disadvantage by establishing a list of topics that the report authors agreed should be included in their individual chapters. These topics were specified in a way that ensured comparisons between the countries were possible yet allowed the inclusion of specific national issues. This latter facility was particularly important because the participating countries had quite diverse reasons for participating in PIRLS.

### 1.3.4 The Analytical Framework

The report authors used the following analytical framework for their respective chapters:

1. A short country description
2. The national education system
3. The country's experience in large-scale assessments
4. National results, impact, and long-term effects of PIRLS 2001
5. Future activities
6. Concluding remarks.

Topics 1 to 3 provide contextual information necessary for understanding and interpreting the national PIRLS results and their impact within each country. Topics 4 and 5 are at the heart of each country chapter, and of this publication. Topic 4 required the authors to detail the important findings of PIRLS 2001 within their respective countries, to document dissemination of the PIRLS results to the press and public, to describe the reactions of these agencies to that information, and to outline the study's impact in relation to publications, educational governance, and the functioning and work of schools. The authors were also asked to identify the first visible long-term effects of the study in their respective countries. "Future activities" (Topic 5) required the authors to provide information on ongoing or planned research related to PIRLS, to list and describe major publications in progress, and to outline literacy-related initiatives planned by educational policy-makers and administrators. As the national chapters reveal, the authors varied in what they chose to include under these topics.

### 1.3.5 The Synthesis

For this chapter, the comparative education expert took the information presented in the national reports and detailed how the countries were similar in their experience of the impact of PIRLS and how they were different. The chapter author also endeavored to explain these similarities and differences. She structured this chapter according to the analytical framework of the country reports, and took account of the different emphases paid by the report authors to the framework topics. This approach allowed her to draw out aspects of and insights into the impact of PIRLS that had not been anticipated *ex ante* by the framework, but which *ex post* turned out to be of importance in one or more of the reports.

## 1.4    Structure of this Publication

The publication comprises 17 chapters, the first of which is this introductory chapter. Chapter 2, directed primarily at readers unfamiliar with the PIRLS 2001 assessment, outlines the design and major findings of this study. The country reports (Chapters 3–15), presented alphabetically according to country name, follow. Chapter 16 synthesizes and discusses the information contained in the country reports, while Chapter 17 offers a concise reflection on the anticipated outcomes of this publication and on methodological options for the future documentation of the impact of PIRLS. Readers interested in further reading or background information will find a bibliography of all international PIRLS literature at the end of the book.

Last, but not least, it is important to acknowledge the contribution of the authors who wrote chapters for this book. They did this despite the enormous workload they have to manage in relation to their "everyday" participation in PIRLS. Without their continued commitment to the Impact of PIRLS Project, this publication would not have been possible. I would also like to thank Paula Wagemaker for proof-reading the manuscript with great care, and Martin Goy for skillfully assisting me in coordinating and editing this volume and for doing the layout.

### References

Campbell, J. R., Kelly, D. L., Mullis, I. V. S., Martin, M. O., & Sainsbury, M. (2001). *Framework and specifications for PIRLS Assessment 2001* (2nd ed.). Chestnut Hill, MA: Boston College.

Döbert, H., Klieme, E., & Sroka, W. (Eds.). (2004). *Conditions of school performance in seven countries.* Münster: Waxmann.

Döbert, H., & Sroka, W. (Eds.). (2004). *Features of successful school systems.* Münster: Waxmann.

Husén, T., & Postlethwaite, T. N. (1996). A brief history of the International Association for the Evaluation of Educational Achievement (IEA). *Assessment in Education, 3*(2), 129–141.

Lankes, E.-M., Bos, W., Mohr, I., Plaßmeier, N., Schwippert, K., Sibberns, H., et al. (2003). Anlage und Durchführung der Internationalen Grundschul-Lese-Untersuchung (IGLU) und ihrer Erweiterung um Mathematik und Natur-wissenschaften (IGLU-E) [Design and implementation of the Progress in International Reading Literacy Study in Germany and its national extension by mathematics and science]. In W. Bos, E.-M. Lankes, M. Prenzel, K. Schwippert, G. Walther, & R. Valtin (Eds.), *Erste Ergebnisse aus IGLU: Schülerleistungen am Ende der vierten Jahrgangsstufe im internationalen Vergleich [First results from PIRLS-Germany: International comparisons of student achievement at the end of grade 4]* (pp. 7–28). Münster: Waxmann.

Mullis, I. V. S., Martin, M. O., Gonzalez, E. J., & Kennedy, A. M. (2003). *PIRLS 2001 international report: IEA's study of reading literacy achievement in primary schools in 35 countries*. Chestnut Hill, MA: Boston College.

Mullis, I. V. S., Martin, M. O., Kennedy, A. M., & Flaherty, C. L. (Eds.). (2002). *PIRLS encyclopedia: A reference guide to reading education in the countries participating in IEA's Progress in International Reading Literacy Study (PIRLS)*. Chestnut Hill, MA: Boston College.

Robitaille, D. F., Beaton, A. E., & Plomp, T. (Eds.). (2000). *The impact of TIMSS on the teaching and learning of mathematics and science*. Vancouver, BC: Pacific Educational Press.

Wagemaker, H. (2001). Preface. In J. R. Campbell (Ed.), *Framework and specifications for PIRLS assessment 2001* (pp. v–vii). Chestnut Hill, MA: Boston College.

# Chapter 2
# PIRLS 2001 in Brief

*Knut Schwippert and Martin Goy*

## 2.1  Introduction

This chapter provides a concise overview of PIRLS 2001, with the aim of providing a context within which to consider the results from the 13 countries that participated in the Impact of PIRLS Project. The overview details the theoretical framework used to assess reading literacy, the population tested, the assessment procedures used, and the assessment results. We stress that our documentation and interpretation of the results are relatively general, as our intention is to give readers unfamiliar with the PIRLS 2001 assessment some background information sufficient to aid their interpretation of the detailed information contained in the national reports. The following presentation is based upon two central PIRLS publications, the *Framework and Specifications for PIRLS 2001 Assessment* (Campbell, Kelly, Mullis, Martin, & Sainsbury, 2001) and the *PIRLS 2001 International Report* (Mullis, Martin, Gonzalez, & Kennedy, 2003), which provide a more detailed account of the PIRLS assessment. Readers interested in further reading or background information will find a bibliography of all international PIRLS literature at the end of the book.

The present chapter starts with a description of the theoretical framework underpinning the development of the reading ability tests that form the core of the PIRLS assessment. The PIRLS target population is then introduced, and some information on the participating countries is provided. Next, this chapter documents the major findings from the study, paying particular attention to differences in the distribution of the results for reading ability found between and within the 35 participating countries. The chapter concludes with a concise presentation of the achievement findings in relation to certain factors, such as student gender, immigrant background, and socio-cultural/economic background, that seem to account for the variance between and within countries, and that also have particular relevance to the discussions on the impact of PIRLS in the national reports.

## 2.2  The Development of the PIRLS 2001 Assessment

### 2.2.1  The Importance of Reading

Reading is one of the most important cultural techniques enabling students to become successful members of society. Within this socio-cultural view, reading refers not only to the ability to decode words but also to the ability to reflect on what is read and to use the understanding gained from that reflection as a tool for attaining individual and societal goals. With explicit reference to the reading experience of young children, the IEA accordingly defines reading literacy as

> . . . the ability to understand and use those written language forms required by society and/or valued by the individual. Young readers can construct meaning from a variety of texts. They read to learn, to participate in communities of readers, and for enjoyment. (Campbell et al., 2001, p. 3)

For young readers, acquiring reading literacy, as defined here, is of essential importance for their academic and general success in life. Nine-year-olds, the target population of PIRLS, are at a point when most of them have stopped learning to read and are starting to read to learn. Students who fail to achieve to learn to read let alone read to learn face enormous problems in coping with the demands of school and society. Only by reading to learn can children become autonomous learners. This autonomy is important for their progress in school and their sustained participation in a global society that increasingly requires people to engage in lifelong learning. Once students are able to read to learn, they have a tool for acquiring and evaluating an increasing amount of diverse information. This literacy helps them become independent thinkers and educated members of society. It also helps them make informed and able use of other media such as television and internet. The above definition of reading literacy reflects two major reasons why young people read. These are reading to learn and reading for enjoyment (Campbell et al., 2001, p. 15).

## 2.2.2   The Components of the Theoretical Framework

With these considerations in mind, the PIRLS Reading Development Group (RDG) agreed that PIRLS 2001 should assess three aspects of reading literacy (Campbell et al., 2001, p. 4):

1. Processes of comprehension
2. Purposes of reading
3. Students' reading behaviors and attitudes.

The first two aspects formed the basis of the written test of reading ability, and a student background questionnaire addressed the third.

Figure 2.1 illustrates the theoretical framework within which the test of reading ability was developed. This figure shows that the PIRLS 2001 reading literacy test rested on two purposes of reading and four processes of comprehension. The *purposes of reading* relate to the two types of reading that students most commonly engage in whether inside or outside school. These are (1) reading for literary experience, and (2) reading to acquire and use information. In the test, narrative fiction was used to assess the former and various informational texts were used to assess the latter. The *processes of comprehension* concern how readers construct meaning from text. When comprehending text, readers focus on and retrieve specific ideas, make inferences, interpret and integrate ideas and information, and examine or evaluate features of the text (Campbell et al., 2001, p. 9 ff.).

**Figure 2.1:  The PIRLS 2001 reading assessment: purposes and processes**

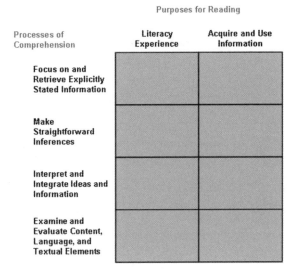

Source: Campbell, Kelly, Mullis, Martin, & Sainsbury (2001, p. 4).

Under this schema, the German PIRLS group conceived reading comprehension as involving two main abilities: (1) the ability to use text-based information, and (2) the ability to draw upon general or external knowledge (Bos et al, 2003, p. 78 ff.). The ability to use text-based information relies not only on extracting information from the text but also on identifying relationships between the parts and passages of the text. The ability to draw upon outside knowledge requires ability to reflect on the content of the text and on the structure of the text. Each of these abilities in turn relates directly to the processes of comprehension (see Figure 2.2).

### 2.2.3   The Nature of the Reading Literacy Test

The achievement test used in PIRLS 2001 involved eight different text passages and four informational and four literary passages, which combined to create 10 different test booklets. Each student was required to work on one booklet containing two passages and to answer an average of 12 questions for each passage. Students had 40 minutes to read one of the text passages and to answer the related questions. After a break of 10 minutes, the students had another 40 minutes to read the second passage and answer the questions. When working through the test questions, the students could continue to look back at the texts, since the focus of the assessment was reading ability, not ability to remember.

**Figure 2.2:  Reading comprehension abilities assessed in PIRLS 2001 and their relationship to the purposes and processes of reading—theoretical framework used by the German PIRLS group**

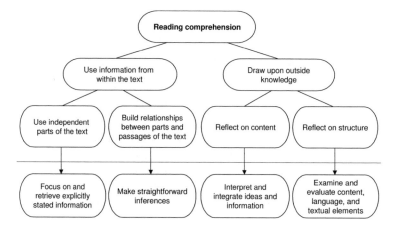

Source: Adapted from Bos et al. (2003, p. 79).

The test questions were a mixture of multiple-choice and constructed-response items. For answering a multiple-choice question correctly, a student received one point. For answering a constructed-response question correctly, he or she received one, two, or three points, depending on the level of difficulty of the question and on how well he or she answered it. The number of levels for these items depends on the number of clear levels of good discrimination. A three-parameter logistical model was used to scale the multiple-choice items, and a partial credit model was used to scale the constructed-response items. To measure both measurement and sampling errors correctly in the later analysis of population parameters for each student, five plausible values were estimated. These took into account not only the student's performance on the reading achievement test but also background information about him or her (Gonzalez, 2003).

### 2.2.4   Piloting of the Test and Construction of the Literacy Scales

The test developed in relation to this framework was piloted in 30 countries. The students' scores on the test showed a strong relationship between all aspects of reading ability and allowed, though the use of structural equation modeling, formulation of a general reading literacy scale, which was titled the combined reading literacy scale. The piloting also confirmed the appropriateness of formulating two component scales related to the two purposes of reading: the literary subscale and the informational subscale (Bos et al., 2003). The combined literacy scale is the scale that the countries participating in PIRLS generally utilize when comparing the reading ability of their students internationally.

## 2.3   The PIRLS 2001 Target Population

The target population of PIRLS 2001 was defined as:

> All students enrolled in the upper of the two adjacent grades that contain the largest proportion of 9-year-olds at the time of testing. (Foy & Joncas, 2003, p. 54)

In most of the participating countries, this was Grade 4. However, because the age of formal school entry and the age at which schools introduce children to formal reading are not the same in all the countries, the selected grade and the average age of the students across the countries varied slightly. Table 2.1 shows, for each of the participating countries, the name of the selected grade and the number of years of formal schooling in the schools attended by the tested students. It also shows the mean age of the students in each country. Detailed information about the school system of each country participating in PIRLS is available in an international encyclopedia edited by Mullis, Martin, Kennedy, and Flaherty (2002).

As Table 2.1 shows, the mean age of the national samples varies. Since the ability to read is positively related to the age of students and to the number of instructional years, this information has to be kept in mind in relation to descriptions of differences between countries. The correlation can but does not necessarily have to be substantial; its size will depend on the group of PIRLS countries one chooses for comparison. This confounding factor is not a problem as long as it is taken into account when interpreting national achievement scores in comparison to other countries, as is necessary, for example, when interpreting the information in Figure 2.3 (see page 28).

**Table 2.1: Details about the target population in each of the countries tested in the PIRLS 2001 assessment**

| Country[1] | Country's name for grade level tested | Years of formal schooling | Mean age of students tested |
|---|---|---|---|
| Argentina | 4 | 4 | 10.2 |
| Belize | Standard II | 4 | 9.8 |
| Bulgaria | 4 | 4 | 10.9 |
| Canada (O, Q)[2] | 4 | 4 | 10.0 |
| Colombia | 4 | 4 | 10.5 |
| Cyprus | 4 | 4 | 9.7 |
| Czech Republic | 4 | 4 | 10.5 |
| England | Year 5 | 5 | 10.2 |
| France | Cours Moyen 1 | 4 | 10.1 |
| Germany | 4 | 4 | 10.5 |
| Greece | 4 | 4 | 9.9 |
| Hong Kong, SAR | Primary 4 | 4 | 10.2 |
| Hungary | 4 | 4 | 10.7 |
| Iceland | 4 | 4 | 9.7 |
| Iran, Islamic Rep. of | 4 | 4 | 10.4 |
| Israel | 4 | 4 | 10.0 |
| Italy | 4 | 4 | 9.8 |
| Kuwait | 4 | 4 | 9.9 |
| Latvia | 4 | 4 | 11.0 |
| Lithuania | 4 | 4 | 10.9 |
| Macedonia, Rep. of | 4 | 4 | 10.7 |
| Moldova, Rep. of | 4 | 4 | 10.8 |
| Morocco | 4 | 4 | 11.2 |
| Netherlands | 6th Group | 4 | 10.3 |
| New Zealand[3] | Year 5 | 4 | 10.1 |
| Norway | 4 | 4 | 10.0 |
| Romania | 4 | 4 | 11.1 |
| Russian Federation | 3 (Stream I); 4 (Str. II) | 3 or 4 | 10.3 |
| Scotland | Primary 5 | 5 | 9.8 |
| Singapore | Primary 4 | 4 | 10.1 |
| Slovak Republic | 4 | 4 | 10.3 |
| Slovenia | 3 | 3 | 9.8 |
| Sweden | 4 | 4 | 10.8 |
| Turkey | 4 | 4 | 10.2 |
| United States | 4 | 4 | 10.2 |

1. The highlighted countries are those participating in the Impact of PIRLS Project.

2. Canada is represented by the provinces of Ontario and Quebec only. Note that the national country report in this volume is based on Ontario only.

3. The official nomenclature used in New Zealand since 1996 refers to students' years of schooling rather than to a class/grade level. Year 5 students are at a class level equivalent to Grade 4.

Source: Joncas (2003, p. 114).

## 2.4    Trends in IEA's Reading Literacy Study

At this point, it needs to be mentioned that those countries participating in PIRLS 2001 and which also participated in IEA's 1991 Reading Literacy Study (RLS) had the option of re-administering the RLS tests as well as the PIRLS tests in order to determine progress in student reading performance across the 10 years. This study within a study was called the Trends in IEA's Reading Literacy Study. The countries that participated in the trends study were Greece, Hungary, Iceland, Italy, New Zealand, Singapore, Slovenia, Sweden, and the United States. Of these countries, three (Hungary, Slovenia, and Sweden) provide details about their participation in the trends study in their national chapters in this book. For more detailed information about the trends study, see Martin, Mullis, Gonzalez, and Kennedy (2003).

## 2.5    Main Findings of the PIRLS Assessment

### 2.5.1    Distribution of Reading Achievement across and within Countries

Across the participating countries, reading ability varied between students within classes, between schools, between tracks (streams), and between the countries themselves. Figure 2.3 depicts the distribution of student achievement on the combined reading literacy scale for the 35 countries that participated in PIRLS 2001. As mentioned before, the mean age of the sampled students is included as additional information with the purpose of easier interpretation of the relative rank order. The scale has a distribution with an international average of 500 and a standard deviation of 100. Given the sampling plan within each country, the confidence interval for this distribution was planned to be less than one tenth of the international standard deviation within each country. Nearly all the countries met this requirement. Within a country, a mean difference of between one third and one half of a standard deviation was estimated to approximate one school year. As such, the students in the highest performing countries were reading at a level about one year ahead of the international average.

Because PIRLS involved a sample design, inferences about the tested population within the countries involve some degree of uncertainty. Consequently, in Figure 2.3, the mean achievement (M) of students for each country is accompanied by the standard error (SE) for that mean. The confidence interval for the amount of error was set at 95% and is depicted in the black-shaded central part of the shown distribution for each country.

**Figure 2.3: Distribution of average combined reading literacy scale scores of students tested in PIRLS 2001, by percentiles, by country**

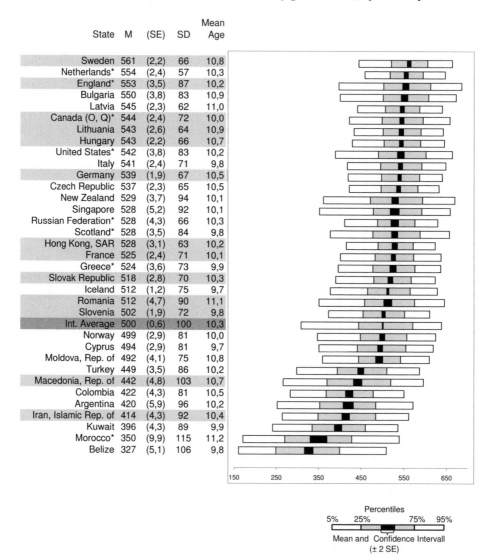

| State | M | (SE) | SD | Mean Age |
|---|---|---|---|---|
| Sweden | 561 | (2,2) | 66 | 10,8 |
| Netherlands* | 554 | (2,4) | 57 | 10,3 |
| England* | 553 | (3,5) | 87 | 10,2 |
| Bulgaria | 550 | (3,8) | 83 | 10,9 |
| Latvia | 545 | (2,3) | 62 | 11,0 |
| Canada (O, Q)* | 544 | (2,4) | 72 | 10,0 |
| Lithuania | 543 | (2,6) | 64 | 10,9 |
| Hungary | 543 | (2,2) | 66 | 10,7 |
| United States* | 542 | (3,8) | 83 | 10,2 |
| Italy | 541 | (2,4) | 71 | 9,8 |
| Germany | 539 | (1,9) | 67 | 10,5 |
| Czech Republic | 537 | (2,3) | 65 | 10,5 |
| New Zealand | 529 | (3,7) | 94 | 10,1 |
| Singapore | 528 | (5,2) | 92 | 10,1 |
| Russian Federation* | 528 | (4,3) | 66 | 10,3 |
| Scotland* | 528 | (3,5) | 84 | 9,8 |
| Hong Kong, SAR | 528 | (3,1) | 63 | 10,2 |
| France | 525 | (2,4) | 71 | 10,1 |
| Greece* | 524 | (3,6) | 73 | 9,9 |
| Slovak Republic | 518 | (2,8) | 70 | 10,3 |
| Iceland | 512 | (1,2) | 75 | 9,7 |
| Romania | 512 | (4,7) | 90 | 11,1 |
| Slovenia | 502 | (1,9) | 72 | 9,8 |
| Int. Average | 500 | (0,6) | 100 | 10,3 |
| Norway | 499 | (2,9) | 81 | 10,0 |
| Cyprus | 494 | (2,9) | 81 | 9,7 |
| Moldova, Rep. of | 492 | (4,1) | 75 | 10,8 |
| Turkey | 449 | (3,5) | 86 | 10,2 |
| Macedonia, Rep. of | 442 | (4,8) | 103 | 10,7 |
| Colombia | 422 | (4,3) | 81 | 10,5 |
| Argentina | 420 | (5,9) | 96 | 10,2 |
| Iran, Islamic Rep. of | 414 | (4,3) | 92 | 10,4 |
| Kuwait | 396 | (4,3) | 89 | 9,9 |
| Morocco* | 350 | (9,9) | 115 | 11,2 |
| Belize | 327 | (5,1) | 106 | 9,8 |

Percentiles
5%   25%        75%   95%

Mean and  Confidence Intervall
(± 2 SE)

\* For the specific accounts of these countries' samples, refer to Mullis, Martin, Gonzalez, & Kennedy (2003, p. 42).

The highlighted countries are those countries participating in the Impact of PIRLS 2001 Project.

Israel was not included since the overall student exclusion exceeded 20%. For further details, see Martin, Mullis, Gonzalez, & Kennedy (2003, p. 115).

Source: Adapted from Bos et al. (2003, p. 102).

Significant differences in performance across the countries can be discerned by comparing the extent to which the confidence intervals overlap. If the confidence intervals of two countries overlap, it can be assumed that no significant differences were observed. If the confidence intervals do not overlap, the observed mean achievement of both countries can be interpreted as significantly different. (For exact calculations of differences and multiple comparisons, see Mullis, Martin, Gonzalez, & Kennedy, 2003.)

Countries are shown in Figure 2.3 in decreasing order of average (mean) scale score, and also whether they were above or below the international average. Sweden had the highest average reading literacy achievement score of the 35 countries (mean age of students: 10.8). It and 22 other countries achieved above the international average, two countries (Slovenia and Norway) achieved at about the international average, and the remaining 10 countries achieved below the international average. The performance gap between the highest performing country and the lowest was considerable, ranging from an average score of 561 for Sweden to an average score of 327 for Belize (mean age: 9.8).

As is evident from Figure 2.3, the countries participating in the impact project spread across the range of achievement. This diversity can be regarded as being beneficial to the Impact of PIRLS Project, as it offers more chances for readers of this publication to identify contexts that suit their own tasks and settings than would be the case with a very homogeneous group of countries.

In some countries, students performed significantly better on literary texts than on informational texts, while in other countries, students performed significantly better on informational than on literary texts (see Figure 2.4). In Figure 2.4, 11 of the 35 countries (Scotland to Argentina) have a numerical but statistically non-significant difference between both subscales. In the countries in the upper part of the figure (United States up to Canada (Ontario, Quebec)), it is apparent that the students of these countries were significantly better at reading for literary purposes than for informational purposes.

Notable is that most English-speaking countries are in this group as are most of the west-European countries. In contrast, most of the east-European countries can be found in the group of countries where students were better at reading for informational than for literary purposes. The countries with significant differences in favor of informational reading can be observed in the lower part of the figure (Turkey to the Republic of Moldova). The authors of some of the national reports touch on these differences, especially in terms of endeavoring to account for them.

**Figure 2.4:  Differences between the average scores of students tested in PIRLS 2001 on the literary subscale and on the informational subscale, by country**

| State | Mean literary reading | Mean inform. reading | Difference | Informational higher / Literary higher |
|---|---|---|---|---|
| United States* | 550 | 533 | 17 | |
| Iceland | 520 | 504 | 16 | |
| Norway | 506 | 492 | 14 | |
| England* | 559 | 546 | 14 | |
| Iran, Islamic Rep. of | 421 | 408 | 12 | |
| Hungary | 548 | 537 | 11 | |
| Cyprus | 498 | 490 | 8 | |
| Italy | 543 | 536 | 7 | |
| Greece* | 528 | 521 | 7 | |
| New Zealand | 531 | 525 | 7 | |
| Lithuania | 546 | 540 | 6 | |
| Canada (O, Q)* | 545 | 541 | 3 | |
| Scotland* | 529 | 527 | 2 | |
| Colombia | 425 | 424 | 2 | |
| Singapore | 528 | 527 | 1 | |
| Sweden | 559 | 559 | 1 | |
| Int. Average | 500 | 500 | 0 | |
| Netherlands* | 552 | 553 | -1 | |
| Romania | 512 | 512 | -1 | |
| Czech Republic | 535 | 536 | -1 | |
| Germany | 537 | 538 | -2 | |
| Bulgaria | 550 | 551 | -2 | |
| Belize | 330 | 332 | -3 | |
| Argentina | 419 | 422 | -3 | |
| Turkey | 448 | 452 | -4 | |
| Slovenia | 499 | 503 | -4 | |
| Macedonia, Rep. of | 441 | 445 | -4 | |
| Russian Federation* | 523 | 531 | -8 | |
| Kuwait | 394 | 403 | -9 | |
| Latvia | 537 | 547 | -10 | |
| Slovak Republic | 512 | 522 | -10 | |
| Morocco* | 347 | 358 | -11 | |
| France | 518 | 533 | -15 | |
| Hong Kong, SAR | 518 | 537 | -20 | |
| Moldova, Rep. of | 480 | 505 | -25 | |

The international average was based on all 35 participating countries.

*For the specific accounts of these countries' samples, refer to Mullis, Martin, Gonzalez, & Kennedy (2003, p. 42).

The highlighted countries are those participating in the Impact of PIRLS 2001 Project.

Israel was not included since the overall student exclusion exceeded 20%. For further details, see Martin, Mullis, Gonzalez, & Kennedy (2003, p. 115).

Source: Adapted from Bos et al. (2003, p. 112).

## 2.5.2   Gender Differences

In all the participating countries, girls' achievement on the reading tasks was significantly higher than that of the boys, with the advantage ranging from 8 points (Italy) to 48 points (Kuwait) on the combined literacy scale. On average, the girls' performance was 20 points higher than the boys' (Mullis et al., 2003, p. 30). The girls' advantage over the boys' was slightly higher for literary texts (21 points; SE 0.7) than for informational texts (18; 0.8) (Mullis et al., 2003, p. 43). Figure 2.5 shows the extent to which the girls outperformed boys for both reading purposes in the participating countries.

**Figure 2.5:  Girls' advantage in PIRLS 2001 over boys in achievement on literary and informational texts, by country**

| State | Literary | Informa-tional |
|---|---|---|
| Italy | 11 | 6 |
| France | 11 | 12 |
| Colombia | 12 | 12 |
| Czech Republic | 14 | 9 |
| Russian Federation* | 14 | 9 |
| Germany | 14 | 10 |
| Hungary | 20 | 10 |
| Romania | 13 | 13 |
| Netherlands* | 17 | 11 |
| Slovak Republic | 14 | 16 |
| Canada (O, Q)* | 19 | 16 |
| Lithuania | 18 | 16 |
| Scotland* | 19 | 14 |
| Argentina | 21 | 15 |
| United States* | 16 | 16 |
| Hong Kong, SAR | 21 | 17 |
| Iceland | 21 | 16 |
| Turkey | 22 | 16 |
| Morocco* | 19 | 20 |
| Int. Average | 22 | 18 |
| Greece* | 23 | 15 |
| Macedonia, Rep. of | 22 | 17 |
| Norway | 24 | 14 |
| England* | 30 | 17 |
| Latvia | 21 | 22 |
| Slovenia | 19 | 21 |
| Sweden | 25 | 18 |
| Bulgaria | 28 | 20 |
| Cyprus | 26 | 20 |
| Singapore | 25 | 21 |
| Moldova. Rep. of | 23 | 23 |
| Belize | 20 | 32 |
| Iran, Islamic Rep. of | 28 | 24 |
| New Zealand | 30 | 21 |

The international average was based on all 35 participating countries

* For the specific accounts of these countries' samples, refer to Mullis, Martin, Gonzales, & Kennedy (2003, p. 42).

The highlighted countries are those participating in the Impact of PIRLS 2001 Project.

Israel was not included since the overall student exclusion exceeded 20%. For further details, see Martin, Mullis, Gonzalez, & Kennedy (2003, p. 115).

Source: Adapted from Bos et al. (2003, p. 116).

The figure shows that, in most of the countries, the advantage girls had over boys in relation to both reading purposes was numerically bigger for literary than for informational texts, with the biggest gaps evident in England, Norway, Hungary, and New Zealand. Only six of the 35 countries showed the advantage working in reverse for girls (that is, a bigger gap for informational than for literary texts). However, Belize was the only country where this advantage was substantial (12 points—about one-tenth of a standard deviation).

### 2.5.3   Students with/without Immigrant Background

The students' reports of where their parents were born revealed that, on average, just over three-quarters (77%) of the students across the countries had parents who had both been born in the country in which they were residing. Nine percent of the students reported that one of their parents was born in the country, and 9% that neither parent was born there. Some countries had very little immigration, and some had at least 15% of the students reporting that neither parent was born in the country.

Because of the considerable variability in the composition (for example, ethnic/racial) and nature of immigrant populations (for example, reason for immigrating), and in how well these populations integrate into their new country, it is difficult to make meaningful comparisons across the participating countries about the achievement of students with or without an immigrant background. However, student achievement tended to be higher for students who reported *both* parents born in the country. This difference was significant for those countries listed at the top of Figure 2.6 (Bulgaria to Morocco), but non-significant for the countries in the lower part of the figure (France to Kuwait).

In a small number of countries, students from families with an immigrant background outperformed students from autochthonous families. Future in-depth analysis of students from these immigrant groups seems desirable so that it can be determined if the achievement difference is simply random, or if it is the result of immigration policies, or successful integration strategies.

**Figure 2.6: Advantage in reading literacy achievement of students tested in PIRLS 2001 whose parents were both born in the country compared with students whose parents were both born abroad, by country**

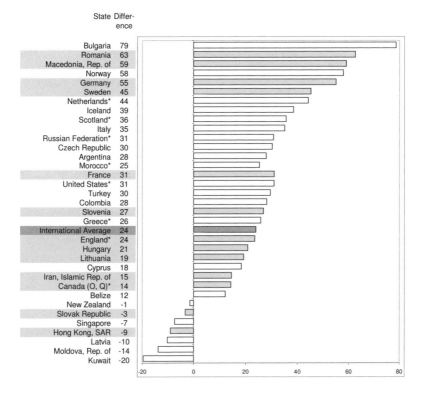

The international average was based on all 35 participating countries.

*For the specific accounts of these countries' samples, refer to Mullis, Martin, Gonzales, & Kennedy (2003, p. 42).

The highlighted countries are those participating in the Impact of PIRLS 2001 Project.

Israel was not included since the overall student exclusion exceeded 20%. For further details, see Martin, Mullis, Gonzalez, & Kennedy (2003, p. 115).

Source: Adapted from Schwippert, Bos, & Lankes (2003, p. 296).

### 2.5.4 Influence of Socio-cultural and Socio-economic Background

As a single indicator of the educational, social, and, to some extent, economic status of the students' home backgrounds, the students were asked to indicate on the background questionnaire how many books they had at home. Although simple, this indicator has been proven in several IEA studies, including RLS and TIMSS, as a reliable means of ascertaining these aspects of home background. Figure 2.7 shows the advantage in reading ability (in score points) of students from families with more than 100 books compared with students with fewer than 100 books at home.

**Figure 2.7:  Advantage in reading literacy achievement of students tested in PIRLS 2001 from families with more than 100 books at home compared with students from families with fewer than 100 books at home, by country**

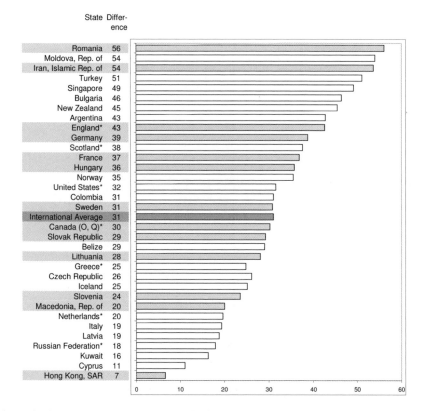

The international average was based on all 35 participating countries.

* For the specific accounts of these countries' samples, refer to Mullis, Martin, Gonzalez, & Kennedy (2003, p. 42).

The highlighted countries are those participating in the Impact of PIRLS 2001 Project.

Israel was not included since the overall student exclusion exceeded 20%. For further details, see Martin, Mullis, Gonzalez, & Kennedy (2003, p. 115). Morocco was not included since the difference between both groups was negative (-6).

Source: Adapted from Schwippert, Bos, & Lankes (2003, p. 295).

The ratio of students who belong to one of the two groups as opposed to the other varied greatly between the countries, a point that needs to be considered during further in-depth analyses. Details about the distribution can be taken from Mullis et al. (2003, p. 107). The reported difference was significant in the top-listed countries in the figure (Romania to Greece), but non-significant in the bottom-listed countries (Czech Republic to Hong Kong, SAR).

## 2.6 Conclusion

This chapter offered a short introduction to PIRLS 2001 by setting out the theoretical framework of the assessment of reading literacy, the population tested, the assessment procedures, and some of the major results. Some explanations for achievement diversity were given in terms of differences between boys and girls, differences between students with and without an immigrant background, and differences between students from different socio-cultural and socio-economic backgrounds. Readers should find it useful to take differences such as these into account when comparing the national PIRLS findings and their impact in the following reports.

**References**

Bos, W., Lankes, E.-M., Schwippert, K., Valtin, R., Voss, A., Badel, I., et al. (2003). Lesekompetenzen deutscher Grundschülerinnen und Grundschüler am Ende der vierten Jahrgangsstufe im internationalen Vergleich [Reading comprehension of German primary school students at the end of grade four in international comparison]. In W. Bos, E.-M. Lankes, M. Prenzel, K. Schwippert, G. Walther, & R. Valtin (Eds.), *Erste Ergebnisse aus IGLU: Schülerleistungen am Ende der vierten Jahrgangsstufe im internationalen Vergleich [First results from PIRLS-Germany: International comparisons of student achievement at the end of grade 4]* (pp. 69–142). Münster: Waxmann.

Campbell, J. R., Kelly, D. L., Mullis, I. V. S., Martin, M. O., & Sainsbury, M. (2001). *Framework and specifications for PIRLS assessment 2001* (2nd ed.). Chestnut Hill, MA: Boston College.

Foy, P., & Joncas, M. (2003). PIRLS sampling design. In M. O. Martin, I. V. S. Mullis, & A. M. Kennedy (Eds.), *PIRLS 2001 technical report* (pp. 53–65). Chestnut Hill, MA: Boston College.

Gonzalez, E. J. (2003). Scaling the PIRLS reading assessment data. In M. O. Martin, I. V.S. Mullis, & A. M. Kennedy (Eds.), *PIRLS 2001 technical report* (pp. 151–168). Chestnut Hill, MA: Boston College.

Joncas, M. (2003). PIRLS sampling weights and participation rates. In M. O. Martin, I. V. S. Mullis, & A. M. Kennedy (Eds.), *PIRLS 2001 technical report* (pp. 113–133). Chestnut Hill, MA: Boston College.

Martin, M. O., Mullis, I. V. S., Gonzalez, E. J., & Kennedy, A. M. (Eds.). (2003). *Trends in children's reading literacy achievement 1991–2001: IEA's repeat in nine countries of the 1991 Reading Literacy Study*. Chestnut Hill, MA: Boston College.

Mullis, I. V. S., Martin, M. O., Gonzalez, E. J., & Kennedy, A. M. (2003). *PIRLS 2001 international report: IEA's study of reading literacy achievement in primary schools in 35 countries*. Chestnut Hill, MA: Boston College.

Mullis, I. V. S., Martin, M. O., Kennedy, A. M., & Flaherty, C. L. (Eds.). (2002). *PIRLS encyclopedia: A reference guide to reading education in the countries participating in IEA's Progress in International Reading Literacy Study (PIRLS)*. Chestnut Hill, MA: Boston College.

Schwippert, K., Bos, W., & Lankes, E.-M. (2003). Heterogenität und Chancengleichheit am Ende der vierten Jahrgangsstufe im internationalen Vergleich [Heterogeneity and equality of opportunity at the end of grade four in international comparison].In W. Bos, E.-M. Lankes, M. Prenzel, K. Schwippert, G. Walther, & R. Valtin (Eds.), *Erste Ergebnisse aus IGLU: Schülerleistungen am Ende der vierten Jahrgangsstufe im internationalen Vergleich [First results from PIRLS-Germany: International comparisons of student achievement at the end of grade 4]* (pp. 265–302). Münster: Waxmann.

# Chapter 3
# The Impact of PIRLS in Ontario, Canada

*Hervé Jodouin*

## 3.1 Ontario, Canada at a Glance[1]

Occupying the northern half of the North American continent, Canada's land mass is 9,093,507 square kilometers, making it the second-largest country in the world after Russia. It also has the longest coastline of any country. Canada shares an 8,891-kilometer boundary with the United States to the south. Due to Canada's harsh northern climate, most of the country's 30 million people live within a few hundred kilometers of the southern border, where the climate is milder. It is estimated that Canada has one-seventh of the world's fresh water. Canada is made up of 10 provinces and three territories. Two of these provinces, Ontario and Quebec, represent 60% of Canada's population and are part of the PIRLS project.[2]

The population of Canada in 2001 was 31,081,887, with a population density of 3.1 residents per square kilometer. Ontario's population is about 11.8 million and Quebec's is over seven million. About 78% of Canada's population lives in urban areas, 3% live in rural farming areas, and 19% live in rural non-farming areas.

Canada's gross domestic product in 2000 was CAN$M1,076,577. Ontario's gross domestic product (GDP) was CAN$M440,759. Quebec's gross domestic product was CAN$M224,928.

Education is the second-largest public expenditure in Canada, at CAN$B68.6 in 2001/02 ($2,207 per capita). Only spending on health exceeds the country's spending on education. In terms of the percentage of total public expenditure, Canada spent approximately 14.3% on education in 2001/02, with Ontario's expenditure being about the same percentage as the national average (Education Indicators in Canada, 1996).

## 3.2 Canada's Education System as Context for PIRLS 2001

### 3.2.1 Structure of the Education System

Canada's 10 provinces and three territories are each responsible for education within their own jurisdictions up to the end of secondary school. Each province or territory

---

1  This introduction is based on Canada's country profile in the *PIRLS 2001 Encyclopedia* (Jaques & Gaudreault, 2002).
2  Note that this national country report is based on Ontario only.

sets its own policies for curriculum, teacher certification, accreditation of schools, and reporting of student progress. Within the parameters set by the provincial Ministry of Education, school boards set local policy in such areas as operation of schools, implementation of curriculum, and hiring of teachers and support staff. Individual teachers and schools make decisions about instructional techniques and classroom processes (Robitaille, 1997).

At the national level, the ministers of education from the provinces and territories have established the Council of Ministers of Education, Canada to ensure communication on issues such as funding, programs, and assessment. The council also occasionally undertakes national education projects, primarily in the area of student assessment (School Achievement Indicators Program, 1998).

Public education is provided free to all Ontario citizens and permanent residents up to the age of 21. School is compulsory from age six to age 16.

### 3.2.2   Levels of Education

The public education system in Ontario is divided into two levels: elementary and secondary. Elementary is subdivided into primary, junior, and intermediate divisions. Secondary is divided into intermediate and senior divisions.

#### *Pre-Elementary Education*

The province offers a one-year program for children before they start Grade 1. Most schools boards, however, offer a two-year program (junior and senior kindergarten) for children ages three to six (Education Indicators in Canada, 1996). Ontario's pre-elementary enrolment of four-year-olds is 82% of this cohort.

#### *Elementary Education*

The primary division comprises Grades 1 to 3. The age range of students in these grades is typically six to nine years. In the junior division, students are in Grades 4 to 6, and are nine to 12 years of age. In the intermediate division, students are in Grades 7 to 10 and are 13 to 16 years old. The students in Grades 7 and 8 are usually in elementary schools. In 2000, 98% of all Ontario children of elementary school age attended school.

#### *Secondary Education*

Secondary or high school usually comprises Grades 9 to 12. The age range of students in these grades is typically 13 to 18 years. In 2000, 93% of 13- to 16-year-olds in Ontario were enrolled in school. Students who fulfill the provincial graduation requirements are awarded an Ontario Secondary School Diploma after

Grade 12. They can then proceed to college, university, and apprenticeship programs. Some students who are planning to enter the workforce directly may not complete all the requirements for a diploma. Instead, they may earn an Ontario Secondary School Certificate. This certificate is not accepted for entrance into college or university but informs prospective employers that the student has completed the equivalent of approximately two years of secondary school education.

### 3.2.3   Types of Schools

In 2000/01, Ontario's provincial government funded public schools, which include Roman Catholic schools. Of the 4,793 public schools in Ontario that received government funding, 3,174 were non-denominational schools (66% of the total) and 1,619 were Roman Catholic schools (34%). In 2000/01, 68% of students in government-funded schools were enrolled in the non-denominational system, while 31% were enrolled in the Roman Catholic system. There were also 743 Ministry-recognized private schools in Ontario, with a total enrolment of 109,904 students. Private schools do not receive government funding.

### 3.2.4   Duration and Timing of the School Year

The school year in Ontario is a minimum of 190 instructional days, beginning in September and ending in June. Most schools close for two weeks in December and one week in March. In addition to these closures, there are several national or local holidays throughout the school year, during which schools are closed (Robitaille, 1997).

### 3.2.5   Classroom Organization and Class Size

In Ontario, local school boards or schools determine how and when to group students for instruction purposes. There is no typical class size for a Canadian classroom. Class size may range from fewer than 10 students to more than 40. In Ontario, the majority of elementary school classes ranges from 21 to 28 students. In 2001/02, kindergarten class sizes ranged from 18 to 20 students; Grade 1 classes, from 18 to 25 students; Grade 2, from 25 to 27; and Grades 3 to 6, from 27 to 29 students.

The provincial government has recently introduced an initiative to limit class sizes in the pre-elementary and primary divisions (Junior Kindergarten to Grade 3) to 20 students. The initiative will start by targeting schools with larger class sizes; later, all class sizes will be reduced. Additional primary teachers will be hired and funded with new money, so that school boards will not need to increase class sizes in Grades 4 to 8 to offset the cost (Government of Ontario/Ministry of Education, 2004).

### 3.2.6   Reading Curriculum and Instruction

#### *Language Policy*

The Ontario language curriculum for Grades 1 to 8 (Government of Ontario / Ministry of Education, 1997) includes expectations for each grade level in writing, reading, and oral and visual communication. The curriculum document (p. 555) stresses the importance of language learning:

> ... [S]tudents acquire skills that are essential in the workplace; for example, they learn to analyse ideas and information and to communicate them clearly, both orally and in writing. Through a study of literature, they come to understand other people and themselves and to appreciate the power of words and the many different uses of language. By examining media productions, they develop the ability to understand and interpret a range of media messages.

The curriculum defines an effective reader as one who can grasp the essential ideas in a piece of writing and can also use and apply these ideas. Students develop the skills needed to process, analyze, and absorb information and to think clearly, creatively, and critically. The underlying belief is that exposure to a variety of reading activities and experiences will engender a love of reading, which is seen as one of the most valuable resources a student can take into adult life (Government of Ontario/Ministry of Education, 1997).

The curriculum further defines reading as the process of understanding the relationship between written language and speech and relating ideas and information encountered in reading to one's knowledge and experience (Government of Ontario/Ministry of Education, 1997, p. 27). Some essential aspects of the reading process cited in the curriculum document (Government of Ontario/Ministry of Education, 1997, p. 28) are:

- reading for particular purposes,
- examining a piece of writing in preparation for reading,
- using a range of reading strategies to understand what is being read,
- critically examining the ideas, and
- summarizing and explaining the main ideas.

#### *Content Standards*

Ontario's language curriculum details the content standards or expectations for student learning for each subject or course and for each grade. Expectations are classified as "overall" or "specific". For example, an overall expectation for Grade 4 reading is that "Students will state their own interpretation of a written work, using evidence from the work and from their own knowledge and experience" (p. 32).

Specific expectations for Grade 4 reading include the following:

> Students will: identify the main idea in a piece of writing, and provide supporting details, they will identify various forms of writing and describe their main characteristics, they will use their knowledge of oral and written language structure and elements of grammar to understand the meaning of sentences. (p. 32)

Language expectations are further classified as follows:

- reasoning and critical thinking, such as research skills,
- form and style, such as knowing the difference between biography and fiction,
- language structures, including grammar,
- writing conventions, including punctuation, and
- vocabulary (p. 32).

### Achievement Standards

All curriculum documents also contain achievement charts that define the achievement standards. Each chart provides criteria for four levels of achievement for four categories of knowledge and skills. The four categories of knowledge and skills are reasoning, communication, organization, and application of language conventions. The provincial standard or expected level of achievement is set in the curriculum language document at Level 3, described as "the level at which teachers and parents can be confident that students are well prepared for work in the next grade or the next course" (p. 8).

Level 1 identifies achievement that is well below the provincial standard, and Level 2 identifies achievement that approaches the provincial standard. Level 4 identifies achievement that surpasses the standard.

### Reading Materials

The Ontario language curriculum states:

> The reading program should include a variety of materials, both fiction and non-fiction. Students should read both classic and contemporary literature of a high standard, including works produced by Canadians. Frequent exposure to writing of high quality will inspire students to work towards high standards in their own writing and to develop an appreciation for the power and beauty of the written word. (p. 28)

The curriculum also recommends different types of materials for different grade levels. For example,

- In Grades 1 to 3, students should read poetry, folk tales, picture books, alphabet and counting books, pattern books, etc.,
- In Grades 4 to 6, students should read fables, myths, adventure and mystery stories, humor, children's classics, etc.,
- In Grades 7 and 8, students should read myths and legends, short stories and novels, historical fiction, classics, non-fiction, reports, etc. (p. 28)

### *Curriculum Match*

The content of the Progress in International Reading Literacy Study assessment reflects the expectations up to and including Grade 4 in the Ontario language curriculum document. The two general PIRLS "purposes for reading" categories— "demonstrate literary experience" and "acquire and use information"—reflect the overall expectation in the Ontario curriculum that students should read a variety of fiction and non-fiction materials for different purposes. The expectations in specific areas of the Ontario language curriculum reflect the four processes of comprehension defined by the PIRLS assessment framework.

### *Instructional Time*

In Canada, elementary students usually attend school for 30 hours a week. Of these, 23 to 24 hours are spent on instruction, and the rest is divided among daily opening exercises, lunch, and recess (Robitaille, 1997). In Ontario, local school boards, and often schools themselves, determine the amount of time teachers dedicate to language instruction and activities. There are currently no provincial directives about the length of time teachers must spend in these areas; however, the Ministry strongly recommends organizing dedicated blocks of time for reading.

## 3.3    Experience in Large-scale Assessments

### 3.3.1    International Assessments

Ontario students participate in a variety of international, national, and provincial assessments. Internationally, Ontario students have participated in the assessments cited in Table 3.1.

**Table 3.1: Ontario's participation in international large-scale surveys of educational achievement, 1980–2003**

| Year(s) of data collection | Name of survey | Organization in charge | Target population |
|---|---|---|---|
| 1980 | Second International Mathematics Study (SIMS) | IEA | Thirteen-year-old students (Grades 7 and 8) and a sample in the final grade of the secondary school |
| 1983 | Second International Science Survey (SISS) | IEA | Thirteen-year-old students (Grades 7 and 8) and a sample in the final grade of the secondary school |
| 1994–1996 | International Adult Literacy Survey (IALS) | OECD | Ages 16–64 |
| 1995–1999 | Third International Mathematics and Science Study (TIMSS) | IEA | Thirteen-year-old students (Grades 7 and 8) and three different samples in the final grade of the secondary school. |
| 1999–2000 | Second Information Technology in Education Study (SITES): Module 1: Principal and IT Directors Survey Module 2: School Case Studies | IEA | Principals and teachers from selected schools |
| 2000–2003 | Program for International Student Assessment: PISA 2000 Reading Literacy PISA 2003 Mathematics Literacy | OECD | Fifteen-year-old students |
| 2001 | Progress in International Reading Literacy Survey 2001 (PIRLS 2001) | IEA | Nine-year-old students (Grade 4) |

### 3.3.2 National Assessments

In terms of national assessments, samples of 13- and 16-year-old students across Canada have participated in the Council of Ministers of Education, Canada (CMEC) School Achievement Indicators Program (SAIP), beginning in 1993. SAIP assesses mathematics and problem-solving, reading and writing, and science on a three-year cycle (see Table 3.2).

In 1996, Ontario established its Education Quality and Accountability Office (EQAO) to ensure the quality and effectiveness of elementary and secondary education and to make recommendations for improvement. Every year, all Grades 3 and 6 students in the province participate in reading, writing, and mathematics assessments, and Grade 9 students participate in a mathematics assessment. The assessments all reflect the expectations for student achievement outlined in the provincial curriculum.

**Table 3.2:  Ontario's participation in national large-scale surveys of edu-cational achievement since 1993**

| Year(s) of data collection | Name of survey | Organization in charge | Target population |
|---|---|---|---|
| 1993–1997–2001 | School Achievement Indicators Program—Mathematics | CMEC | Thirteen- and 16-year-old students |
| 1994–1998–2002 | School Achievement Indicators Program—Reading and Writing | CMEC | Thirteen- and 16-year-old students |
| 1996–1999–2004 | School Achievement Indicators Program—Science | CMEC | Thirteen- and 16-year-old students |

To obtain an Ontario Secondary School Diploma, all secondary students must meet a graduation literacy requirement. Beginning in Grade 10, students can meet this requirement by passing the Ontario Secondary School Literacy Test (OSSLT). The test measures the basic reading and writing skills Ontario expects all students to have acquired by the end of Grade 9. Students who fail the OSSLT may rewrite it or enroll in the Ontario Secondary School Literacy Course (OSSLC). Students who improve their literacy skills through the course and pass it also meet the graduation literacy requirement.

## Commercial Standardized Tests

In Ontario, individual school boards or schools determine whether and when they will use commercial tests of reading achievement. Commonly used tests include the Canadian Cognitive Abilities Test, the Canadian Test of Basic Skills, the Canadian Achievement Test, the Developmental Reading Assessment, Reading Recovery, and First Steps.

## Diagnostic Testing and Screening

In Ontario, local school boards are required to have procedures in place to identify each child's level of development, learning abilities, and needs. The procedures must be initiated by the time the student begins Grade 1. Usually, a combination of screening tools and teacher observations identify students with learning difficulties. Students are referred for assessments by a specialized teacher or by professional resource staff. Appropriate educational programs are developed for the students.

# 3.4 National Results and Impact of PIRLS 2001

## 3.4.1 Results of PIRLS 2001

Ontario Grade 4 students performed near the top in overall reading achievement compared to 35 countries worldwide. Only Sweden performed significantly better than Ontario in overall reading achievement and in achievement in reading for literary purposes. Only Bulgaria, the Netherlands, and Sweden outperformed Ontario in achievement in reading for informational purposes. Ontario students performed statistically better in reading for literary purposes than in reading for informational purposes.

Ontario Grade 4 French-language students scored significantly lower than Ontario Grade 4 English-language students in overall reading achievement, achievement in reading for literary purposes, and achievement in reading for informational purposes.

Approximately one-fifth (19%) of Ontario Grade 4 students reached the top 10% benchmark. Forty per cent reached the upper quarter benchmark, defined as the 75th percentile. Statistically, only Sweden, Bulgaria, and England outperformed Ontario on these indicators.

In all countries and provinces, Grade 4 girls performed significantly better than Grade 4 boys in reading achievement. In Ontario, there was a 20-point difference favoring the girls. This trend was found in Ontario in both reading for literary and reading for informational purposes.

Reference to a categorization based on parents' responses to statements about the activities "read books", "tell stories", "sing songs", "play with alphabet toys", "play word games", and "read aloud signs and labels" placed 67% of Ontario students in the high "early home literacy activities" (EHLA) category. The average achievement of these students was significantly higher than that of students who were in the medium or low EHLA categories. This positive relationship was found in every country.

In Ontario, as well as in most other countries, there was a strong relationship between speaking the language of the PIRLS test at home and performance on the PIRLS test.

In all countries, Grade 4 students from high "home educational resources" (HER) homes (number of books and children's books in the home, available educational aids such as computer, desk, and daily newspaper, and parents' education) had higher reading achievement than did students from low HER homes. This was also true in Ontario, where a significant difference was found between students from high HER homes and students from medium or low HER homes.

Internationally, average reading achievement was considerably higher (40 scale-score points) for students from homes with incomes less than 10% below the national average than for students from homes with incomes more than 50% below the national average. This trend was also found in Ontario, where almost half the students were in the first category.

Ontario students who had attended more than two years of pre-primary education performed significantly better than students who had attended one to two years, attended one year or under, or not attended pre-primary education. Internationally, average reading achievement was highest among those who had attended preschool for more than two years (523 points).

In Ontario, approximately 60% of students attended schools that were in the high category in an index based on principals' characterizations of school climate. These students had significantly higher average achievement than students who attended schools where the perception of the school climate was less positive. This trend was also found internationally.

About half of Ontario students (54%) had a positive attitude toward reading. As in all other countries, students with the most positive attitudes and with a positive reading self-concept had the highest reading achievement.

### 3.4.2   Publication of PIRLS Results

The EQAO and the Ministry released the Ontario results simultaneously with the international results. The EQAO also included a short discussion of the PIRLS results in its annual report to the province. These documents are available on the Ministry's and the EQAO's websites.[3]

Several national and local newspapers ran stories highlighting the performance of Ontario students on the PIRLS assessment. One teachers' federation and a school trustees' association mentioned the results in their newsletters (Ontario Secondary School Teachers' Federation, 2003). The PIRLS results, as well as other international assessment results, have been quoted in several academic papers discussing the performance of Ontario students on large-scale assessments (see, for example, Sweetman, 2003).

### 3.4.3   Impact of PIRLS 2001

*Impact on Administrative and School Levels*

The Ontario Ministry of Education uses a variety of data sources to help in its decision-making process. One important data source is the performance of Ontario students on international assessments such as PIRLS. These data are used as external

---

3   Ontario Ministry of Education website (www.edu.gov.on.ca). EQAO website (www.eqao. com).

indicators to inform discussion about the impact of policy and program changes on student learning.

For example, the province plans to amend the curriculum to put a clear daily focus on reading, writing, and mathematics to provide the necessary learning intensity. This will include a dedicated literacy hour and mathematics time each day. Future large-scale assessments will help determine the effectiveness of this policy initiative. The present government has introduced a wide range of initiatives to improve students' literacy skills.

### Second-Language Instruction

The Ontario Ministry of Education states that the role of the school is to assist students for whom English is a second language acquire the language skills that will allow them to participate on an equal footing with their peers. The Ministry accordingly requires that programs and assessment methods be adjusted to accommodate the needs of these students and to support them in their learning (Government of Ontario/Ministry of Education, 2001). The decisions about how to meet the needs of these students are made at the local school board level.

### Students with Special Education Needs

In Ontario, local school boards determine the programs and services for students with special education needs. As noted earlier, a combination of screening and classroom teacher evaluation is commonly used to initially identify students having problems learning to read and write. Some school boards require that these students receive an intensive reading intervention program. If, through further assessments, specific learning problems become evident, the student may be identified as requiring special education programs and services. An Individual Education Plan (IEP) is then created to meet the student's needs. An IEP identifies accommodations that will help the student access the regular curriculum and/or outlines modifications to the regular curriculum that would be appropriate for the student's instructional levels in reading and writing. Specific policies and regulations provide for continuous review of the progress made by students with special education needs.

Each school board is required to have a special education advisory committee to advise it on the establishment, development, and delivery of special education programs and services. These committees include elected school board trustees and representatives from provincial parent associations that further the interests and well-being of children with special needs.

At the provincial level, the Minister's Advisory Council on Special Education provides advice to the Minister of Education. The Council includes spokespersons for people with different types of exceptionalities and professionals who provide special education programs and services.

### *Early Reading Strategy*

*Expert Panel on Early Reading*

- In 2003, the Expert Panel on Early Reading, K–3 released its research report to all elementary school teachers and principals. The Expert Panel's findings influenced the kind of resources purchased for K–3 students, the instructional guidance materials for teachers, and a professional development program for teachers and principals on effective literacy instruction and on school leadership (see details below).

*Supports for Teachers and Principals, K–3 Reading*

- Instruction guides: The Ministry is producing and distributing to all elementary K–3 teachers *A Guide to Effective Instruction in Reading*. This comprehensive guide includes practical advice and tools for implementing effective instructional practices and assessment strategies in the classroom.
- Professional development: A professional development program, based on *A Guide to Effective Instruction in Reading*, has been designed for teachers and principals. It focuses on effective teaching methods, assessment, interventions for students having difficulties, and the use of school and other achievement data to guide instruction and set improvement targets. In total, there are now close to 200 members of school board-based teams, training teachers, and elementary school principals in literacy. The teachers, principals, and consultants on the team are selected by their boards for their knowledge and expertise in literacy and school leadership.
- Electronic learning modules: The Ministry is developing, for all elementary teachers and principals, web-based learning modules for literacy and school leadership. The modules feature case studies of learning gaps in reading, writing, and school leadership, combined with model practices to resolve the problems. TV Ontario is the Ministry's partner in producing the modules and hosting the website.

*Student Supports*

- School boards are allocated ongoing targeted funding to purchase learning resources to support early literacy in the classroom (e.g., appropriate grade-level storybooks, material to set up book rooms).

*Parent Supports*

- The Ministry has produced and distributed *Helping Your Child Learn to Read: A Parent's* Guide. This handbook, written in plain language, gives parents tips on helping their children with reading.
- The Ministry has translated the guide into eight other languages: Arabic, Chinese, Hindi, Portuguese, Punjabi, Somali, Tagalog, and Tamil. The Ministry is also working in partnership with the WaWaTay Native Communications Society to translate the guide into Cree, Ojibway, and Ojicree.
- A Family Literacy Kit has been developed by the Ministry to provide schools, public libraries, and community organizations with assistance and guidance on organizing literacy events for parents.

*Accountability*

- Target setting: Since 2001/02, school boards and schools have been required to set three-year improvement targets based on EQAO test results for Grade 3 reading and to submit them to the Ministry of Education.

### Excellence for All Plan

The Government is working to ensure that students have high-level skills in literacy and numeracy at the critical age of 12. The Excellence for All Plan states that, by 2008, 75% of students will meet or exceed provincial standards on province-wide tests. Only 82,000, or slightly more than half of students, were achieving at this level in 2004 on the EQAO Grade 6 Assessment of Mathematics (Education Quality and Accountability Office, 2005).

### Education Foundations Program (a province-wide literacy initiative)

Announced in 2004, this four-year program is designed to assist more students each year reach high levels in reading, writing, and comprehension. The main components are as follows.

*Reduced Class Size*

- A reduction in class size in primary grades (Junior Kindergarten to Grade 3); school boards had added more than 1,100 new teachers by September 2004.

*Intensive Teacher Development and Support*

- Training for 8,000 lead teachers on reading and writing instruction so that they can provide on-site capacity and work with other classroom teachers in schools.

- Providing all teachers from Junior Kindergarten to Grade 6 with specialized training guides and e-learning modules.
- Early assessment tools for reading and writing so that educators can find out which kindergarten students need extra help.

*Focused Curriculum*

- Ongoing funding for new textbooks, computers, and resource material to ensure that students have cutting-edge resources and technology.
- Amending expectations to enable a more intense focus on literacy.

*Targeted Supports*

- A special fund for innovative approaches based on best practices, to address the needs of students who need extra help.
- An increase in the number of turnaround schools in Ontario (from 43 to 100).
- Targeted supports for students struggling with low literacy skills.

*K–6 Literacy*

- The Kindergarten to Grade 6 Literacy Strategy is aimed at improving student learning and achievement in Grades K–6 through focused professional development for teachers on effective instruction in the classroom, and for principals on the leadership skills and knowledge needed for school improvement.
- An advisory committee on Grades 4 to 6 literacy was established in 2004 to report on the core knowledge and skills teachers need to teach reading and writing effectively in junior grades.

## Resources for Parents

There is a strong link between students' readiness to learn and their parents' encouragement of literacy. The Ontario Government provides parents with resources to encourage and support early reading at home. It has released an easy-to-use guide for parents on how to help children read. This guide is available to parents of children in Junior Kindergarten to Grade 3.

## Turnaround Teams

In 2004, the Ontario Government increased to 100 the number of struggling schools receiving extra support from 'turnaround teams' of experienced teachers, administrators, and literacy experts. Teams of experts provided struggling schools with direct intervention and support in developing an individualized school improvement plan. They also supported schools as they moved through the three years of the plan's implementation. Lessons learned from a successful demonstration program highlighted the fact that struggling schools require additional support in order to make effective use of lead literacy teachers and professional development. Struggling schools also require a dramatic shift in the culture of the school, direct and targeted skills training for principals and classroom teachers, capacity building focused on leadership at the school level, and individualized improvement planning

### *Long-term Effects*

It is always difficult to predict the long-term effects of any assessment program on programs, curricula, and pedagogy. In Ontario, the results of all large-scale assessments are integrated into the total picture of student performance. Although there is much pride in the performance of Ontario students, the province is not resting on its laurels but continuing to work on those areas of the programs that it has identified as not adequately serving students' needs.

## 3.5    Future Activities

Ontario will participate in the PIRLS 2006, PISA 2006, and TIMSS 2007 assessments as well as the Pan-Canadian Assessment Program (PCAP). This new assessment program is due to start its assessment cycle with the assessment of reading, science, and mathematics of 13-year-old students in 2007. The Ministry of Education and the EQAO will continue to analyze student performances and background information from the international, pan-Canadian, and provincial assessments to determine the effects of the current program on student learning as well as changes to programs that may be suggested by the data.

### 3.5.1    Research

Several independent university researchers are using Ontario data from a variety of assessments to identify factors that affect student performance.

### 3.5.2    Publications

The EQAO makes available on its website all international, pan-Canadian, and provincial reports for the large-scale assessments administered in Ontario. The site also has links to the EQAO research series, where independent researchers, who have used Ontario data to look into the factors that influence student achievement and education quality, publish their results. The EQAO research series provides information and analysis on a wide range of educational matters and encourages further probing of educational issues.

## 3.6    Concluding Remarks

Ontario has been participating in large-scale assessment activities for several decades. The information gleaned from these assessments was and will continue to be used to help policy-makers decide on the best course of action to take to ensure the Ontario school system permits all students to reach their full educational potential. The changes in the system that have occurred in the past few years, based on the data collected through a variety of assessments, will continue to be revisited and updated as new data are available. The province is committed to improving student performance on large-scale assessments by providing timely and appropriate resources to the educational community.

### References

Education Indicators in Canada. (1996). *Report of the Pan-Canadian Education Indicators Program*. Toronto: Canadian Education Statistics Council.

Education Quality and Accountability Office (EQAO). (2005). *The Grades 3, 6 and 9 provincial report 2004–2005: English language schools*. Toronto: Queen's Printer for Ontario.

Government of Ontario/Ministry of Education. (1997). *The Ontario Curriculum: Languages, Grades 1–8*. Toronto: Queen's Printer for Ontario.

Government of Ontario/Ministry of Education. (2001). *September reports*. Toronto: Queen's Printer for Ontario.

Government of Ontario/Ministry of Education. (2004). *Building the Ontario education advantage: Student achievement (April 2004)*. Toronto: Queen's Printer for Ontario.

Jaques, F., & Gaudreault, L.-P. (2002). Canada. In I. V. S. Mullis, M. O. Martin, A. M. Kennedy, & C. L. Flaherty (Eds.), *PIRLS 2001 encyclopedia: A reference guide to reading education in the countries participating in IEA's Progress in International Reading Literacy Study (PIRLS)* (pp. 23–34). Chestnut Hill, MA: Boston College.

Robitaille, D. F. (Ed.). (1997). *National contexts for mathematics and science education: An encyclopedia of the education systems participating in TIMSS*. Vancouver: Pacific Educational Press.

School Achievement Indicators Program. (1998). *Report on reading and writing assessment*. Toronto: Council of Ministers of Education, Canada.

Sweetman, A. (2003). *Ontario's Kindergarten to Grade 12 education system: Some thoughts for the future. Submission to the Ontario panel on the role of government*. Kingston: School of Policy Studies, Queen's University.

# Chapter 4
# The Impact of PIRLS in England

*Liz Twist*

## 4.1  England at a Glance[1]

England is part of the United Kingdom of Great Britain and Northern Ireland. It is separated from mainland Europe by the English Channel and the North Sea, and borders Wales to the west and Scotland to the north. The Republic of Ireland is to the west, across the Irish Sea, and beyond that is the Atlantic Ocean. England has a surface area of approximately 130,422 square kilometers, with a population density of 381 persons per square kilometer.

The national census in 2001 gave a population in England of 49.1 million, and the population is growing at a rate of 0.4% per annum. A large proportion of the population (7.2 million) lives within the London area.

The GDP per capita (UK) in 2001 was US$24,700 (US$26,715 PPP Intl.). Great Britain joined the European Union (then the European Economic Community) in 1973, but has not adopted the euro and retains the pound sterling as the official currency.

Funding of schools is largely determined by the number and age of students on roll. Public expenditure on education in the UK was 4.9% of GDP in 2001/02.

## 4.2  England's Education System as Context for PIRLS 2001

The education system in England is organized into primary and secondary phases, with most students transferring to secondary school at the age of 11. Within this system, compulsory schooling starts at age five, although many children enter school at four. In Key Stage 1 (five to seven years) and Key Stage 2 (seven to 11 years), students are mostly taught by a class teacher. In Key Stages 3 and 4 (11 to 14 years and 14 to 16 years, respectively), much of the teaching is by subject specialists.

A national curriculum was introduced in 1989. This requires all students of primary age to be taught three core subjects (English, mathematics, and science), and seven foundation subjects (art and design, design and technology, geography, history, information and communications technology, music, and physical education). Religious education is also included in the curriculum. Students are

---

1  This introduction is based on England's country profile in the *PIRLS 2001 Encyclopedia* (Twist, 2002).

assessed in the core subjects at the end of Key Stages 2 and 3, and in English and mathematics at the end of Key Stage 1. Most students take public examinations at the end of compulsory schooling at age 16.

At the time of the PIRLS 2001 survey, the education system in England was beginning to settle down after more than a decade of large-scale and often radical reform. In that environment, it was perhaps inevitable that the results of the survey would be interpreted widely as an evaluation of those reforms.

Many people in England saw the results of PIRLS 2001 as an endorsement of the National Literacy Strategy. It is difficult to overestimate the influence of the two national strategies, in literacy and numeracy, on primary education in England in recent years. To understand the reaction to and impact of PIRLS, it is necessary to consider the educational context into which the strategies were introduced in the 1990s.

After the launch of the national curriculum in England and Wales in 1989, an ambitious program of large-scale national assessments was devised. This led to the statutory assessment of almost all students in a cohort (each amounting to about 620,000 in England) at the ages of seven, 11, and 14. By 1996/97, the results of these assessments were being made available at both national and local levels to enable conclusions to be drawn about more or less effective schools and local education authorities.

The results of the 1996 national assessments in English for students aged 11, in the final year of primary education, indicated that 56% were achieving at what was considered the target level for that age group. The equivalent figures for mathematics and science were 53% and 61% respectively. This led to expressions of horror amongst politicians and in the media about the proportions of 11-year-olds "leaving primary school unable to read and write" (a chorus that echoes every autumn when national results are published).

The government of the day set up a large-scale pilot of a new approach to literacy teaching in the first six years of schooling, called the National Literacy Project. This was influenced by, amongst others, the First Steps approach to literacy teaching introduced in Western Australia (Sainsbury, 1998). The project was focused in 18 local education authorities, targeting schools identified from national test results to be lower achieving.

The most novel aspect of the National Literacy Project was the expectation of a distinctive teaching methodology, operationalized in what became known throughout the primary teaching force as "the literacy hour". The national curriculum had provided a broad outline of expected achievement at particular points in a child's educational career, but signally failed to promote one particular pedagogical approach above any other. In addition to detailing the pedagogy, this new approach provided highly specific teaching objectives (Department for

Education and Employment, 1998). Nevertheless, the strategy at this point was a five-year research exercise, evaluated by the National Foundation for Educational Research (NFER) and also by OFSTED, the national school inspection agency.

The next chapter in the story is an example of political imperative overriding the researcher's ideal. The National Literacy Project had been introduced during a Conservative government, in 1996. The following spring saw a general election and the Labour Party returned to power with a stated priority policy area of "education, education, education". The new administration decided, one year into the pilot, that the project should be introduced nationally and known as the National Literacy Strategy. This was despite the fact that no clear evaluation evidence was yet available. Although the strategy had no legal status, it was made clear to head teachers in all primary schools that they were expected to adopt the approaches specified in the National Literacy Strategy and, subsequently, the National Numeracy Strategy. These included a much higher proportion of whole-class teaching than had been common previously.

Since 1997, a high level of resources has been focused on literacy and numeracy (the National Numeracy Strategy was introduced in 1999). There has been substantial investment in teachers' continued professional development, and resources to support the strategy's implementation in the classroom are now provided at a level previously unseen in England.

Alongside the strategies has been a focus on target setting, at school, local, and national levels. A former secretary of state for education, who was also the minister who had introduced the strategies nationally in 1997, promised to resign if national targets, set for 2002 in English and mathematics, were not met. In fact, he had already been moved to another cabinet post when the 2002 results showed that both targets had been missed, but his successor did resign soon after, partially because of this failure.

The national tests, taken by almost all children in England at the end of their primary education, have therefore become very high stakes for teachers and schools, and for politicians, although they are of lesser significance for students. These tests have continued alongside the national strategies, and it is argued that they should be seen as assessing the national curriculum and not the strategies. Schools have become data rich, being able to compare their performance on various measures with that of other schools. A current focus is developing ever more sophisticated "value added" measures in order to evaluate better the effectiveness of a school within the context in which it operates. Parents are able to access a great deal of information about their local schools. National test results for any school, for example, are available annually in local and national newspapers and on the web. These can be compared to those of other schools in the area and to the national picture. Reports from inspections are available from individual schools and from OFSTED's website.

Before the results of PIRLS were published in 2003, the only external evaluation of the two national strategies had been through a study commissioned by the Department for Education and Skills (DfES). This was conducted by the Ontario Institute for Studies in Education (OISE) and was not an evaluation in the conventional sense. The OISE team acted as a "critical friend" to the branch of the DfES overseeing the strategies and produced three annual reports, the final one of which was published in January 2003, in advance of the release of the PIRLS results. It was inevitable, therefore, that the national results of the tests for seven- and 11-year-olds, published annually in the autumn, would be seen as an ongoing evaluation of the approaches elaborated in the literacy and numeracy strategies. From 1998 to 2000, a steady annual improvement was evident in English (reading and writing), but from 2001 results appeared to have reached a plateau (DfES, 2004).

This, then, was the educational context in which the results of PIRLS 2001 were interpreted.

## 4.3   Experience in Large-scale Assessments

In the 1970s and 1980s, the Assessment of Performance Unit (APU) ran national surveys of attainment in Great Britain of students at ages 11 and 15. These surveys sampled student attainment in schools across England, Wales, and Northern Ireland, and provided reports on trends over time as well as detailed reports about national attainment on each dimension assessed. The APU was abolished, at the end of the 1980s, with the introduction of the national curriculum and its system of assessment. The emphasis shifted from regular sampling of schools using the same instruments from one administration to the next, to the annual assessment of complete cohorts and the development of the notion of school-level accountability.

The involvement of England in international surveys in the 1990s and the first decade of the 21st century can be seen as complementing the interest in comparing educational outputs *within* the country. England's and/or the UK's participation in such surveys since 1993 is shown in Table 4.1.

**Table 4.1: England's and/or the UK's participation in international large-scale surveys of educational achievement, 1993–2003**

| Year of data collection | Name of survey | Organization of survey | Target population |
| --- | --- | --- | --- |
| 1993 | The Language Education Study | IEA | Nine-year-olds (Grade 4) |
| 1994 | Civic Education Study (CivEd) | IEA | Fourteen-year-olds (Grade 8/Year 9) |
| 1995 | Third International Mathematics and Science Study (TIMSS) | IEA | Nine-year-olds (Grade 4/Year 5) and age 14 (Grade 8/Year 9) |
| 1999 | Fourth International Mathematics and Science Study (TIMSS) | IEA | Nine-year-olds (Grade 4/Year 5) and 14-year-olds (Grade 8/Year 9) |
| 1999 | Second Information Technology in Education Study Module 2 (SITES-M2) | IEA | Primary and secondary schools (case studies) |
| 1999 | Second Civic Education Study (CivEd) | IEA | Fourteen-year-olds (Grade 8/Year 9) |
| 2000 | Trends in Mathematics and Science Study 2003 (TIMSS 2003) | IEA | Nine-year-olds (Grade 4/Year 5) and 14-year-olds (Grade 8/Year 9) |
| 2000 | Program for International Student Assessment (PISA) | OECD | Fifteen-year-olds (Years 10 & 11) |
| 2001 | Progress in International Reading Literacy Study 2001 (PIRLS 2001) | IEA | Nine-year-olds (Grade 4/Year 5) |
| 2003 | Fifth International Mathematics and Science Study (TIMSS) | IEA | Nine-year-olds (Grade 4/Year 5) and age 14 (Grade 8/Year 9) |
| 2003 | Program for International Student Assessment (PISA) | OECD | Fifteen-year-olds (Years 10 & 11) |

England has participated in TIMSS on all four occasions the study has been conducted. The messages from TIMSS were relatively positive with regard to science, where England performed significantly better than most economic competitors, but much less positive with regard to mathematics. The results of the third study (1994–1995) gave some evidence of a slight deterioration in attainment compared to previous surveys, relative to some other countries, including the United States, Canada, and Ireland. Attainment was significantly lower than that of half of the participating countries, not significantly different from about a quarter of the countries, and significantly better than a quarter.

The consistently high performance of several of the Pacific Rim countries on TIMSS, combined with the evidence of their thriving economies, led to a desire to identify their distinctive educational practices with the intention of "importing" these. This strategy may be linked with the approach to school effectiveness research current at the time, which tried to link a country's educational outputs and its economic health by identifying key educational processes—strategies that could then be borrowed and used to drive up attainment (Alexander, 1999; Steedman, 1999). An example of this influence at a local level is in the London Borough of Barking and Dagenham, a socially deprived part of outer London. This authority adopted the published mathematics curriculum of the canton of Zurich in Switzerland in 1996 and now markets this approach to other local authorities. The emphasis is on a highly structured and methodical building up of mental strategies, with a high proportion of whole-class teaching. The pedagogy espoused by the National Literacy and Numeracy Strategies does echo some of these approaches—in the advocacy of whole-class and highly interactive teaching, for example.

England had originally been expected to participate in the IEA 1991 Reading Literacy Study (RLS), but a dispute about the approach to assessing reading adopted by the study led to England withdrawing. A study was published several years later (Brooks, Pugh, & Schagen, 1996) that used the 1991 instruments within England and suggested that, had England taken part, it would have been ranked broadly average.

The OECD-PISA study of 15-year-olds was conducted in 2000. The United Kingdom participated, with students in England the most numerous, but also including Northern Ireland, Scotland, and Wales. Politicians interpreted the results as a positive endorsement of the educational reforms of the past few years. In the crude league table of participating countries, the UK was ranked in the top 10 for all three areas assessed (reading, mathematical, and scientific literacy), with a fourth place for science being the highest placement.

The timing of PIRLS 2001 meant that it was the first international survey to include children in England who had, for most of their primary education, been taught using the approaches detailed in the National Literacy Strategy. In fact, because England did not participate in the 1991 IEA Reading Literacy Study, PIRLS was the first primary literacy survey since the introduction of the national curriculum.

With the exception of the OECD-PISA study, all international surveys involving England have been conducted for the DfES by the NFER. The most challenging aspect of all these surveys has been, and continues to be, meeting the sample participation rates. Decisions on participation are made at school level, and there are many demands on teachers' time. It is necessary for researchers to emphasize the unique opportunities provided by international comparative surveys to supplement the information available nationally.

## 4.4    National Results and the Impact of PIRLS 2001

The results of the survey were reported in England just after they were made available, but it was only in 2004 that references started to appear in official documents and academic papers. This lapse was inevitable, given the time required for the findings to become familiar, and also because PIRLS was a new survey, in contrast to TIMSS. The names of both PISA and TIMSS continue to be more readily recognized in education circles in Britain, perhaps because these surveys include the results for students of secondary-school age.

### 4.4.1    Results of PIRLS 2001

Children in England did well in PIRLS in 2001, with only children in Sweden scoring significantly higher. Performance was significantly better than that of all other participating English-speaking countries. For England, this was the best outcome to date from its participation in an international survey. Performance was better on literary reading in PIRLS than on reading for information. This was somewhat surprising given the emphasis in both the national curriculum and the National Literacy Strategy on ensuring children receive exposure to a variety of text types. Two other aspects of performance in England were the subject of some discussion in the national report: the range in performance, and the relatively poor attitudes to reading apparently held by children.

### *Range in Attainment*

In discussions of education in England, references are sometimes made to a "long tail of underachievement". This term summarizes a phenomenon seen in both international and national surveys of attainment, where the results of a substantial group of children are lower than might be expected. It was very clear from PIRLS 2001 that England again had a notably wide spread of achievement, although it was recognized that the high achievement of the top quartile was highly significant in creating this spread.

It is instructive to compare the results of the Netherlands with those of England. In terms of overall attainment, the results are very similar (the Netherlands with a mean scale score of 554 and England with 553). However, the pattern of attainment across the range is markedly different (see Table 4.2).

**Table 4.2:  Comparison of performance of students in England and students in the Netherlands in PIRLS 2001**

| | 5th percentile | | 25th percentile | | 50th percentile | | 75th percentile | | 90th percentile | |
| --- | --- | --- | --- | --- | --- | --- | --- | --- | --- | --- |
| | Scale score | Rank | Scale score | Rank | Scale score | Rank | Scale score | Rank | Scale score | Rank |
| **England** | 395 | 14 | 501 | 7 | 559 | 2= | 612 | 1 | 685 | 1 |
| **Netherlands** | 458 | 1 | 517 | 2 | 556 | 4 | 593 | 6= | 645 | 12= |

The best 25% of students in England were amongst the best readers in the survey. The scale score of these students at the 90th percentile was a full 40 score points higher than that of the equivalent group in the Netherlands. Conversely, a look at the weakest 25% of students in the two countries shows students at the 25th percentile in the Netherlands scored 16 points higher than did those in England. At the fifth percentile, students in the Netherlands scored 63 points higher than did the students in England.

The high attainment of the most able readers in England greatly contributed to the spread of attainment observed. This group consisted of both boys and girls. Scrutiny of the data from PIRLS suggested that this range of achievement was also a feature of the results of other countries testing in English (New Zealand, Scotland, and the United States). Further analyses indicated that the spread may be related to the English language, recognized as complex to master (Twist, Sainsbury, Woodthorpe, & Whetton, 2003; Whetton & Twist, 2003).

*Attitudes to Reading*

The second notable aspect of the PIRLS results for England was the relatively poor attitudes held by children about reading. Over 40% of the children sampled in England indicated a positive attitude, but a comparison of this proportion with the results of other countries shows it is low. In particular, 18% of boys had poor attitudes to reading. This finding encouraged researchers to gather additional information about reading attitudes by re-running a Reading Survey questionnaire previously used in 1998 (Sainsbury, 2003; Sainsbury & Schagen, 2004). This survey found that children's attitudes to reading in England had significantly declined since 1998, with a greater fall in the attitudes of boys, from a baseline that was already lower than that for girls. However, the survey also found children's confidence and independence as readers had significantly improved in the same period. It is not possible to attribute these findings unambiguously to the introduction of the

National Literacy Strategy, although such a link must be considered. Other changes in children's use of their leisure time is evident in the same period, especially their greater access than previously to new technologies, both for school and homework, and their use of computer games and toys.

This PIRLS finding can be compared to the outcomes of TIMSS. The results of the 1999 survey of 14-year-olds, in which attainment in England was near the international average, showed that students' attitudes were better than the international average and had not changed from 1995. In contrast, the results of the 2003 survey revealed some deterioration in attitudes to mathematics among both Grade 4 and Grade 8 students, compared to previous surveys (Ruddock, Sturman, Schagen, Styles, Gnaldi, & Vappula, 2004).

### 4.4.2   Publication of the PIRLS Results

The results of PIRLS were published in April 2003. A national report for England was published simultaneously, made available as a priced publication in hard copy, and freely available on the web (Twist et al., 2003). With a teaching profession that is increasingly gaining information from internet, the DfES ensured that links to the NFER site, where the national report could be found, were placed on several sites popular with teachers.

### 4.4.3   Impact on the Primary Curriculum

It has been argued above that the operationalization of the primary curriculum, especially regarding the teaching of literacy, underwent massive reform in England in the 1990s. There was little appetite for further reform when the results of PIRLS 2001 were published. But despite the success, there were still very clear messages from PIRLS. This section outlines some of the public pronouncements made since April 2003, showing the impact of the PIRLS findings in the short and medium term.

The announcement of the PIRLS results was low key, with other education stories receiving greater attention. The national report was made available to the media ahead of the release of the findings. The press notice included a statement from the Secretary of State for Education in which he explicitly linked success in PIRLS with government reforms:

> The fact that our 10-year-olds are reading at a higher level than almost every other country is a credit to them and our education system. It shows that the National Literacy Strategy we set up five years ago to raise standards in primary schools is working. (DfES, 2003b)

In addition to the national report, the DfES produced a leaflet summarizing the PIRLS results. This full-color, glossy publication, titled *England's Success*, was distributed to a large number of primary schools. In the foreword, the Secretary of State again made a clear link between the PIRLS results and the National Literacy Strategy and also drew attention to other findings of PIRLS:

> The study . . . shows that the combination of breadth and rigour offered by the National Literacy Strategy has had tangible benefits . . . However, while I congratulate the pupils and teachers for their achievement, I know that we still have much to do before we can be confident that every child is fulfilling his or her potential . . . The new study teaches us other important lessons. While pupils in England scored well, their confidence in their reading ability remained comparatively low. And they are less likely to read for fun than children in other countries. (DfES, 2003a)

All serious daily newspapers in Britain included a piece about PIRLS, focusing on the high attainment but often also referring to the findings about attitudes or the range in performance. One finding, that girls outperformed boys in all participating countries, was cited as a potential source of reassurance given that, each summer and autumn in England, announcements of the same finding in the majority of public examinations and national tests are accompanied by national hand-wringing and debates about boys' underachievement and the feminization of the curriculum.

Politicians also capitalized on the PIRLS findings during 2003 and 2004. The teacher trade unions traditionally hold their annual conferences in the spring, and some publicity for ministerial speeches to the delegates is guaranteed. The opening paragraphs in the speech given in April 2003 by the Minister for School Standards show how the findings from PIRLS—and from PISA—were selected for this particular audience of teachers:

> This is a vital time for education in England. Ofsted say we have the best generation of teachers ever—and the best generation of teacher trainees. International studies show our ten year olds achieving more than every other country in the industrialised world except Sweden and the Netherlands. At 15, students achieve in the top quartile in international comparisons. This is world class performance. And it is only possible because of world class teaching. Day in, day out, idealistic, motivated, determined teaching. Every child helped to develop their potential, helped to fill their minds and open their eyes, is a tribute to their teachers. (Miliband, 2003, p. 1)

Later in the speech, the Minister used some of the findings from PIRLS to discount arguments that the primary curriculum was too full and had too much testing:

> I have to look at the evidence, like last week's international study of reading in primary schools. In 1996 10-year-old pupils in England performed at the international average. Now, out of 35 countries, we are third from top. English

pupils have more books of a wider range, more access to specialist staff and a richer curriculum experience than in most other countries. That is not a cramped curriculum. (Miliband, 2003, p. 5)

Miliband's speech anticipated the publication of a new guidance document for primary schools. Titled *Excellence and Enjoyment* (DfES, 2003c), it was sent to all primary schools. The document outlined the government's view that primary schools were now in a position to look beyond literacy and numeracy, the subjects of the two national strategies, and to build on their success "with improving results and good comparisons internationally" (p. 4). The document emphasized that primary schools should not only ensure providing their students with a rich curriculum but also feel able to develop their own distinctive strengths. This advice was a clear shift from the philosophy espoused in the national strategies over the past six years, which had expected schools to follow a prescriptive diet and common methodology.

By 2004, the results of PIRLS were being used more selectively. In December 2004, OFSTED published a report titled *Reading for Purpose and Pleasure* (OFSTED, 2004), which received considerable media attention. The report was based on an investigation by inspectors into the range of attainment and poor attitudes to reading in primary schools—two of the key findings of PIRLS discussed in England's national report. Inspectors tried to identify the distinctive features of teaching in schools deemed, through reference to the results of national assessments of seven-year-olds, "more" or "less effective". In his press conference to launch the report, the Chief Inspector of Schools commented on both the range in achievement in England revealed in PIRLS and also the attitudinal findings:

> The gap between competent . . . readers and those who struggle still persists. Research published in [PIRLS] recognised that English 10-year-olds were among the best readers in the world. However, the gap between those who could, and those who couldn't, read was wider than in many other developed countries. And although many of our children could read well, this research also reported that they did not necessarily read for pleasure and enjoyment. (Bell, 2004, p. 1)

## 4.5   Future Activities

England is committed to participating in PIRLS in 2006, and the results will be scrutinized for any changes in reading attainment and various other measures. There is continued interest in studying children's attitudes to reading, given the evidence of relatively poor attitudes held by a proportion of children in England. Comparisons are being drawn with the outcomes of TIMSS 2003 in this regard.

A second strand of work relates to the current interest in value-added analyses. Two further elements of attainment data have been collected for the group of students involved in PIRLS 2001: their attainment on the national tests for seven-year-olds in 1998; and their attainment on the national tests in 2002, the year after PIRLS. The potential of this data-set has yet to be tapped, but linking this attainment data to the background data available in the various questionnaires should lead to some interesting analyses.

## 4.6   Concluding Remarks

England's relative success in PIRLS 2001 means that the results have been seen primarily as an endorsement of an innovative national strategy. This can be contrasted with previous international surveys, especially in mathematics, where the tendency, following the publication of results, has been to try to reproduce some of the pedagogy and practices observed in countries that performed well. It will be interesting to see how the results of TIMSS 2003 are interpreted.

## References

Alexander, R. (1999). Introduction. In R. Alexander, P. Broadfoot, & D. Phillips (Eds.), *Learning from comparing: New directions in comparative educational research: Vol. 1: Classrooms, contexts and outcomes* (pp. 7–11). Oxford: Symposium Books.

Bell, D. (2004). *Speech at the launch of "Reading for Purpose and Pleasure". OFSTED press conference, 14 December.* Retrieved February 3, 2005, from http://www.ofsted.gov.uk/publications/index.cfm?fuseaction=pubs.displayfile& id=3806&type=pdf

Brooks, G., Pugh, A. K., & Schagen, I. (1996). *Reading performance at nine.* Slough: NFER.

Department for Education and Employment. (1998). *The national literacy strategy framework for teaching.* Retrieved February 3, 2005, from http://www. standards.dfes.gov.uk/literacy/teaching_resources/?nls=ed

Department for Education and Skills (2003a). *England's success.* London: Author.

Department for Education and Skills. (2003b). *English primary pupils are among the best readers in the world* (DfES Press Notice, 8 April). Retrieved February 3, 2005, from http://www.dfes.gov.uk/pns/DisplayPN.cgi?pn_id=2003_0060

Department for Education and Skills. (2003c). *Excellence and enjoyment: A strategy for primary schools.* Retrieved February 3, 2005, from http://publications. teachernet.gov.uk/default.aspx?PageFunction=productdetails&PageMode=publi cations&ProductId=DfES+0377+2003&

Department for Education and Skills. (2004). *Pupil achievement tracker: National summary results.* Retrieved February 3, 2005, from http://www.standards. dfes.gov.uk/performance/word/KS2nsr2004_Summary.doc?version=1

Miliband, D. (2003). *Teachers and trade unions: Making a difference.* (Speech made at the ATL Conference, Blackpool, April 15, 2003.) Retrieved February 3, 2005, from http://www.dfes.gov.uk/speeches/search_detail.cfm?ID=68

Office for Standards in Education. (2004). *Reading for purpose and pleasure: An evaluation of the teaching of reading in primary schools (HMI 2393).* Retrieved February 3, 2005, from http://www.ofsted.gov.uk/publications/index.cfm? fuseaction=pubs.displayfile&id=3805&type=pdf

Ruddock, G., Sturman, L., Schagen, I., Styles, B., Gnaldi, M., & Vappula, H. (2004). *Where England stands in the Trend in International Mathematics and Science Study (TIMSS) 2003.* Retrieved February 3, 2005, from http://www.nfer.ac.uk/research/timms/Section7.pdf

Sainsbury, M. (1998). *Literacy hours: A survey of the national picture in the spring term of 1998.* Slough: NFER.

Sainsbury, M. (2003). *Children's attitudes to reading (research summary).* Retrieved February 3, 2005, from http://www.nfer.ac.uk/research/outcome _popup.asp?theID=RAB

Sainsbury, M., & Schagen, I. (2004). Attitudes to reading at ages nine and eleven. *Journal of Research in Reading, 27*(4), 373–386.

Steedman, H. (1999). Measuring the quality of educational outputs: Some unsolved problems. In R. Alexander, P. Broadfoot, & D. Phillips (Eds.), *Learning from comparing: New directions in comparative educational research: Vol.1: Classrooms, contexts and outcomes* (pp. 201–216). Oxford: Symposium Books.

Twist, L. (2002). England. In I. V. S. Mullis, M. O. Martin, A. M. Kennedy, & C. L. Flaherty (Eds.), *PIRLS 2001 encyclopedia: A reference guide to reading education in the countries participating in IEA's Progress in International Reading Literacy Study (PIRLS)* (pp. 59–78). Chestnut Hill, MA: Boston College.

Twist, L., Sainsbury, M., Woodthorpe, A., & Whetton, C. (2003). *Reading all over the world: Progress in International Reading Literacy (PIRLS): National report for England.* Slough: NFER.

Whetton, C., & Twist, L. (2003). *What determines the range of reading attainment in a country?* Paper presented at the 29th International Association for Educational Assessment Conference, Manchester, England, October 6–10, 2003. Retrieved February 3, 2005, from http://www.nfer.ac.uk/research/ papers/PIRLScwlt.doc

# Chapter 5
# The Impact of PIRLS in France

*Marc Colmant*

## 5.1   France at a Glance[1]

France, western Europe's largest country, is located on the edge of the Eurasian continent. Forming a hexagon of which no side is longer than 1,000 kilometers, France shares its borders with eight neighboring countries: Andorra, Belgium, Germany, Italy, Luxembourg, Monaco, Spain, and Switzerland. Excluding the overseas administrative divisions, the area of mainland France is 550,000 square kilometers with over 3,400 kilometers of coastline (the North Sea, English Channel, Atlantic Ocean, and Mediterranean Sea).

In January 2000, mainland France had a population of 58.7 million—the 21st largest population in the world and third largest in the European Union. Inclusion of the more than two million inhabitants of the overseas departments and territories gave a population for France of 60.4 million in 2000. These data reflect the demography of France at the time of PIRLS 2001; the last available figures indicate that in January 2004, the total French population had reached 62 million.

France experiences a light population growth of about 0.4% a year. However, the number of young people under 25 years of age and the proportion of this age group in the total population are on the decline. Today, the 19 million people in this age group in mainland France comprise 32% of the overall population, compared with 35% during the census of 1990, and 40% around 1970. There is thus a slow ageing of the population, but this trend is less pronounced than in other nearby countries (Germany, Italy) owing to an increase in the birth rate from the end of the 1990s.

The student population is 15 million, that is, a quarter of the population. A little more than two million students are engaged in higher education.

At the beginning of 2003, France counted 27 million "active" persons. Of them, 2.6 million were unemployed: the unemployment rate is close to 10%. Approximately 1.5 million jobs, involving 6% of the working population, involve teaching and training. Of the people engaged in these jobs, one million are civil servants.

---

1   This introduction is based on France's country profile in the *PIRLS 2001 Encyclopedia* (Colmant, 2002).

In 2003, the national wealth (GDP) exceeded €B1,500, that is, €25,000 per capita. Of this total, €B110 (7.1% of GDP) are dedicated to educational spending for initial and lifelong training.

## 5.2    France's Education System as Context for PIRLS 2001

The education system of France is largely the responsibility of the State and, therefore, of the Ministry of Education. The Government is responsible for the definition and implementation of educational policies.

The State holds an important role as guarantor of the functioning of the public system and of the coherence of education. The State defines educational direction and the curricula. It recruits, trains, and manages education staff, establishes the status and administrative rules of the schools, and appoints teachers and administrative staff. Only the State may define and establish diploma levels.

State education is free to all students, which means that families do not have to pay schooling fees. At primary school level, parents also do not have to pay for schoolbooks and stationery. Schools occasionally ask families for money towards the costs of excursions or special classes (for example, to the seaside, mountains, country), but even here, the amount requested is based on ability to pay, with municipalities, parents' associations, and the schools contributing the difference.

Compulsory schooling encompasses elementary school and lower-secondary school (which children attend between the ages of six and 16). In France, the target population for PIRLS corresponds to students of the fourth grade of the elementary school. This level is called CM1. French elementary school comprises five years of education, which means that students assessed under PIRLS have to complete another year of schooling before entering secondary education. Given that PIRLS focuses on a particular school level, the average age at which students experience this assessment differs across the participating countries. For France, this average age is 10.1 years.

Before entering elementary school, children can attend pre-elementary or nursery school, which is known as the *maternelle*. This school is free of charge, but is not compulsory. The State runs these schools along the same lines as elementary schools, with teachers in both having the same professional status and qualifications. The teachers themselves decide which level to teach in, and they can change from one level to the other during their career. All *maternelle* schools have access to specialists recruited by the municipalities and charged with helping teachers and overseeing all aspects of classroom life.

The *maternelle* schools accept children from ages two to five. Some children therefore experience four years of pre-elementary education before beginning compulsory school. Although children are not required to attend the *maternelle* schools, 100% of youngsters between the ages of three and five do. This figure compares with a 63% attendance rate in the 1960s. The rate increased year by year to reach 100% in 1994.

The proportion of children two years of age attending *maternelle* schools is restricted by the number of such schools in their area and the ability of these schools to provide places for the children. In 2000, 35% of the children in this age group were enrolled in these schools.

Children in the *maternelle* schools are grouped in three sections: junior, middle, and senior. This distribution is flexible, taking into account the progress of each child, his or her maturity level, and the competencies that he or she has acquired. The general objective of the schools is to help children develop, to form their personalities, and to prepare them for success at the elementary school. A particular emphasis is mastery of language. Children progressively learn to speak, build their own language, and write. Art also has an important place at this level, and is directed towards helping children develop sensibility, imagination, and creativity.

Nursery (*maternelle*) school (encompassing up to four years) and elementary school (five years) together form the primary school. In 2003/04, just over 6,550,000 students were attending the French elementary school.

Since 1989, the primary school has included three cycles of learning, each lasting three years:

1. *First learning cycle*: for children two years of age and incorporating the junior and middle sections of the *maternelle*;
2. *Fundamental learning cycle*: this begins in the senior section of the *maternelle* and continues through the first two years of elementary school; and
3. *Consolidation of learning cycle*: this includes the last three years of elementary school.

Students assessed in PIRLS 2001 were thus in the second year of the third cycle of primary school.

Although this three-cycle framework generally governs the curriculum, individual students may take one year longer or one year less to complete it, depending on their knowledge and abilities. A team of educationists decides at the end of each cycle which students should repeat a year and which students should jump a year. Some sense of this pattern can be discerned from Table 5.1, which shows the distribution of ages among the 800,000 students enrolled in Grade 4 (the PIRLS target grade), in France, in 2000.

**Table 5.1:  Age distribution of students in Grade 4, France, 2000**

| Age in Grade 4 | Percentage |
| --- | --- |
| Eight years and under | 2 |
| Nine years | 80 |
| Ten years | 16 |
| Eleven years and more | 2 |

Of the students enrolled in Grade 4, current estimates show that about one in six (17.5% of the total) will have repeated a year. The practice of requiring students to repeat a year is not unusual within the French education system, although rates have declined at elementary school level, particularly since 1989 with the introduction of the cycles. At that time, about one student in four (23.1% of the total) enrolled in Grade 4 had repeated a year. The present-day rate of one in six is nevertheless still very high, especially when we realize that students are only in their fourth year of compulsory schooling.

Studies investigating the effects of this practice all point to its negative aspects. The most recent study is that conducted by Cosnefroy and Rocher (2005), who examined the issue with reference to various sources of data, in particular, students' performance in large-scale studies. They found that the practice is inequitable and ineffective in terms of student progress, that it amplifies disparities, that it is ineffective in lifting student performance across the education system, and that it decreases student motivation, confidence, and ambition. Students who repeat also tend to be stigmatized. They tend, for example, to be directed towards vocational rather than general studies. Students cannot "hide" the fact they have repeated one or more years, as the repeats are noted on their school records.

In each of the 100 French departments, primary schools are under the responsibility of a chief education officer, who organizes the recruitment and the administrative and educational management of the teaching personnel of this level. Every department is divided into districts, each of which is under the responsibility of a primary school inspector.

State education in France is non-denominational. Eighty-six percent of students at the primary level attend State schools. Private schools are primarily denominational. Most are Roman Catholic. In the private sector, families pay school fees, which vary from school to school. However, private-sector schools generally operate under a contract with the State, which grants them a substantial income. They are either under simple contract, association contract, or without contract. Simple contract means the State pays only the teachers' salaries and their pre- and in-service training. With an association contract, the State also pays for the operating expenses of the school. Without contract is extremely rare. Private schools under contract have to respect the schedules (opening hours and holidays) and curricula applicable in public schools.

The school year encompasses 36 weeks distributed in five periods of work of comparable duration, separated by four periods of holidays. Since 1992, the duration of a primary school week has been 26 hours. Generally, students are in school four and a half days per week. They have Wednesdays free of schooling, but not so Saturday mornings. Three-quarters of French schools follow this traditional organization. For the remaining quarter, students attend school on four days only and have Wednesdays and Saturdays free. However, to meet the State-prescribed number of hours of schooling per annum, these schools have shorter holiday periods.

The total instructional time in primary school is usually six hours per day, including two 15-minute breaks. A normal school day runs from 8:30 a.m. to 11:30 a.m. and from 1:30 p.m. to 4:30 p.m. Outside of school hours, schools often offer a service of supervised studies, mostly overseen by teachers, for children whose parents work in paid employment. Local authorities and/or associations also often offer sports, artistic, and cultural activities outside standard school hours.

In France, the term "class" normally corresponds to a group of students taught at the same level during a school year. However, a number of schools in which student numbers are insufficient to form separate grades offer composite classes comprising two or more grade levels. In 1999, composite classes represented nearly 22% of all French classes. Some schools, mostly rural ones, have only a single class made up of all the levels. In 2000, 2.4% of classes in French schools were of this kind, and the mean size of classes was 25.5 students in pre-elementary schools and 23 or fewer in elementary schools.

Students enter secondary school after Grade 5. The first stage of secondary education is called *collège* (lower secondary school). This stage lasts four years. Students receive automatic promotion to secondary school once the pedagogical team responsible for assessing progress confirms they have acquired the knowledge and skills specified for the third cycle of the primary school.

Today, for almost all students, this promotion has no influence on their future academic and vocational orientation. The first year of *collège* is an observation and adaptation cycle, followed by two years of a central cycle. The fourth year corresponds to the orientation cycle, so it is only at the end of the lower secondary school that students' educational and vocational futures truly begin to take shape.

# 5.3    Experience in Large-scale Assessments

## 5.3.1    History

During the last 40 years, large-scale assessments of students' competencies have been developed and conducted with increasing success. In their recent report, Bottani and Vrignaud (2005) identified three factors they think have favored France's participation in international assessments:

1. *The unprecedented expansion of the educational system during this period, with greater numbers of students enrolled in and graduating from secondary and tertiary education*: This increase has fuelled differentiation of course content in these sectors and is requiring educational policy- and decision-makers to find ways of managing the growth.
2. *Increasing standardization across the educational system*: The different sectors of the system have evolved in the same direction over the 40-year period, albeit at different speeds. Alignments have been particularly noticeable in pedagogy and curricula.
3. *Guidance for politicians and educationists*: The findings of the assessments are not only giving those who direct education in France a better understanding of how well the educational system is achieving its teaching and learning objectives but also highlighting areas in need of change.

For France, participation in the large-scale international studies of educational achievement has shown it is possible to gain a better knowledge of one's own education system by comparing it with the systems of other countries. This, in turn, has marked a renewal of comparative studies in education. "Comparison is both an instrument of knowledge and a change control lever, because it serves to legitimize teaching's reforms, by bringing scientifically validated proofs of the utility of a method or of the necessity of a reform, thwarting ideological resistance to comparative studies" (Bottani & Vrignaud, 2005, p. 32 ).

The official agency responsible for conducting comparative international studies in France, on both a bilateral and a multilateral basis, is the *Direction de l'évaluation et de la prospective* (the Department for Assessment and Forecasting of the French Ministry of Education, or DEP). The DEP's work applies to students in both the general and vocational streams of the education system, to teachers and other educational staff, to the overall education system, and to individual schools and universities.

In general terms, the DEP is responsible for maintaining and refining statistical information collected at the national and local levels and for analyzing the outcomes of the education system. The Department's work can more particularly be summarized as follows:

- *Forecasting*: The DEP carries out quantitative and qualitative short-term, medium-term, and long-term analyses, and forecasts the development of the education system over time and space.
- *Knowing*: The DEP is in charge of collecting information throughout the education system, from kindergarten through to doctoral studies and research.
- *Evaluating*: The DEP is responsible for assessing the state of the education system and for promoting a culture of evaluation at all levels (primary, secondary, higher).

The DEP's objectives are to:

- Provide ministers, political advisers, and departments responsible for curricula and teaching personnel with data that will allow them to formulate and implement policy.
- Provide (chiefly) teachers and head teachers with assessment tools and outcome results (for example, mass diagnostic testing, assessment item banks, school management indicators) to help them improve their professional practices.
- Actively participate in activities that allow comparison of the national education system with the systems of other developed countries. This work is achieved through bilateral and multilateral co-operation, particularly with international institutions such as the European Union, the OECD, and UNESCO.

The Department is heavily involved with the OECD Educational Indicator Project (INES), and with PISA and IEA studies, as well as with EUROSTAT, the OECD, and UNESCO, in the field of statistics. It is also increasingly developing its role in European Union projects.

## 5.3.2 International System-monitoring

During the 40 years between 1964 and 2003, France's presence in international assessments of students was constant but irregular. France took part in the first UNESCO/IEA pilot study, which took place between 1959 and 1962. Of the 28 large-scale assessments undertaken since that time and which invited France's participation, France has chosen, after careful consideration, to participate in 14 (see Table 5.2).

**Table 5.2:   France's participation in international large-scale surveys of educational achievement, 1959–2006**

| Year(s) of data collection | Name of survey | Organization in charge | Target population |
|---|---|---|---|
| 1959–1962 | Pilot Twelve-Country Study | UNESCO/ IEA | Thirteen-year-old students |
| 1964 | First International Mathematics Study (FIMS) | IEA | Thirteen-year-old students, 13-year-old grade-level students, and pre-university students |
| 1970/71 | First International Science Study (FISS), part of the Six Subject Study | IEA | Fourteen-year-old students and students in the final grade of the secondary school |
| 1982 | Second International Mathematics Study (SIMS) | IEA | Thirteen-year-old students and students in the final grade of secondary education |
| 1989 | Computers in Education Study (Stage 1) | IEA | Three populations: modal grade for 10-year-old students, modal grade for 13-year-old students, and students in a final year of secondary education |
| 1991 | International Assessment of Educational Progress 2 (IAEP 2) | ETS | Thirteen-year-olds |
| 1991 | International Reading Literacy Study (RLS) | IEA | Two populations: nine-year-old students and 14-year-old students |
| 1994–2000 | International Adult Literacy Study (IALS) | OECD | Population aged 15–64 |
| 1995 | Third International Mathematics and Science Study (TIMSS) | IEA | Students enrolled in the two grades containing the largest proportion of students (Grades 7 and 8 in most countries), and students in their final year of secondary education |
| 1998/99 | Second Information Technology in Education Study Module 1 (SITES-M1) | IEA | School principals and technology coordinators from primary, lower secondary, and upper secondary schools |
| 2000 | Program for International Student Assessment (PISA) Reading | OECD | Fifteen-year-olds |
| 2001 | Progress in International Reading Literacy Study 2001 (PIRLS 2001) | IEA | Upper of the two adjacent grades with the most nine-year-olds. In most participating countries, this was Grade 4 |
| 2003 | Program for International Student Assessment (PISA) Mathematics | OECD | Fifteen-year-olds |
| 2006 | Progress in International Reading Literacy Study 2006 (PIRLS 2006) | IEA | Students in the grade that represents four years of schooling, counting from the first year of ISCED, Level 1. The minimum average age at the target grade set as not falling below 9.5 years of age |

France's participation in international large-scale assessments was, until the end of the 1980s, overseen by three centers: the University of Caen, the INETOP (National Institute of Study on Work and Vocational Guidance), and the CIEP (International Center of Educational Studies) in Sèvres. Today, the Department for Assessment and Forecasting of the French Ministry of Education (DEP) has responsibility for these studies in France. The Ministry of Education provides funding for all aspects of France's participation in the surveys (for example, financing of the French data collection and contribution to the international budget of the study).

Analysis shows that the international studies in which France has systematically chosen to engage itself are those relating to the fundamental disciplines, that is, mathematics, sciences, and reading. Of the pertinent studies, France has missed only the first Reading Literacy Study in 1970/71. The only exceptions France has made to its general rule on which discipline areas to involve itself are the two studies of school use of new technologies (Computers in Education Study and SITES). The first study took place in 1988/89 and the second 10 years later, in 1998/99.

It seems that French participation in the international surveys is driven by a particular pedagogical orthodoxy, which limits French researchers and/or authorities from involvement in the more "experimental" or innovative studies, such as preschool education, written composition, and civics. France has also neglected international studies with a focus on research issues in education and methodological innovation. The only exception has been France's participation in the International Study on Adult Literacy (IALS) in 1994. This study was a world first in terms of testing populations of adult participants in their homes.

France's decision to take part in IALS had major repercussions. After participating in the development of the study and collecting data from a representative sample of adults 16 to 65 years of age, France disputed the validity of the results and demanded not to appear in the study's report. This decision, taken by the Minister of Education, was highly controversial. Since then, France has sought to justify this decision by undertaking a long process of validity checks of the study, and mobilizing the national and international research community as well as the European Union to examine the study's methodological reliability.

France's shock withdrawal from the IALS study signified a change of direction for the nation's participation in large-scale international surveys (Haut Conseil à l'Évaluation de l'École, 2005). During the 30 years between 1964 and 1994, France maintained a relatively low profile on the large-scale assessments scene, with its communities of educational authorities and educational researchers keeping to their own spheres of interest and not playing a leading role internationally. As a result of contesting the methodology and the results of IALS and then withdrawing from it (events that were widely exploited by the media), France was forced to "leave the shadows".

In 1995, during the French presidency of the European Union, France was instrumental in creating the European Network of Policy Makers for the Evaluation of Education Systems (known, in short, as the European Network). Mindful that education is not a community prerogative, this inter-governmental network, which meets twice a year, includes members designated by their states. France, through the DEP, is responsible for the administration, presidency, and secretariat of the network.[2]

Since 1996, the Network has organized several comparative studies. The first, an assessment of 15-year-old students' skills in English (1996, three countries), was replicated in 2003 with eight countries. The second was an assessment of 15-year-old students' reading performances in their respective countries, and it used tests that had not been translated, as is usually the case in international surveys of reading performance. This assessment, known as the C-BAR Project (Culturally Balanced Assessment of Reading), was conducted in 2004 and involved eight countries. The third study looked at reading skills at the end of primary education. It was conducted in 2002 and involved three countries. Other projects led by the Network were directed by Ireland, Scotland, and Greece.

France also intervenes in the French-speaking domain, either to participate in comparative studies or to promote them. One example is a study focused on the writing skills of Grade 9 students in several French-speaking populations (Belgium, France, New Brunswick, Québec, Senegal, and Switzerland) (Colmant & Desclaux, 1996; Groupe DIEPE, 1996).

### 5.3.3   National Large-scale Surveys

In France, the system used to evaluate students' skills is conducted by the DEP. The system, which was gradually set up from the end of the 1970s, today rests on two types of assessment: diagnostic and monitoring.

#### *Diagnostic Assessments*

These permit close examination of each student's strengths and weaknesses. Prepared by the DEP, the assessments are used in class and are intended as professional tools containing benchmarks against which teachers can identify and

---

2   Information about the Network's surveys, projects, and publications can be found on the following website (in English and in French) : http://cisad.adc.education.fr/reva/english/index.htm

respond to any difficulties their students are experiencing. These assessments comprise the following:

- *Start-of-year tests*: At the beginning of the school year, test-based assessments provide a systematic and compulsory assessment of the levels of mastery in French and mathematics of all Grades 3 and 6 students in public and private schools (over 800,000 students at each grade).
- *Bank of assessment tools*: These tools, provided by the DEP, allow teachers from the *maternelle* level up to secondary school determine how well students have mastered diverse skills in numerous disciplines. The tools are available in paper format, on CD-ROM, and as downloadable files on an Internet site.

### Monitoring Assessments

These are used to assess the competencies of representative samples of students at key points of the education system. The Ministry uses the findings of these assessments to monitor how well the education system is meeting its objectives, to direct and implement national educational policy, and to identify the factors that need to be addressed to improve student achievement. The extent to which students have mastered the French language and acquired linguistic skills in English and German is assessed at the end of primary school. General curriculum-wide skills and linguistic skills in English, German, and Spanish are assessed at the end of the lower secondary school. The regular replication of these assessments not only permits monitoring but also comparisons across time, which is why the content of the tests is confidential and not made public. The findings of the assessments are set within the contexts in which teaching and learning take place. These contexts are elucidated from information obtained from student, teacher, and school principal questionnaires administered to these groups at the time of each assessment. Figure 5.1 shows the variety of assessments used within the French school system and how these are used across the levels of that system. It also shows how the large-scale international assessments align with these national assessments. What is clear here is the close integration of the two, with the international assessments providing information complementary to that obtained from the national monitoring assessments.

Access to a national assessment tool that functions well and supplies regular information on students' skills has favorably influenced the French attitude towards international assessments. In his book on monitoring of education systems, de Landsheere (1994) praises France's national monitoring assessment as "an exemplary development".

**Figure 5.1:  Assessments used to monitor educational performance in France: two types of assessments for two complementary goals**

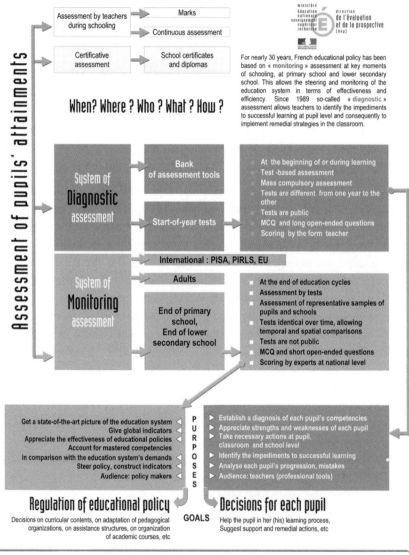

Source:    Poster prepared by J. Levasseur and P. Cosnefroy of the DEP for the general assembly of the Association for Educational Assessment Europe (AEA-Europe), 2004.

France reviews the information it obtains from the international assessments against the information it already has from its own assessments. It also subjects its international data to the same scrutiny and critique it pays to all other data it gathers on its education system. The international assessments therefore are seen not as the premier source of information about the French education system. Rather, they are seen as an additional important source of information that allows specific aspects of the education system to be identified, appraised, and compared at set moments of time and over periods of time both internally and cross-nationally. The advantage of this dual system of assessment is particularly evident when we consider that many countries had no national sets of data on their students' skills until their participation in PISA and/or PIRLS. France's long-term practice of collecting national assessment data has meant that it can use both its national and international sets not only to cross-assess the reliability and validity of each set, but also to view its international performance within the context of understanding gained over time from scrutiny of the results of the national assessments.

### 5.3.4 Feedback System

To facilitate the dissemination of information useful for practitioners and policy-makers at all levels of the education system, and to promote a wide and informed debate on education among the general public, the DEP publishes a number of documents. These include the following:

- *Repères et Références Statistiques sur les enseignements et les formations (Landmarks and Statistics on Education and Training)*, an annual volume that synthesizes all available official educational statistical data;
- *L'état de l'école and Géographie de l'école (The State of the School and Geography of the School)*, published once a year to provide, respectively, 30 national and 37 regional indicators on the education system;
- *Note d'Information and Note d'Évaluation (Information Note and Evaluation Note)*, each issued one or more times every week, and offering updated raw figures and basic commentaries on a variety of educational matters;
- *Les Dossiers (The Files)*, which features detailed accounts and findings of recent surveys; and
- *Education et Formations (Education and Training)*, a quarterly journal that presents individual articles on specific educational subjects.

Most of these documents and most of the data they contain are also available on the DEP Internet site: http://www.education.gouv.fr/stateval/

Three types of publication offer commentary specifically related to the results of the international studies. These are: (1) presentation reports for educational policy-makers and teachers; (2) academic research reports that aim to analyze and discuss the results; and (3) publications prepared for the general public and generally disseminated through the media (newspapers, radio, television).

### Publications for Educators

Since the DEP became responsible, in the early 1990s, for overseeing the evaluation of education throughout France, it has published the results of the main international assessments in which France has participated primarily in *Note d'Information* and *Note d'Évaluation*. For examples citing the findings of TIMSS, see Jouvanceau (1992), Servant (1997), and Servant and Murat (1996). For PISA 2000, see Bourny, Dupé, Robin, and Rocher (2001); for PIRLS, see Colmant and Mulliez (2003); and for PISA 2003, see Bourny, Fumel, Monnier, and Rocher (2004). The DEP has also published details of the studies, the students' achievement results, and discussion of several hypotheses concerning those results in special issues of *Les Dossiers*. The other publication in which the DEP disseminates results findings to educators is *Education et Formations*.

Details of work undertaken by the European Network are also available to educators through these publications. Two other published sources of information on the international studies available to educators are the biannual newsletter *Évaluation* (*Evaluation*) and reports prepared at the request of the *Haut Conseil de l'Évaluation de l'École* (the *High Council of the Evaluation of Schools* or HCÉÉ).

### Academic Publications

These include journal articles, reports, and books, reports and proceedings arising out of national and international conferences and congresses, and university papers and theses. They also include reports commissioned by the DEP to address methodological aspects of the studies and to analyze and discuss the findings of these studies. Publication in refereed journals has been particularly evident in relation to the French TIMSS data. Another sphere of publishing activity for France is reviews and articles on the methodology of cross-national comparative studies (see, for example, Murat & Rocher, 2004; Rocher, 2003; Vrignaud, 2002). A seminar held in 2003 by Jean-Richard Cytermann, at the School of Higher Studies in Social Sciences, concerned the international studies and their links with the educational policies of various European countries.

Before the 1990s, French researchers did not publish on topics relating to the international studies. Since then, publications featuring the TIMSS data have been produced by and for French academics, although the number of publications arising out of IALS and PISA is increasing. These latter works are written mostly by psychologists and sociologists and frequently adopt a critical position towards the results of the studies.

### Publications for the General Public

Until the release of the results for IALS, information on the international studies did not appear in the French press, although some brief mention was made of the results in specialist magazines and periodicals such as *Le Monde de l'Éducation* (*World of Education*) and *Sciences et Avenir* (*Science and Future*).One reason why IALS attracted media attention may have been because of the OECD's widespread promotion of this study. PISA (conducted by the OECD) and PIRLS (IEA) were also systematically promoted through press conferences, with the results of the studies subsequently reported in the main media, although this was more the case for PISA than for PIRLS. Daily newspapers such as *Le Monde* and *Le Figaro* provided reasonably detailed coverage of the studies, but most other media tended to provide only brief summaries of the findings relating to French students.

## 5.4    National Results and Impact of PIRLS 2001

### 5.4.1    Results of PIRLS 2001

### General Considerations

In PIRLS 2001, the overall average achievement score for French students of 525 was significantly above the average (500) for all participating countries. This score gave France a median ranking in the study, with 12 countries, among them Sweden, England and Scotland, Netherlands, Italy, Germany, and the United States, having significantly better results than France. Fifteen countries performed less well than France; seven had comparable performances.

A comparison of the average performance of the French students against the average performance of students in PIRLS countries with which France has geographic and economic ties, notably those of the European Union and the OECD countries, showed that French students performed below the averages for these groupings. Comparison with countries where students' average level of performance was similar to that of the French students showed the standard deviation for the French students to be smaller than that for the students of these countries. This characteristic was also evident in the PISA results for 15-year-old students.

French students' achievement was better on some of the activity items in the PIRLS assessment test than on others. On nine of the total 98 test items, student achievement set France amongst the top five countries. However, for 11 other items, student performance situated France in the last 10 countries. Looked at another way, the performance of French students on the 98 items of the test was significantly lower than the international averages for 19 of the items and significantly superior than the international averages for 64 items. In general, then, the performance of French students deviated significantly from the international averages for 85% of the test items. However, these observations need to be viewed cautiously, as they are based on the aggregation of disparate results.

For both reading purposes (informational and literary), France's position was above the international average. French students performed better on test items related to informational texts (13th place in the international ranking) than on items related to literary texts (19th place). When constructing meaning from the texts, French students were reasonably consistent in their ability to "retrieve explicit information", "make straightforward inferences", "interpret information", and "evaluate textual elements". France's cross-country ranking on these comprehension processes ranged from 20th place for "interpret information" to 16th for "make straightforward inferences".

When considering these results, it is important to remember that performance variability across countries may not relate simply to the purposes and processes of reading processes but also to cultural sensibilities to the texts. For example, in France, the test items on which the students scored most highly were (1) an advertising leaflet that presented the services of a rent-a-bike shop and included a map of a cycle trail (informational text), and (2) an animal fable (a narrative literary text). France's across-country ranking for the first item was third and for the second was 10th. However, for another narrative text, France's ranking was much lower, at the 26th position. In Québec, the only other French-speaking community in PIRLS, student performance on these three texts followed the same hierarchy. It seems that language and culture maintain some influence on students' comprehension of what they are reading despite all the methodological efforts to reduce it.

The French students also showed they are highly influenced by the question format. They did better when they did not have to construct a response to a question, and this applied no matter what the comprehension process involved. Certainly, French students have a strong tendency to refrain from answering open-ended questions. This sensibility to question format was evident in all countries, with those answers requiring written elaboration attracting the highest rate of non-response, and the rate of non-response increasing with the degree of elaboration required. This sensibility was particularly marked in France.

Analysis of variance showed that "comprehension processes" and "question formats" could explain 35% of the variance in performance, a percentage that is considerable. The influence of question formats is thus weaker than the influence of processes, which, by itself, explains more than 30% of the variance.

The French students' non-response rate on all the PIRLS assessment multiple-choice questions was 1%; only six countries had a lower rate. However, when we consider only the items requiring an open-ended response, France's position falls to 23rd place, and falls lower again, to 26th place, for items requiring the most elaborated answers. This pattern was also evident for the results for France in PISA 2000.

For historic reasons (see 5.3.2), France has not taken the results from the international studies at face value, an attitude that became particularly evident after France's withdrawal from IALS. France now systematically scrutinizes the findings for any one study against the results of the other international studies. Even though the target populations of each study are different, even though each looks at different subjects and issues, and even though the methodological procedures vary slightly, the accrual of information across the studies builds to provide a more realistic and valid picture of the effectiveness of the French education system. This process is evident in France's decision to examine how well its interpretation of the country's PISA 2000 results holds up against what has been discovered through its participation in PIRLS.

### Specific Considerations

#### Gender Differences not as Pronounced

In PIRLS, as in PISA, girls achieved better results than boys in all participating countries. In both studies, the difference between girls and boys in France was lower than the international average. The difference between the genders in France was even less marked in PIRLS, where the girls scored 11 points higher than the boys (531 for girls and 520 for boys) against 19 points internationally. France was at second position amongst the countries revealing the weakest difference between girls and boys.

#### Strong Performance on Information-Based Tasks

In all countries that participated in PIRLS, students obtained a better score on literary texts than on informational ones. In France, the distance between these two texts categories was not as pronounced as in all but two other countries, reinforcing the notion that French students perform better on informational texts than do students in most other countries. Analysis of the French students' performance in PISA sheds further light on this finding, by strongly suggesting that these students have a particular ability in those tasks requiring technical competency and precision. This ability was particularly evident on test items dealing with spatial location, maps, and plans. For example, on the three items in PISA where students needed to track their way through maps or carry out similar tasks involving spatial locations, French students performed at rates significantly superior to the international averages. It would seem that activities involving these skills are widely represented in the French education system.

## Weaker Performance on Interpretation Tasks

French students' generally poorer performance relative to many other participating countries on tasks that required them to "interpret information" (as in PIRLS) and "to react" (as in PISA) revealed their relative weakness in expressing personal opinions about the content of texts. France needs to examine what is happening in classrooms in order to explain this phenomenon. Is it simply that students do not have sufficient opportunity to practice this competence in class? Or is their reticence to give opinions a function of teachers leaving little room for personal expression? Unless teachers actively encourage students to consider and discuss points, students are unlikely to do so.

## Underestimation of Ability

In addition to measuring competency in reading, PIRLS solicited the students' attitudes to reading, including their perceptions of their own reading skills. French students sharply underestimated their ability, to the extent that only one other country had students who gave a lower estimation. Although French students had an average score on the reading literacy scale a little higher than the international average (525 as against 500), only 28% of the students had a very good opinion of their ability, against 40% at the international level.

It seems that this lack of assurance, aligned with fear of being discredited for not giving a correct answer, may be why French students prefer not to answer test questions. This situation could be because schools tend to see errors not as a necessary part of learning, but as a fault, and to stigmatize them as such.

## Ill at Ease with Writing Tasks

Students' non-response was particularly evident in both PIRLS and PISA in relation to open-ended questions, particularly those requiring a long answer. This finding suggests that it is in written expression rather than in reading that French students meet the most difficulties.

In PIRLS, French students were above the international average in terms of answering questions that either did not require writing (such as multiple choice questions) or asked them to do tasks like linking objects by arrows or ordering sentences numerically. As soon as they encountered questions requiring written answers, the students' non-response rate increased relative to the international level. Similarly, the longer the required answer, the more likely the French students were not to answer it. On the questions asking for the longest answers, nearly one-fifth

(19.3%), on average, of the French students refrained from answering, against one-tenth (9.9%) of the students at the international level.

These observations pose questions about the teaching of writing in French schools. Texts and programs all emphasize mastery of writing as an essential component of French education. However, possibly because teachers find it difficult to teach students writing skills, they tend to assume students gain this mastery early in their school career. It also seems that teachers then see students' writing ability throughout their education as implicit. Although educational programs and texts clearly emphasize written expression as an integrated part of students' ongoing education, and require students to have frequent daily opportunity to practice writing, the everyday reality in classes seems quite different. Writing competency appears to be seen purely from the point of view of form and correct grammatical usage. Students who find their written expression assessed only in this way may consider that writing is a risky exercise, full of constraints, and so better avoided. The lack of frequent and progressive practice may also cause students to see writing as an arduous exercise.

*French Schooling in General*

What we have learned about the students schooled in France from our participation in PIRLS and PISA has allowed us to form several hypotheses about the nature of French primary and secondary schooling. Our observations suggest that practice in French classrooms leaves little room for interaction and that teachers tend to treat the errors students make as faults rather than as a necessary part of learning. In general, French schools seem to be places where students tend more towards the passive in their learning and whose thoughts and ideas on what they are learning are not sufficiently sought. However, both studies show that French students are relatively at ease with the "technical" mechanisms of reading, seen in the tasks requiring them to extract information from a document.

**Dissemination of PIRLS Results**

The DEP released the French results of PIRLS 2001 simultaneously with the international results, on April 2003. All major national and local newspapers, television channels, and the AFP (France Press Agency) were invited to attend a press conference, and most did. The conference not only presented the French and international results and France's performance relative to the other participating countries, but also carefully explained the aim of the study, outlined its methodology, and provided examples of the test tasks. All those attending the conference received a six-page document containing this information (see Colmant & Mulliez, 2003).

On the same day as the press conference, French public television presented a brief item during its midday news. In the followings days, all newspapers contained short articles on the subject but not feature ones, perhaps not surprising given that world media attention at the time was on US troops entering Baghdad. Most of the articles gave information only about the countries' "success lists" and supplied little additional detail. Later, some professional and specialized newsletters (for example, teacher trade unions, student–parent associations) also provided information about the findings.

In the months that followed, the DEP tried to enhance interest in the results, in particular among education professionals. The Ministry sent about 2,500 copies of its *Note d'Information* to subscribers, among them school inspectors, local authorities, and teachers. The schools that had participated in PIRLS also received copies of this document. The French National Research Coordinator for PIRLS presented the results in a series of sessions open to Ministry staff, and the National Formation Center organized a special conference for primary school inspectors. PIRLS-related information was also made freely available on the web, a particularly useful medium of dissemination, since teachers, even at primary school level, increasingly are sourcing information from the Internet.

### 5.4.2   Impact of PIRLS 2001

Despite these efforts, the public paid little attention to the PIRLS results, let alone debated them. Certainly, the findings did not engender strong feelings or controversy, as occurred in Germany, perhaps because people were not overly concerned about them, given that student performance was above the international average. Also, the performance of French students in previous large-scale studies of educational achievement had not been unexpected or overly concerning, so PIRLS had nothing new to say. For much of the French media and the public, the results of PIRLS were neither a source of pride nor a source of disquiet.

#### *Impact on School Administration and Pedagogy*

With only a few years having elapsed since the release of the PIRLS results, it seems too early to determine the study's true impact on the administration and pedagogy of schools. It is also difficult to find a reliable means of assessing the impact. What we can say at this point is that because the performance of French students was average, and so created little concern, there was no driving impetus to impose immediate change in the education system. Also, as Figure 5.1 above showed, France embeds the international studies in its system of monitoring assessment. The outcomes of such assessments give global indicators for educational policy-makers; they do not help teachers directly in their work within schools and classes, as the pedagogical information given is too weak for that. This is not a criticism, but simply acknowledgement that the studies are not designed for this purpose. Only the diagnostic assessments can have a straightforward influence on pedagogical practices. This is because they are designed to identify student strengths and weaknesses and what impedes or enhances successful learning. This information, in turn, allows the development and implementation of remedial strategies.

### Long-term Effects

PIRLS provides information in a domain that is dear to policy-makers, namely reading comprehension. For the past 16 or so years, all French students have received diagnostic testing at the beginning of Grades 3 and 7 (the latter being the first year of secondary school). These nationwide assessments are designed to provide quality information about children's strengths and weaknesses in French and mathematics. The assessments involve a considerable annual investment of resources (time, people, and money), and so the DEP expects teachers and policy-makers to use the assessment results to good effect. Studies of the usefulness of the national diagnostic assessments show they are having the desired impact. In particular, they have given teachers a clearer understanding that how they teach influences student learning, and this knowledge has helped them modify their teaching practices to better meet the needs of their students. This process is one that is leading to an attitudinal change amongst teachers. Little by little, teachers are engaging in a culture where assessment is viewed as part of the learning process, not simply as the giving of good or bad marks. Although this change is taking time, it is important to persevere with it, as its ultimate goal is to help teachers help students learn to read, and read to learn.

During PIRLS 2001 and afterwards, those associated with the study began to realize that France needed to do more to enhance the reading literacy of its students, especially those with poorer ability. Questions were asked as to whether Grade 4 (PIRLS) or Grade 3 (French diagnostic assessment) were the best points at which to make skills comparisons or identify problems, especially given the attitude that the sooner difficulties were identified and remedied, the better. These considerations led France to develop two new assessments.

The first, known as the *Grande Section/Cours Préparatoire*, was given to teachers at the beginning of the 2002 school year. The tools that make up this assessment comprise hard copy, a CD-Rom, and a website, and are designed for students in their last year at the *maternelle* and their first year of elementary school, times that together represent a key period in young children's reading learning. Validated and calibrated to make sure of their reliability, the tools can be used by teachers in accordance with the needs and characteristics of their students. Along with the assessment package, teachers also receive pedagogical guidance and information on how to promote learning opportunities for individual children and small groups.

The second assessment tool is for use with students with poor reading ability. Tested in 2004, the assessment was implemented nationwide at the beginning of the 2005/06 school year. It is designed not only to detect these students but also to give a very detailed knowledge of their difficulties. Administered at the beginning of Grade 2, the assessment consists of a test booklet containing about 30 items and taking students only about 20 minutes to complete. Students identified as having weak abilities undertake a second assessment, which takes about an hour and is more in-depth than the first in its coverage of different domains (word recognition, comprehension, phonology, syntax, dictation, writing). The first assessment is designed to direct about 20% of children nationwide to the second assessment. However, in some schools, the percentage of children moving to the second step can, of course, be much higher or lower than this average. The results are organized so that teachers can interpret student ability by domains and by competencies. At the end of the process, teachers know exactly which students require attention, and what type of attention each needs.

## 5.5   Future Activities

### 5.5.1   Research

To date, France has considered that overcoming poor reading literacy skills amongst its students requires early and speedy detection of reading difficulties (diagnosis) and teacher-directed measures designed to remedy those difficulties. However, the PIRLS results suggest that more needs doing to meet the needs of students whose reading ability is particularly poor. The French Minister of Education accordingly decided to trial a completely new approach.

His proposal is premised on the idea that the lower the number of students in a class, the higher the benefits for student learning. However, a review of relevant research on the benefits of reducing class size was inconclusive. The Minister then decided to reduce class size during the first grade of elementary school in order to gain hard data on the learning benefits or otherwise of reducing class size.

The study will last several years to allow for investigation of long-term effects, and the DEP is conducting it in association with researchers from five French universities. The schools participating in the study have had to meet three characteristics. First, the reduction has to be in the first grade of school. Second, the reduction has to be significant.[3] Third, the classes must be in schools within low socio-economic areas and have students whose performance was poor on the national evaluations. The Ministry accordingly selected, using information relevant to the criteria furnished by inspectors, 100 Grade 1 classes from throughout France for participation in the study. The Ministry selected another 100 Grade 1 classes in the same socially deprived areas but with traditional class numbers to serve as a control group.

Preliminary results from the study were released in April 2005 (DEP, 2005). They showed that, at the end of Grade 1, the progress of students in the experimental classes was a little higher than that of their schoolmates in the control classes. Unfortunately, this difference, even though statistically significant, was very moderate. Also, inequalities in ability among the members of the experimental class evident at the beginning of the year were still evident at the end, and when the students went into the usual class size of Grade 2, the small improvement in ability they had gained in Grade 1 disappeared. The results also indicated that reducing class size had little effect on teachers' practices, offering another explanation for the lack of impact on student performance.

The fact that student achievement at the end of Grade 1 is, irrespective of class size, on a similar level to that at the beginning of Grade 1 confirms that inequalities are already strongly ingrained by the beginning of elementary school. As such, diagnosis and remedy should focus not only on Grade 1 but also on the *maternelle* school, and particularly on the last year of pre-elementary.

## 5.5.2  Publications

In addition to the PIRLS-related information in the aforementioned *Note d'Information*, more detailed published interpretations of the PIRLS 2001 data are in progress. This material will be published in *Les Dossiers*, which is widely disseminated throughout the French education world.

## 5.5.3  Programs

During 2000, there was considerable debate in France about education in the primary schools. This debate reinforced the idea that it is an absolute priority to preserve the national language. Language is the basis of social integration, and knowledge of the French language is indispensable to knowledge attainment. In order to achieve in other disciplines, students must comprehend their own language:

---

3   In France, Grade 1 classes have, on average, 23 students. The study requires participating classes to have no more than 12 students in each class.

it is the backbone of learning. In line with this concern, a new curriculum, made public in February 2002, emphasized two aspects of reading: the diversity of written language, and the diversity of written documents. This diversity is evident in the skills needed to learn to read across specific courses, and in the variety of texts that students encounter across disciplines. The new curriculum thus rests on the assertion that students learn to read in all disciplines and through different written documents, such as works of fiction, stories, historical documents, geographical descriptions, and reports of scientific experiments.

For France, the PIRLS 2001 main survey took place just before the new curriculum became effective. France is also participating in PIRLS 2006, and a comparison of the performance of the 2001 students with that of the 2006 students will provide a valuable indication of the effectiveness of the new curriculum's focus on language skills, especially (within the context of PIRLS) reading comprehension.

## 5.6   Concluding Remarks

The impact of PIRLS 2001 has made an important contribution to the field of education evaluation in France. The methodology used in this large-scale study has helped the DEP think about and refine the way it organizes and analyzes its own assessments. The study results have provided a valuable additional source of information to that usually collected on the education system, and have enabled the DEP and its parent body, the Ministry, to conduct analyses and formulate hypotheses useful to advancing knowledge of France's education system.

The results of the study created little interest or debate amongst parents and members of the general public. The reason for this is probably because French students scored above the international average, and so people saw no reason to be particularly concerned.

French educational policy-makers and administrators and the teachers themselves have at hand a consistent and highly capable system of collecting and analyzing student achievement information, so they were not unduly surprised by the PIRLS results. Also, from a pedagogical point of view, teachers have access to professionally prepared assessment tools, the use of which has a stronger impact on their practices than does participation in assessments such as PIRLS.

As for the role of French research in education, the situation is summed up in this quote from the HCÉÉ report:

> Psychometry and 'edumetry' are domains that are little developed in the French landscape of research. It is the same for the applications of those disciplines (tests development, surveys). This lack of knowledge has doubtless played on the little interest shown in the international studies. (Bottani & Vrignaud, 2005, p. 91)

France is involved in the next cycle of PIRLS (2006). It is likely that the results of this second phase of the study will have much more impact than those of PIRLS 2001 because the time lapse will allow us to examine the evolution of French students' achievement in reading literacy over time. The word "Progress", denoted by the upper-case P in the acronym PIRLS, has particular resonance in this regard. We trust that the PIRLS 2006 results will supply answers to a question that in recent years has frequently been asked during debates on the effectiveness of schooling and education in France: does the level of student achievement rise, or does it fall?

## References

Bottani, N., & Vrignaud, P. (2005). *La France et les évaluations internationales. Rapport établi à la demande du Haut Conseil de l'Évaluation de l'École, Nr. 16 [France and the international assessments: Report made at the request of the HCEE]*. Retrieved 2005, from http://cisad.adc.education.fr/hcee

Bourny, G., Dupé, C., Robin, I., & Rocher, T. (2001). Les élèves de 15 ans: Premiers résultats d'une évaluation internationale des acquis des élèves (PISA) [Fifteen-year-old students: First results of an international assessment (PISA)]. *Note d'Information*, 01.52, December, 6 pages.

Bourny, G., Fumel, S., Monnier, A.-I., & Rocher, T. (2004). Les élèves de 15 ans: Premiers résultats de l'évaluation internationale PISA 2003 [Fifteen-year-old students: First results of the international assessment PISA], *Note d'Evaluation*, 04.12, December, 6 pages.

Colmant, M. (2002). France. In I. V. S. Mullis, M. O. Martin, A. M. Kennedy, & C. L. Flaherty (Eds.), *PIRLS 2001 encyclopedia: A reference guide to reading education in the countries participating in IEA's Progress in International Reading Literacy Study (PIRLS)* (pp. 69–78). Chestnut Hill, MA: Boston College.

Colmant, M., & Desclaux, A. (1996). *Écrire en fin de scolarité [Writing at the end of schooling]* (Vol. 59). Paris: Ministère de l'Éducation nationale–Direction de l'évaluation et de la prospective.

Colmant, M., & Mulliez, A. (2003). Les élèves de CM1: Premiers résultats d'une évaluation internationale en lecture (PIRLS) [Grade 4 students: First results of an international assessment in reading (PIRLS)]. *Note d'Information*, 03.22, 6 pages.

Cosnefroy, O., & Rocher, T. (2005). *Le redoublement au cours de la scolarité obligatoire. Nouvelles analyses, mêmes constats [Repeating during compulsory schooling: New analysis, same findings]* (Vol. 166). Paris: Ministère de l'éducation nationale, de l'enseignement supérieur et de la recherche–Direction de l'évaluation et de la prospective.

de Landsheere, G. (1994). *Le pilotage des systèmes éducatifs [Monitoring of educational systems]*. Brussels: De Boeck Université.

DEP. (2005). L'expérimentation d'une réduction des effectifs en cours préparatoire: Les résultats [The effect of a reduction in class size on students' performance in Grade 1: The results]. *Note d'Évaluation*, 05.03, April, 6 pages.

Groupe DIEPE. (1996). *Savoir écrire au secondaire [Knowing how to write at secondary school].* Collection "Pédagogie en développement, Problématiques et recherché". Brussels: De Boeck Université.

Haut Conseil à l'Évaluation de l'École. (2005). *La France et les évaluations internationales des acquis des élèves [France and the international assessments of students' knowledge].* Avis No. 16 du HCEF. Paris: Ministère de l'éducation nationale, de l'enseignement supérieur et de la recherche–Direction de l'évaluation et de la prospective.

Murat, F., & Rocher, T. (2004). The method used for international assessment of educational competencies. In J. Tarsh (trans.), *Comparing learning outcomes: International assessment of education policy* (190–214). London: Routledge Falmer.

Rocher T. (2003). La méthodologie des évaluations internationales de compétences [Methodology of international evaluations of skills], *Psychologie et Psychométrie: Numéro spécial: Mesure et Education, 24*, 117–146.

Servant, A. (1997). Évaluation internationale en mathématiques et en sciences des élèves de cinquième et de quatrième [International assessments of students in maths and sciences (TIMSS)]. *Note d'Information*, 97.06, February, 6 pages.

Servant, A., & Murat, F. (1996). Les connaissances des élèves en mathématiques et sciences en terminale [Student achievement in maths and science]. *Note d'Information*, 96.49, December, 6 pages.

Vrignaud, P. (2002). Les biais de mesure: Savoir les identifier pour y remédier [Biased measures: Knowing how to identify them to remedy them]. *Bulletin de Psychologie, 55*(6), 625–634.

# Chapter 6
# The Impact of PIRLS in Germany

*Knut Schwippert*

## 6.1    Germany at a Glance[1]

Germany is situated in the heart of Europe and borders nine other European countries. From north (the border with Denmark) to south (the Alps), Germany has a length of 876 kilometers and covers an area of about 357,000 square kilometers. In the north, Germany has access to the North Sea and to the Baltic Sea. With its northern lowlands, densely wooded low mountain ranges, and high mountain range (the Bavarian Alps), Germany has a great variety of landscapes.

Germany has 82 million inhabitants. Population density in the former West Germany is 235 persons per square kilometer; in the former East Germany, it is 145 persons per square kilometer. Despite the high population density, only three cities—Berlin, Hamburg, and Munich—have more than one million inhabitants. Eighty-seven per cent of the population lives in rural areas, most of them in communities with fewer than 100,000 inhabitants. After reunification, Berlin once again became the capital of Germany, in the summer of 1999.

Germany, a member of both the OECD and the G7 Economic Group of countries, is rated as a high-income country by the World Bank. The gross national product per capita in 2000 was US$25,620 (US$23,510 PPP Intl.). The gross national product comprises mainly manufacturing, industry, catering, financing, renting, and business services as well as public and private services. The majority of the country's export earnings are from vehicles, machinery, and chemicals.

Public expenditure on education in 2000 was about €M79.264 (US$B95.34),[2] 3.91% of the GNP (Bundesministerium für Bildung und Forschung, 2004).

## 6.2    Germany's Education System as Context for PIRLS 2001

The German school system is organized by the State. Because Germany consists of 16 independent federal states, the education system is also under their administrative control. With the exception of only a few private schools, which are under the control of the State, schooling is free for all children and compulsory until the age of 18. Only in some federal states are parents required to buy school-books, but

---

1    This introduction is based on Germany's country profile in the *PIRLS 2001 Encyclopedia* (Lankes, Bos, & Valtin, 2002).
2    Exchange rate as of October 2, 2005: €1= $US1.203.

throughout the system, parents can be charged for excursions or special programs. However, parents from socially disadvantaged backgrounds who cannot afford such payments generally receive reimbursement from the states.

Some German students attend some form of day care or a kindergarten before entering the primary school. Parents who are both employed find it difficult to procure regular and professional day care for children younger than three years, and generally have to organize and pay for care privately. The situation is similar for children of age three and above whose parents wish them to attend kindergarten. Parents also have to pay for this service, the cost of which is prohibitive for some. Those parents who can afford such care often find the hosts do not offer a full-day service. Some kindergartens close in the early afternoon, which is not appropriate for most employed parents.

In general, most children start primary school at age six. Some students enter school earlier or later than this, because, under German tradition, parents can choose to hold their children back. They may want their children to have a longer childhood or they may be convinced their children are not ready to start school. Once in school, students who do not perform as expected may be required by their teachers to repeat a grade. Because of this, the ages of students in Grade 4, the grade from which the students who participated in PIRLS 2001 were drawn, can vary widely.

In general, students in the first four grades of the primary school attend school during the morning, although the amount of time given over to lessons varies from day to day, which means the time of day at which children return home also varies daily. Afternoon child care is not compulsory. Some federal states are moving towards a system where all children stay at school until the same time every day. In some federal states, schools have specific pedagogical programs for after school hours. In other states, the children are only supervised, either by teachers, parents, or other trained pedagogical personnel.

In 14 of the 16 federal states, students move on to secondary school after Grade 4. However, students in Brandenburg and Berlin attend primary school for six years. In Bremen, students leave the primary school after Grade 4 and enter a two-year intermediate level (*Orientierungsstufe*). In most of the German federal states, students are tracked into one of three secondary school types, each with different academic demands. Some states also have a compulsory school (*Gesamtschule*), which sits alongside the tracked system. Every school type gives different certificates. Students who complete *Hauptschule* (Grades 5–9 in most states, and the least demanding school type academically) generally enter apprenticeships and trades-based employment after leaving school. The *Realschule* (Grades 5–10 in most states) offers a certificate that is necessary for entry to more demanding occupations, while the *Gymnasium* (Grades 5–13 in most states) offers a certificate that is necessary for entry to university. The *Gesamtschule* offers all certificates.

In all federal states, the primary school teacher recommends which secondary school a child should enter, but parents can go against the recommendation and send their child to another school type. Empirical research shows that, in Germany, parents who have higher educational qualifications favor sending their children to schools demanding higher academic performance while parents with lower educational qualifications favor sending their children to the more vocationally directed schools (Avenarius et al., 2003, p. 209). The practice of having students of all levels of ability remaining together as a group during their primary schooling and then entering different ability tracks for their secondary schooling is one of the most important and controversial aspects of the German education system.

## 6.3    Experience in Large-scale Assessments

### 6.3.1    History

During the 1970s and 1980s in Germany—or more precisely in West Germany— many educational policy-makers were intent on reforming the education system. Education for all, equal chances, even a change in the capitalist society through a new kind of education, were all ideas on the horizon of educational hope. Politicians and educational researchers and commentators fought for the implementation of comprehensive schools, the establishment of a school system that would compensate for social inequalities, and many other well-meant changes.

### *International System-monitoring*

During this period of reforms, no one thought of empirically evaluating the impact of the changes, even though there could have been unintended effects. This lack of formal evaluation tradition testing is a fundamental reason for Germany's limited participation, for many years, in international system-monitoring studies. In the early 1970s, West German students participated in the First International Science Study (FISS). The students' achievement results were far below expectations. Germany consequently started to reform its education system but did not participate with representative samples in international system-monitoring studies for about 20 years. In 1991, educational researcher Rainer Lehmann broke with common research tradition in Germany and facilitated Germany's participation in the International Reading Literacy Study (RLS). Since then, Germany has participated in interna- tional student achievement studies on a regular basis. As Table 6.1 shows, Germany did not participate in the SITES and TIMSS-R surveys because the country had decided to take part in similar studies, namely the *Schulen ans Netz* (Schools to the Web) project (covering SITES) and the OECD-PISA study (covering TIMSS-R).

Germany's participation status relating to national representative samples and non-representative samples, respectively, is summarized in Table 6.1.

**Table 6.1:  Germany's participation in international large-scale surveys of educational achievement, 1964–2001**

| Year(s) of data collection | Name of survey | Organization in charge | Participation status in Germany |
|---|---|---|---|
| 1964 | First International Mathematics Study (FIMS) | IEA | Two federal states |
| 1970/71 | Six-Subject Survey: English French Literature First International Science Study (FISS) Reading Comprehension Civic Education | IEA | Diverse: only reading comprehension in English<br><br>Representative sample<br><br>No participation Only 10 federal states |
| 1985–87 | Study of Written Composition | IEA | One federal state |
| 1985/86 | Classroom Environment Study | IEA | One federal state |
| 1986–89 | Pre-Primary Study | IEA | Representative |
| 1990/91 | International Reading Literacy Study (RLS) | IEA | Representative (first study after reunification) |
| 1989 + 1992 | Computers in Education | IEA | Nine federal states |
| 1994 | International Adult Literacy Study (IALS) | OECD | Representative |
| 1994–96 | Third International Mathematics and Science Study (TIMSS) | IEA | Representative (Pop 2) (one federal state missing) |
| 2000 | Civic Education Study (CivEd) | IEA | Representative |
| 2000 | Program for International Student Assessment (PISA) | OECD | Representative |
| 1998–2001 | Second Information Technology in Education Study (SITES) | IEA | Representative (Module 2 only) |
| 2001 | Progress in International Reading Literacy Study 2001 (PIRLS 2001) | IEA | Representative |

## National Large-scale Surveys

After the mid-1990s, several researchers tried to fill knowledge gaps not only by participating in international large-scale surveys but also by conducting large-scale surveys based on national samples from federal states. Table 6.2 sets out this shift towards empirical educational research in Germany. In the LAU studies (*Lern-Ausgangslagen-Untersuchung*) (Lehmann, Peek, & Gänsfuß, 1997), Grades 5, 7, 9, and 11 students in Hamburg were tested in the main subjects in an assessment process employing a longitudinal design under the direction of Rainer Lehmann. In QuaSUM (Lehmann, Peek, Gänsfuß, Lukat, Mücke, & Barth, 2000), a representative sample of third and eighth graders in Brandenburg was tested in mathematics. In MARKUS (Helmke & Jäger, 2002), all eighth graders in Rhineland-Palatinate (*Rheinland-Pfalz*) were tested in mathematics under the direction of Andreas Helmke. In KESS4 (*Kompetenzen und Einstellungen von Schülerinnen und Schülern*), conducted in 2003, all fourth graders in Hamburg were tested in the main subjects under the direction of Wilfried Bos. Recently, most of the federal states of Germany have planned or carried out studies comparing educational achievement within and across different grades and subjects.

**Table 6.2:** **National large-scale surveys of educational achievement conducted in Germany, 1996–2003**

| Year of data collection | Name of survey | Status of regional extension |
|---|---|---|
| 1996 | Study of Education Basics in Grade 5 (first longitudinal study of the population in one federal state) (LAU 5) | Census of one federal state (Hamburg)—first wave |
| 1998 | Study of Education Basics in Grade 7 (LAU 7) | Census of one federal state (Hamburg)—second wave |
| 1999 | School Quality and Mathematics (QuaSUM) | One federal state (Brandenburg)—representative sample |
| 2000 | Study of Mathematics in Rhineland-Palatinate: competencies and school and teaching environment (MARKUS) | Census of one federal state (Rhineland-Palatinate) |
| 2000 | Program for International Student Assessment (PISA) | Representative samples of all federal states for within-Germany comparisons of 15-year-olds |
| 2000 | Study of Education Basics in Grade 9 (LAU 9) | Census of one federal state (Hamburg)—third wave |
| 2002 | Competencies and Attitudes of Students in Grade 4 (KESS 4) | Census of one federal state (Hamburg)—follow-up study of LAU |
| 2002 | Study of Education Basics in Grade 11 (LAU 11) | Census of one federal state (Hamburg)—fourth wave |
| 2003 | German–English Student Assessment (DESI) | Extension of German PISA study (Grade 9) |

After publication of the results of TIMSS, which showed that German students had performed below expected levels, Germany discussed what was termed the "TIMSS-shock". The TIMSS results should not have been so surprising, however, given that the FISS and RLS results had previously shown German students from across different grades and competencies performing below expectation. With the results of these studies in mind, the German Ministry of Education decided to participate in the Program for International Student Assessment (PISA), conducted by the Organization for Economic Co-Operation and Development (OECD). A consortium, led by Jürgen Baumert, extended the basic design of the study to include a test of additional competencies. More importantly, the consortium also extended the sampling frame to allow comparisons of student achievement across all federal states and the different school types.

In Germany, the names of Rainer Lehmann and Jürgen Baumert are synonymous with the transition to participation in large-scale comparative surveys of educational achievement. Today, this form of empirical research is established in educational institutes and universities and is well on the way to becoming accepted by those researchers who formerly rejected it. However, a 20-year lack of empirical research cannot be remedied quickly, which helps explain why Germany decided to embed its participation in international large-scale surveys within nationally prepared studies, and why it has extended its instruments in all studies since RLS (1991) to collect data specific to Germany's education system. Although the instruments of the international large-scale surveys are well prepared, they can cover only the core interests of the participating countries.

Germany's desire to obtain more in-depth specific information about the performance of the country's education system also explains why Germany conducted national assessments with a qualitative focus. An example of these decisions in operation is that of PIRLS. Germany embedded its participation in this study within its national IGLU study, which focused on the reading ability of fourth graders, as well as on their performance in writing, mathematics, science, and some basic cognitive abilities. Germany also substantially expanded all PIRLS background questionnaires for the purposes of IGLU, a modification that required a second testing day to ensure sufficient time to test the students and gather additional information without overburdening them.

### 6.3.2   Funding of Studies and Freedom of Expression

Funding for Germany's participation in large-scale surveys is covered primarily by the federal Ministry of Education and Research (*Bundesministerium für Bildung und Forschung*), the leading group of educational ministers of the federal states (*Kultusministerkonferenz*), and the German Research Council (*Deutsche Forschungsgemeinschaft*). Although these agencies supply funding, they have no control over the direction and nature of the research. Similarly, the German Research Council has no jurisdiction over the content of the published reports of the research that it funds. However, publications produced under the name of the ministries are read by and modified (generally to a limited degree only) by personnel within those agencies. Research-based publications produced in universities are not subject to political oversight, given that university professors in Germany are entitled to conduct their research and teaching free of political interference. This freedom was granted as a reaction to the Nazi regime in Germany, which exploited universities in order to advance Nazi ideology.

### 6.3.3   Reporting of Survey Results

For Germany, until relatively recently, a significant issue relating to dissemination of the results of the studies of educational achievement concerned the aforementioned resistance within Germany's educational community (from the members of Germany's strong teacher union, in particular) to these studies. This resistance was not surprising, given that the results of the first large-scale surveys in which Germany participated were addressed primarily to the research community and in a form that teachers and educational administrators could not easily understand. Even with the more recently conducted studies of educational achievement, schoolteachers have experienced difficulty reading and interpreting the results because of lack of knowledge of research methodology and statistical reporting. These concerns led to efforts to publish the results of TIMSS more widely, but all this achieved was journalists "interpreting" and publicizing the results in terms of teachers "not doing a good job". Also, for most teachers and principals, the results, as presented for both TIMSS and other studies, have been too general to allow them to see any relationship to their particular classrooms and the work they do within them.

Over the last few years, there has been increased effort to overcome these difficulties, by presenting the results in a more basic and reader-friendly format for teachers, and by presenting the results for individual schools and classes. Teachers and principals who participate in surveys also now receive individual feedback and are offered training and assistance in interpreting the results and remedying deficient pedagogical practices. These measures have been building a useful spirit of trust between those who perform the studies and those to whom the results are presented. In short, resistance to participation in the studies is gradually declining.

Professional curiosity and concern over what the studies have revealed about the performance of German students is also helping break down barriers. PISA, for example, showed that almost one quarter of German students risk leaving school without functional literacy. In general, however, one of the main reasons for the growing acceptance of Germany's participation in large-scale surveys is that the researchers who conduct them now set great store in presenting the results in formats appropriate for teachers and in developing a "feedback culture". Such a culture allows practitioners to see feedback not as a threat but as a means of enhancing their practice and, in turn, ensuring sound educational outcomes for their students.

Today, the strategy behind publication of survey results rests on using publication formats appropriate to the different communities (research, educational, news media) likely to be interested in the results. News media journalists, for example, are invited to attend press conferences, given press kits, and encouraged to question the researchers. These developments have seen journalists presenting more informed and accurate interpretations of the results in the media.

One important reason for Germany's engagement in the surveys is, of course, to provide information that can be directly used to enhance school development. Such information complements insights gained from other evaluations (both internal and external) of the school system. Internal evaluations, conducted by teachers and "guest critics" from related schools, allow individual schools to assess the efficacy of their teaching practice. External evaluations, conducted by agencies outside the school, involve administration of quasi-normative tests that generate information which allows comparisons across schools and classes.

More specifically, these evaluations provide schools and teachers with information about the average achievement of students in their class, and in relation to the achievement of students in similar classes and/or across the school system. Care is taken to present this information as simply as possible and only to present comparative data for which statistically significant differences were observed. These practices help limit the likelihood of teachers, especially those who have little or no experience of empirical studies, of paying undue heed to differences that are close to but not statistically significant.

## 6.4    National Results and Impact of PIRLS 2001

### 6.4.1    Results of PIRLS 2001

German students' average achievement score on the PIRLS literacy scale was 539, significantly above the international average. Only Swedish, Dutch, English, and Bulgarian students outperformed the German students. The mean difference between boys and girls in reading was 13 points, significantly smaller than the international average difference of 20 score points. The difference between German students' average achievement scores on the literary and informational reading subscales was only two points, and so not significant. However, girls significantly outperformed the boys on each subscale (a difference of 14 score points on literary and 10 score points on informational), although the difference was less evident in relation to informational texts.

The PISA results, published some time before the PIRLS results, showed the achievement of the 15-year-old German students who participated in the study to be significantly below the international average. This outcome shocked educational administrators and everyone involved in secondary education and influenced expectations of Grade 4 German students' performance on PIRLS. There were two sets of expectation. The first, held primarily by people in the secondary school system, was that the primary school students' performance would be below average, which would mean that blame for deficiencies within the secondary schools could reside with the primary schools. The second expectation was that all would be well in the primary schools, not only because primary education is compulsory but also because its pedagogical practice is not constrained by the need for students to work towards attainment of formal qualifications (the secondary school certificates). After publication of the PIRLS 2001 results, educational stakeholders decided to look more closely at Germany's education system in relation to some of the other countries that had participated in PIRLS and in PISA.

One research emphasis involved a comparative analysis of the education systems of some of the countries that had participated in PIRLS. The study was based on the notion that comparing Germany's education system with the systems of countries with similar social and migration structures and whose students had achieved better than German students on PIRLS would help Germany identify where its school system and daily teaching practice might benefit from improvement. Comparisons were consequently conducted with Sweden, the Netherlands, and (to a lesser extent) England. While England is, from Germany's perspective, a valuable point of comparison in terms of its use of system-monitoring, the education systems of the two countries differ quite substantially, especially in how they finance their schools. The researchers therefore knew they needed to draw their conclusions from this comparative analysis with caution.

For many people in Germany, one of the most disturbing findings in relation to the results of PISA and PIRLS was that students in primary school seemed to be performing (relatively speaking) much better than their older counterparts. Effort to understand why provided the rationale for the second study. Here, as another research emphasis, the researchers compared German students' performance on PIRLS and PISA with the performance of students in the other countries that had participated in both studies. Fourteen countries were available for this comparison. The comparison could only be qualitative in nature given the lack of commonality between the achievement scales of PIRLS and PISA and between the samples of participating students. Nevertheless, the information obtained was most informative, especially in identifying a group of countries from among the 14 that performed well below Germany in PIRLS but well above in PISA. The question that consequently arose was whether improvement over time in these countries was a "natural" acceleration, or whether it related to significant differences between the primary and secondary sectors of their education systems. At present, answers to this question rely on conducting further qualitative research, which should be possible later in

2006 when, with some limitations, some portions of the PIRLS 2001 populations will be tested in PISA.

### 6.4.2   Publication of the PIRLS Results

Since the release of the international results in spring 2001 in Germany, three books have been published. One (Bos, Lankes, Prenzel, Schwippert, Walther, & Valtin, 2003) gives descriptive results for the representative sample from the German PIRLS population. The second (Bos, Lankes, Prenzel, Schwippert, Valtin, & Walther, 2004) offers an in-depth analysis of the results for extended samples from seven federal states. The third contains in-depth analysis of reading ability, an examination of determining factors, and documentation of further supplemental studies (Bos, Lankes, Prenzel, Schwippert, Valtin, & Walther, 2005). Press conferences held on the days the first two books were released saw German television news reporting the results and many articles published in the press. *Die Zeit*, one of the most respected German weeklies, published a special report on the German PIRLS results over several pages in April 2001. The main findings of the study were summarized on the study's website on the same days as the press conferences. The site also provided example items from the students' tests. Interested people were able to work through some of the questions to test if they could answer them correctly.

More than 60 articles, generally directed at teachers, have been written in educational research and administrative journals since the release of the results. Numerous presentations have also been made. Interested groups have been federal state divisions of the teacher union, industrial associations, and the different political parties. Most of their discussions have focused on the results and their implications for future educational policy and practice. In contrast to the criticism and concern voiced after publication and presentation of the results of the large-scale studies of the mid-1990s, the only criticism evident in relation to publication of the PIRLS concerned the study's design and implementation, and even that was minimal.

### 6.4.3   Impact of PIRLS 2001

PISA attracted considerably more interest than PIRLS in Germany, not only because the PISA results came out before the PIRLS results but also because the PISA results were unexpected. For educational stakeholders and the public, the basic message arising out of the PIRLS results was that "primary schools are doing a good job", while for the media, it was a case of "good news is no news".

After the release of the PISA results, the German KMK decided to spend €B4.0 on enhancing Germany's school system. Several of the seven main foci of the enhancement program centered on the primary school, even though PISA had not addressed this sector of the education system. The decision to effect improvements in the primary schools therefore rested not on empirical evidence but on the assumption that the poor performance of 15-year-olds in PIRLS was in part due to sub-optimal primary schooling. Even publication of the PIRLS results did not alter this stance.

The changes that do seem indicated by the PISA and PIRLS results have to date been addressed in a very rudimentary way. It seems that the long-held traditions of the education system, especially at the secondary level, are continuing to stymie efforts to implement the reforms truly needed. This difficulty is enhanced by the fact that not just one but 16 education systems need to be changed. In addition, party-specific policies are likely to have more effect on the direction of reforms than is empirical evidence about what is needed.

Despite this pessimistic outlook, there is room for optimism. The results of PIRLS and PISA have at least advanced discussion of the issues and encouraged new analyses designed to gain a clearer picture of what is going on in schools, such as the comparative studies noted above. At the primary level, consideration is being given to whole-day schooling and to the implementation of compulsory kindergarten/pre-school education. Some federal states are seriously questioning the advisability of retaining the tracking system, although the higher performing states tend to interpret their good results as confirmation of this system. However, both opponents and advocates of tracking agree that directing students into the different streams at the end of Grade 4 is too early. There also seems to be widespread acceptance of the need to make it easier to redirect students to the other tracks when it becomes obvious, at some stage of their secondary education, that their original placement is wrong. This consideration has also led to debate about the current practice of holding back less able students by not advancing them into the next grade.

As mentioned earlier, Germany's strong teacher union supported for many years those who resisted empirical evaluations of the education system. The reason behind this resistance relates to *Bildung*, a concept not easily explained in English. It is an ideal arising out of Germany's cultural history, and it relates to achievement and knowledge within Germany's cultural and social contexts. However, since the end of the 1990s, the union has changed its position on this matter and has begun to support Germany's participation in large-scale national and international surveys. Suspicions remain in some federal state branches of the union, but even here, opinion is moving towards acceptance of change. Increasingly, too, the relationship between educational researchers and members of the teacher union has been more co-operative and constructive, with branches of the union inviting researchers to explain the results and to discuss their implications. This improvement has been particularly marked since the first presentations of the PIRLS results.

### Impact on School Administration

Since the release of the PISA and PIRLS results, educational standards have been implemented in the school system, recognition has been given to the necessity for greater mobility between the secondary school tracks, and the appropriateness of tracking students at the end of Grade 4 has been the subject of ongoing discussion. Evidence of a substantial number of students (in both the primary and secondary schools) being unable to read at age-appropriate levels has prompted consideration of changing school reading programs and syllabi. One of the most important impacts for school administration, however, is acceptance of the need for ongoing evaluation studies. Certainly, there seems to be no desire to return to the no-evaluation-at-all days of the 1970s and 1980s.

### Long-term Effects

It is uncertain whether the above topics will remain under consideration. Much rests on political will. Concern is heightened by the fact that little was done to remedy the disquiet about Germany's education system that surfaced following Germany's participation in IEA's First International Science (FISS) and Reading Literacy (RLS) studies in the early 1970s and 1990s. Also, although the results of TIMSS and PISA generated serious concern, educational researchers and the public and politicians have yet to reach consensus on what needs remedying and how to effect remedies.

Educational researchers, for example, consider several issues to be particularly important. First, they contend that because learning is cumulative over time, research conducted at the end of primary schools is too late to provide appropriate information about the development of young learners. Consequently, more research is needed at the pre-primary (kindergarten) level. Researchers also consider that the evidence from PIRLS and PISA of too many students performing below expectation and too few performing at the top level indicates a need, in both primary and secondary schools, for special programs for the children performing at these extremes.

A second concern relates to Germany's immigrant populations. During the late 1960s, a booming German economy saw a need for additional labor. Germany consequently invited workers from other countries to work for a few years in Germany before returning to their families in their home countries. However, many of these guest-workers (*Gastarbeiter*) stayed on in Germany and managed to get their families into Germany. Because these workers were seen as temporary residents, little effort was made to integrate them into German society, and this situation was paralleled in the schools, where few, if any, programs existed for several years to integrate migrant children. The whole situation has been exacerbated in recent decades, with many people who were been born in Russia deciding to come to Germany because of having parents or grandparents of German citizenship. Many of these people, known as *Spätaussiedler* (late-resettler), speak little or no German. The PIRLS data showed that one in every five of the German students participating in the study was from a family where at least one parent was not born in Germany. These are often the students whose achievement in schools is poor. As such, researchers have argued the need for remedial programs for such children.

A third area of concern relates to afternoon courses and afternoon child care. Among the many arguments that researchers put forward for these provisions is that children from families from lower socio-economic backgrounds and whose parents have limited formal education gain from professional supervision in an environment that demands more of them cognitively than does an environment where they sit in front of the television or play computer games. In related vein, researchers contend that the PIRLS and PISA results provide a strong rationale for conducting more research specifically related to how students' social and migration backgrounds influence their educational achievement.

Comparisons between teacher-graded student achievement and the large-scale assessments of achievement detected some significant differences in the judgment of students' performance. According to researchers, this fact emphasizes the need for in-depth analysis of teacher training methodology and teachers' diagnostic skills. Finally, to mention but one more of the current topics of interest arising out of the large-scale surveys, researchers argue the need for close observation of professional usage of computers in schools and lessons. PIRLS showed that while computers are widely available in German primary schools, teachers seldom use them in their classroom lessons. The reason why is assumed to be because teachers themselves lack experience in using computers. Researchers consider this lack of use of modern communication technology in schools unacceptable in today's information age and maintain that ways must be found to encourage teachers to discover the value of computers for their work and their students' futures.

## 6.5 Future Activities

The results of PIRLS 2001 have provided researchers, politicians, teachers, and the public with the impetus to think further and widely about the future of primary schooling in Germany. An account of how PIRLS 2001 has influenced planning for Germany's participation in PIRLS 2006 follows. Unfortunately, budgetary constraints mean that some of the mentioned ideas put forward for PIRLS 2006 will not be realized. However, because many educational stakeholders see these ideas as important, they and the ideas that will go forward are noted here.

### 6.5.1  Research

The realized sampling in PIRLS 2001 allowed comparison of only seven of the 16 federal states in Germany. However, publication of the findings of this comparison (Bos et al., 2004) produced sufficient interesting detail to persuade the education ministries of the 16 states to extend their samples in PIRLS 2006 so allowing a comparison of the achievement of students across all the states. Among the hoped-for research initiatives associated with PIRLS 2006 is a longitudinal study of achievement across Grades 3 and 4, videoed observations of pedagogical practice in the classroom studies, with a particular focus on teachers' diagnostic skills, and an investigation into the benefits or otherwise of children learning foreign languages in primary schools.

### 6.5.2  Publications

The fourth and last monograph of the German PIRLS 2001 cycle is planned for late summer 2006. It will present further in-depth analyses and discussion of the PIRLS data in relation to the following student factors: transition from primary to secondary school; gender; and migrant and socio-economic backgrounds. Plans are also afoot to publish not only analyses relating to the extended PIRLS 2001 study (mathematics and science literacy) but also findings from the additional study about the process of learning writing.

### 6.5.3  Programs

One consequence of Germany's abstinence from international large-scale surveys during the 1970s and 1980s was that tuition in research methodology was not part of teacher education programs. Because teachers could not "read" research reports, they became dependent on journalists' interpretations of the findings of the surveys of educational achievement. In 2003, the University of Bielefeld became the first institution in Germany to provide pre-service teachers with systematic training in research methodology. One reason for this decision was to ensure that teachers could read primary sources.

Within Germany, lack of competency among education faculty staff in empirical research methodology has led to a requirement that new chairs of educational faculties must have skills in research methodology. A spread of these skills to all staff in these faculties will increasingly allow useful participation in national and international large-scale surveys.

## 6.6   Concluding Remarks

For Germany, PIRLS 2001 was a success. This study not only received wide acceptance from researchers, politicians, and school staff, but also shed a different light on some findings of previously published studies like TIMSS and PISA. Germany did not participate in the Population 1 study of TIMSS, and this situation contributed to the lack of information about student achievement in primary schools becoming very obvious by the millennium. This led, in turn, to the ministries of the German federal states agreeing to finance the extension of PIRLS 2001 to include mathematics and science tests.

Prior to publication of the PIRLS 2001 results, one main reason that prominent educational stakeholders gave for the unexpected weak performance of German secondary schools students in TIMSS-II, TIMSS-III and PISA 2000 was that the primary schools were not adequately educating students for the requirements of secondary schooling. After the PIRLS 2001 press conference, these people had to revise that opinion. A more accurate explanation now seems to be that it is the secondary schools and not the primary schools that are deficient. Germany's participation in PIRLS has confirmed the need to direct effort towards addressing the weaknesses of the German education system. It has also, in line with the future plans mentioned above, revealed other areas for research in relation to and beyond primary education. PIRLS 2001 thus appears to have served as a starting point for a new and improved era of quantitative educational research in Germany.

**References**

Avenarius, H., Ditton, H., Döbert, H., Klemm, K., Klieme, E., Rürup, M., Tenorth, H.-E., Weishaupt, H., & Weiß, M. (2003). *Bildungsbericht für Deutschland [Educational report for Germany].* Opladen: Leske+Budrich.

Bos, W., Lankes, E.-M., Prenzel, M., Schwippert, K., Walther, G., & Valtin, R. (Eds.). (2003). *Erste Ergebnisse aus IGLU: Schülerleistungen am Ende der vierten Jahrgangsstufe im internationalen Vergleich [First results of PIRLS Germany: Student achievement at the end of grade four in international comparison].* Münster: Waxmann.

Bos, W., Lankes, E.-M., Prenzel, M., Schwippert, K., Valtin, R., & Walther, G. (Eds.). (2004). *IGLU: Einige Länder der Bundesrepublik Deutschland im nationalen und internationalen Vergleich [PIRLS Germany: A number of states of the Federal Republic of Germany in national and international comparison].* Münster: Waxmann.

Bos, W., Lankes, E.-M., Prenzel, M., Schwippert, K., Valtin, R., & Walther, G. (Eds.). (2005). *IGLU: Vertiefende Analysen zu Leseverständnis, Rahmenbedingungen und Zusatzstudien [PIRLS Germany: In depth analysis of reading ability, determining factors and further supplemental studies].* Münster: Waxmann.

Bundesministerium für Bildung und Forschung. (2004). *Grund-und Strukturdaten 2003/2004 [Basic and structural data 2003/2004].* Retrieved August 28, 2005, from http://www.bmbf.de/pub/GuS2004_ges_dt.pdf

Helmke, A., & Jäger, R. S. (2002). *Das Projekt MARKUS – Mathematik-Gesamterhebung Rheinland-Pfalz: Kompetenzen, Unterrichtsmerkmale, Schulkontext [The MARKUS project—mathematics survey in the German federal state Rheinland-Pfalz: Competencies, features of instruction, school context].* Landau: Verlag Empirische Pädagogik.

Lankes, E.-M., Bos, W., & Valtin, R. (2002). Germany. In I. V. S. Mullis, M. O. Martin, A. M. Kennedy, & C. L. Flaherty (Eds.), *PIRLS 2001 encyclopedia: A reference guide to reading education in the countries participating in IEA's Progress in International Reading Literacy Study (PIRLS)* (pp. 79–87). Chestnut Hill, MA: Boston College.

Lehmann, R. H., Peek, R., & Gänsfuß, R. (1997). *Aspekte der Lernausgangslage von Schülerinnen und Schülern der fünften Klassen an Hamburger Schulen [Aspects of educational starting positions of fifth grade students in Hamburg].* Hamburg: Behörde für Schule, Jugend und Berufsbildung, Amt für Schule.

Lehmann, R. H., Peek, R., Gänsfuß, R., Lukat, S., Mücke, S., & Barth, I. (2000). *QUASUM: Qualitätsuntersuchung an Schulen zum Unterricht in Mathematik. Ergebnisse einer repräsentativen Untersuchung im Land Brandenburg [QUASUM: Quality assurance in mathematics lessons. Results of a representative sample of schools in Brandenburg].* Potsdam: Ministerium für Bildung, Jugend und Sport des Landes Brandenburg.

# Chapter 7
# The Impact of PIRLS in Hong Kong, SAR

*Shek Kam Tse and Elizabeth Ka Yee Loh*

## 7.1  Hong Kong at a Glance[1]

The Hong Kong Special Administrative Region (HKSAR), with its superb natural harbor on China's southern coast, is one of the world's major commercial capitals. The total area of the HKSAR is 1,098 square kilometers.

According to the 2001 census, Hong Kong has a population of nearly 6.8 million. Ninety-five percent of its residents are of Chinese descent, and the remainder comes from various countries, including the Philippines, Indonesia, and the United States. Filipinos comprise the largest ethnic sub-group with more than 140,000 people. Hong Kong has a high degree of religious freedom. Although Buddhism and Taoism are the most widely practiced faiths, Confucianism, Christianity, Islam, Hinduism, Sikhism, and Judaism are also practiced.

Hong Kong has three major territorial districts: Hong Kong Island, the Kowloon Peninsula, and the New Territories. Hong Kong's generally hilly landscape has pockets of high-density housing; the overall population density is 6,320 persons per square kilometer. Some 49.2% of the population resides in suburban areas in the New Territories, 20.2% on Hong Kong Island, and 30.5% on the Kowloon Peninsula.

Over the past two decades, the Hong Kong economy has almost tripled in size, with GDP growing at an average annual rate of 5.4% in real terms. Per capita GDP in Hong Kong has more than doubled, making it equivalent to an average annual growth rate of 3.9% in real terms. In 2000, it reached US$24,000 at current market prices, amongst the highest in Asia, and second only to that of Japan.

Public expenditure on education has risen at a constant rate of 4.1% since 1998. In 2000/01, the total expenditure on education in Hong Kong was HK$M54,383, accounting for 18.9% of the total public expenditure and 4.1% of the GDP, respectively. Of the recurrent expenditure on education, secondary education absorbed the highest proportion (32.9%), closely followed by tertiary education (32.3%). The primary education sector accounted for 21.7%, and all other categories accounted for 13.1%.

---

1  This introduction is based on Hong Kong's country profile in the *PIRLS 2001 Encyclopedia* (Tse, 2002).

## 7.2 Hong Kong's Education System as Context for PIRLS 2001

The Hong Kong SAR Government provides nine years of free compulsory education for all children between the ages of six and 15 years. Students in Grades 1 to 9 receive basic education, with 10 months of schooling in each academic year, normally between September and mid-July. Each school year consists of about 200 school days, excluding public holidays (The Government of Hong Kong SAR, 2001). Admission both to aided and government schools is through a centralized system, established to reduce the pressure on children associated with the intense competition for admission to popular schools. To bring more diversity into the school system and give parents more choice, the Government authorized in 1999 the development of Direct Subsidy Scheme schools and non-profit-making private independent schools (The Government of Hong Kong SAR, 2003).

After the normal school day, many parents in Hong Kong send their children for additional private tuition; 42% of Grade 4 students receive these extra lessons. The children are usually asked to complete homework, do extra lesson-based exercises, review texts encountered in class, or prepare for dictation exercises and examinations (Tse, Lam, Lam, & Loh, 2005). Many children also attend interest classes, for example, piano or violin lessons, drawing, dancing, and so on, organized by the child's own primary school, voluntary organizations, or the private sector.

Primary schools are either privately owned or public (The Government of Hong Kong SAR, 2003). After primary education, students in schools participating in the Government's Secondary School Places Allocation System are provided with free secondary school places. Allocation is based on parental choice and internal school assessments. The Government provides free and universal schooling for every child from Grades 7 to 9 and subsidizes schooling from Grades 10 to 12.

### 7.2.1  Literacy, the Reading Curriculum, and Assessment

The Hong Kong SAR Government takes very seriously the aim of having all children able to read confidently for learning and for pleasure. There are two official languages in Hong Kong, Chinese and English, and one of the major goals of education is for all students to acquire the ability to read independently in both languages. Lower primary school students are expected to master basic skills of reading and writing and to develop an interest in and a habit of reading. Upper primary school students are expected to be able to apply their reading and writing skills with fluency, to be able to communicate effectively both orally and in writing, and to be able to use their reading as a tool for learning (Curriculum Development Council, 2000). The promotion of a reading culture among school-age children has been identified as a key means of encouraging lifelong learning (Curriculum Development Institute, 2002).

### 7.2.2 The Reading Curriculum and Standards

The Curriculum Development Council (CDC) laid down clear reading goals for schools in 2000. The whole school is expected to be involved in the promotion of reading and to build up a reading culture in school and at home. Language teachers are expected to focus specifically on the teaching of reading strategies and skills (Curriculum Development Council, 2000).

Schools are allowed to adjust the curriculum and timetable in order to cater for the literacy needs of the students in particular schools. Teachers are encouraged to introduce strategies to motivate students to read with understanding in and after school. The effective use of reading schemes, reading programs, and so on will hopefully help sustain students' interest and effort in reading. At the same time, the availability of quality reading materials in the school library and public libraries is crucial for instilling within students the ability to read with enjoyment both in school and at home (Curriculum Development Council, 2000).

### 7.2.3 Resources for the Teaching of Reading

Before the 2000 Education Reform Act, the focus of teaching reading was on the mastery of prescribed texts. Wong (1984) noted that students focused on textbook exercises so extensively that they had no time to practice and use their language in the classroom. About six to seven lessons per week were assigned for Chinese language teaching, with teachers using most of this time explaining the text, providing background information about the author, and reviewing vocabulary, paragraph themes, and the use of rhetoric (Cheung, 1992). The CDC had already recognized this imbalance, and in 2000 it suggested that teachers expand the range of teaching materials used in lessons to include web-based, audio, and visual materials, as well as a wide range of printed matter. To encourage learning and good reading habits among primary school students, the Government provided, in a series of phased steps, class libraries and a central library in each primary school. A teacher-librarian was assigned to manage the school central library and to organize library activities for students (Education Department, 1997).

### 7.2.4 Literacy Programs

The government had cautiously tried a number of initiatives over the years to improve students' literacy standards. The Extensive Reading Scheme was developed and aimed at improving the reading habits, skills, and techniques of students (Education Commission, 1996). The scheme has been implemented in schools over the past two decades with varying degrees of success.

### 7.2.5   Curriculum Reform and the Monitoring of Standards

Curriculum reform is at the heart of educational development in Hong Kong. One of the major objectives of this reform is to develop within students positive values and attitudes towards learning, enabling them to establish a solid foundation for lifelong learning and whole-person development (The Government of Hong Kong SAR, 2003). The government has also urged teachers to go beyond teaching their own subject to include teaching literacy and numeracy skills to every student. In effect, all teachers are to consider themselves teachers of literacy and numeracy. To widen the focus away from teaching subjects per se, schools have been asked to focus on the basic academic competency of each student. The Basic Competency Assessment (BCA) has been introduced at key stages of learning for Chinese, English, and mathematics. The BCA aims to help teachers better monitor their students' learning needs and areas requiring improvement so that timely assistance can be provided. The Territory (System) Assessment provides the Government and school management with useful information on students' standards at the levels of Grades 3, 6, and 9 on a territory-wide and individual school basis (The Government of Hong Kong SAR, 2003).

The Government has invested heavily in education in order to enhance the competitiveness of Hong Kong students. Education reform has targeted the establishment of a curriculum that meets the needs of a knowledge-based and global economy.

## 7.3   Experience in Large-scale Assessments

Hong Kong has been involved in several large-scale international (IEA or OECD) assessments of educational achievement in mathematics and science (TIMSS and PISA), reading literacy (PIRLS and PISA), information technology in education (SITES), and civic education (CivEd). Hong Kong first participated in a comparative study of reading standards through the International Reading Literacy Study (RLS) in 1991 (see Table 7.1).

Because the University of Hong Kong is the regional centre of the IEA, experts in the University have been responsible for conducting all the studies mentioned above, except for PISA, which was organized by the OECD and conducted by staff in a neighboring university.

The Government has found the results of the large-scale international assessments very useful, especially in providing a baseline for assessing the learning progress of students and permitting comparisons of the performance of students in Hong Kong against that of counterparts in other countries. In addition to supporting the above studies financially and administratively, the Government has carried out its own large-scale annual assessments, for example, the Basic Academic Competency (BAC) tests conducted in Grades 3, 6, and 9. The results of these assessments are fed back as data to participating schools and individual teachers to inform curriculum reviews, teaching materials, and methods.

**Table 7.1:  Hong Kong's participation in international large-scale surveys of educational achievement, 1993–2003**

| Year of data collection | Name of survey | Organization in charge | Target population |
|---|---|---|---|
| 1993 | The Language Education Study | IEA | Age 9 (Grade 4) |
| 1994 | Civic Education Study (CivEd) | IEA | Age 14 (Grade 9) |
| 1995 | Third International Mathematics and Science Study (TIMSS) | IEA | Thirteen-year-old students (Grades 7 and 8) and three different samples in the final grade of the secondary school |
| 1997 | Second Information Technology in Education Study Module 1 (SITES-M1) | IEA | Age 8 (Grade 3), age 14 (Grade 9), and age 17 (Grade 12) |
| 1997 | Third International Mathematics and Science Study Repeat Video Project (TIMSS-R Video) | IEA | Age 14 (Grade 8) |
| 1999 | Fourth International Mathematics and Science Study (TIMSS) | IEA | Age 9 (Grade 4) and age 14 (Grade 9) |
| 1999 | Second Information Technology in Education Study Module 2 (SITES-M2) | IEA | Age 8 (Grade 3), age 14 (Grade 9), and age 17 (Grade 12) |
| 2000 | Trends in Mathematics and Science Study 2003 (TIMSS 2003) | IEA | Age 9 (Grade 4) and age 14 (Grade 9) |
| 2000 | Program for International Student Assessment (PISA) | OECD | Fifteen-year-old students in school |
| 2001 | Progress in International Reading Literacy Study (PIRLS) | IEA | Age 9 (Grade 4) |
| 2003 | Fifth International Mathematics and Science Study (TIMSS) | IEA | Age 9 (Grade 4) and age 14 (Grade 9) |
| 2003 | Program for International Student Assessment (PISA) | OECD | Fifteen-year-old students in school |

## 7.4    National Results and Impact of PIRLS 2001

### 7.4.1    Results of PIRLS 2001

Although Hong Kong students perform admirably in science and mathematics (TIMSS), being ranked among the first three countries worldwide, their reading (PIRLS) scores are less impressive and place them at a rank below their rankings for numeracy and science. The overall mean reading score for Hong Kong students on PIRLS tests was 528, significantly higher than the standardized international average score of 500. Students from Scotland, Singapore, and Russia also performed at this level, sharing with Hong Kong the same rank of 14th out of the 35 participating countries and regions. In terms of the subsections of the reading test, Hong Kong students' processing of informational texts gained a mean score of 537, earning them the rank of 10th out of 35. In terms of processing literary texts, they fared less well, gaining a mean score of 518 and a rank of 20th out of 35 (Tse, Lam, Lam, Loh, & Westwood, in press). Eighty per cent of Hong Kong students achieved mastery level scores in terms of being able to "focus on and retrieve explicitly stated information", and 67% had mastered the ability to "make straightforward inferences". Their reading performance was average in terms of being able to "examine and evaluate content, language, and textual elements", with 50% achieving mastery grades. Performance was below average on the ability to "interpret and integrate ideas and information", with only 40% gaining mastery level scores (Tse et al., 2005).

As was the case in other participating countries, girls in Hong Kong outperformed boys on every reading test. Whereas the overall reading performance scores for girls on reading for literary and informational purposes was 546 and 529 respectively, the mean scores for boys was 538 and 519 (Tse et al., 2005). Rather disappointingly, only 6% of Hong Kong students achieved the "top 10%" benchmark, as against the international average of 10%.

In terms of reading behavior, few students could be said to read habitually or to have an abiding interest in reading for enjoyment. Most students dwell in homes where a home reading environment is not well established. They seldom go to the library or read books outside school. Compared to students at the same age in other PIRLS countries, Hong Kong students seem poorly motivated as readers, and their overall self-concept as readers is relatively low. These characteristics will certainly have had a negative impact on their reading performance (Tse et al., 2005).

Many parents who answered PIRLS survey questionnaires felt that their children had too much homework, leaving them little time to read books for leisure. Parents felt that it was difficult in these circumstances for them to invest much time in enhancing their children's reading competence. Paradoxically, teachers too complained that the children's school timetable allowed insufficient time for them to teach reading for learning and for pleasure. They regarded teaching materials and assessment methods as inadequate, and few considered that they had received appropriate professional training on the teaching of reading. They felt that principals and parents expected them to use textbooks as major teaching materials of reading and admitted that they should use novels and children's readers in class more. They added that school management and parents frowned upon the idea of giving students time to read silently in class, regarding this as a waste of time. "Reading" is not taught as a subject. Students rarely read aloud in class, and encouraging reading across the curriculum is considered a vague, irrelevant concept (Tse et al., 2005).

### 7.4.2   Publication of the PIRLS Results

To sustain the impacts of PIRLS 2001 in the community, a book setting out the background, theories, research methods, results, and implications of the study has been published (Tse et al., 2005) and research articles have been submitted to journals (see, for example, Tse et al., in press). A special website has also been created to disseminate the findings of PIRLS 2001. The dissemination of the PIRLS results has also generated much valuable research data, and related articles are currently being prepared for research journals.

### 7.4.3   Impact of PIRLS 2001

*Long-term Effects*

As mentioned earlier, the findings of the IEA surveys produced a mixed response in Hong Kong. Although Hong Kong students' attainment in science and mathematics was very impressive, their performance on PIRLS (both the 1991 and 2001 studies) was less encouraging. The fact that Hong Kong students achieved above-average standards in terms of reading worldwide offers grounds for celebration, but the finding that students in 2001 were better at reading transactional, informational texts than they were at reading and appreciating literary passages is a concern. The findings have implications for the Government, schools, parents, and the general public, and for how reading is taught.

*Setting out the Implications for the Government*

The PIRLS findings are too important for a response to be left to schools alone. A concerted effort was called for, and it was considered prudent to turn first of all to the Government. PIRLS findings were reported to the Permanent Secretary, officers of the Education and Manpower Bureau (EMB), members of the Standing Committee on Language Education and Research, and members of the Reading Task Force. The research team reported the findings to these bodies and stressed the need to modify practices and policies in order to overcome the deficiencies apparent in the results. It was stressed that it was not simply a matter of asking schools to try harder with the existing syllabus. The whole approach needed to take account of modern theories about the teaching of reading, and schools and curriculum designers needed to reconsider and revise existing practices.

The various government bodies welcomed the PIRLS findings and agreed that such large-scale international monitoring studies are important for identifying areas of performance where Hong Kong students might improve. The competitive nature of Hong Kong students would assist in helping them rise to the challenge, and the Hong Kong research team was encouraged to participate in future PIRLS studies.

The EMB recognized the importance of the "Read to Learn" initiative already in place and agreed that it should be given even greater prominence by emphasizing it as a central element of educational reform. A decision was taken to place more resources in primary schools to help promote the idea of using reading not simply as a tool for learning but also as a means of gaining pleasure and widening cultural horizons. The principal investigating officer in the Hong Kong PIRLS study was invited to be the consultant for a reading website developed by the Government. At the same time, the Curriculum Development Institute decided to include ability to use reading as a vehicle for learning and as a source of pleasure as a main teaching objective and "key learning area" of the Chinese language curriculum of secondary schools.

The PIRLS results were also reported in detail to officers in the Regional Education Office, a section of the EMB. The Office has responsibility for enhancing school development, working with school clusters and teacher networks at district level, disseminating good practice, helping schools implement policies, overseeing the quality of education in schools, and providing professional support. The research team also discussed the findings with researchers and officers of the Library Section of the Bureau.

It was stressed to the Government that parents need to be encouraged to play a more participatory role in teaching children to read, both for learning and for leisure. Such encouragement should commence well before the child enters the kindergarten/school system. In response, the Government plans to distribute a guidebook to parents of newborn babies that sets out the role of parents in fostering children's language skills, especially speaking and listening. The guidebook stresses that reading to children is a vital activity, and it provides outline information about the reading objectives and target levels of reading ability set in schools. The guidebook also tells parents how they can help children develop good reading habits and attitudes, how they can encourage children to read, and what they need to provide for a good home reading environment.

*Setting out the Implications for the General Public*

To capture the interest of the general public and make them aware of the issue of students' reading competence, the PIRLS results were brought to the attention of the wider community. Two press releases were issued, the first reporting the results for Hong Kong and the second setting the Hong Kong results against the wider international context. The first press release led to reports in local newspapers and on television and radio stations. Three newspapers ran special features, as did two radio stations. The second press release prompted reports in 11 Chinese and two English newspapers. Radio stations again reported the findings, and important newspapers presented editorials on the topic. There were also several interview reports in educational journals and magazines.

The findings startled the general public. Most people seemed to think that students' performance should have been better, particularly given their prowess in science and mathematics. Concern was voiced about whether the performance boded well for a society with ambitions to be a central player in the global economy. The press was keen to identify factors affecting students' reading ability and habits as well as their attitudes towards reading as a tool for gaining information, as a means of widening personal horizons, and as a leisure activity.

A key agenda item of a meeting of the Legislative Council was to discuss the PIRLS results. Concern was expressed about whether schools were succeeding in producing graduates able to cope in Hong Kong's tri-literate society. The public seemed to be awakening to the fact that society and parents should not leave the development of children's literacy exclusively in the hands of schools.

*Setting out the Implications for Schools and Teachers*

Schools and teachers awaited the PIRLS results with a degree of apprehension. Many teachers were aware of a mismatch between their usual classroom practice and the expectations of the official curriculum. They also knew that school management and parents expected teachers would daily employ "decoding" methods to the exclusion of more enlightened approaches. It was considered very important that government officers, school principals, teachers, librarians, and parents accept there was room for improvement in the reading performance of students. It was also thought vital that schools and parents accept the need to introduce modern approaches to teaching reading into schools.

The PIRLS research team organized more than 25 talks and workshops for primary schools. Almost 1,600 principals, teachers, and school librarians attended talks and workshops in which new concepts and theories of reading were explained. Reading process theory was clarified, and theoretical strategies for comprehending text were set out. Talks were given to persuade teachers that having students successfully decode words did not mean children were good readers or that they would use reading as a leisure activity. Nor did it imply that the children could understand what they had read or that they possessed the ability to use reading as a vehicle for learning.

The materials and resources habitually used by teachers also came in for criticism. Teachers were asked to expand the range of textual material used in class to include popular fiction, storybooks, and newspapers for children. Schools were encouraged to build up a reading environment and, if possible, to reserve the first lesson every day as a reading for pleasure lesson. In this lesson, students read daily newspapers, storybooks, or other reading materials of interest to them. Many primary schools set up reading corners in corridors and quiet areas of the school so that students could read for pleasure during leisure time.

Some primary schools examined the kinds of skills tested during the PIRLS monitoring investigation and sought to absorb the theoretical framework into the Chinese language curriculum. Reading comprehension tests were redesigned to reflect the PIRLS approach, and Chinese-language-school examinations were similarly modified. Students are now required to read informational texts and texts involving general literacy rather than focusing on transactional text exclusively. Now that the emphasis is on comprehension processes, teachers have been encouraged to modify the various reading assessment methods to include formative (ongoing) tests that help them monitor progress and diagnose reading weaknesses. New end-of-term and annual summative tests have also been introduced in line with the PIRLS approach.

Every school that participated in the PIRLS survey received an individual school report containing an analysis detailing the reading performance of their students, their reading attitudes and behavior, and characteristics of their home reading environments. It was hoped that schools would use this information to tailor programs for extending the reading strategies and power of their own students.

Although we might argue that the superior reading performance of girls over boys was an expected result, the view was there should be no complacency. There is a notorious link between teacher expectations and student performance, and schools have accordingly had to scrutinize practice, resources, and textbooks on an ongoing basis to see that no bias exists against boys. At the same time, parents have needed to be aware that boys may need extra assistance to ensure their literacy performance does not fall unduly behind.

*Setting out the Implications for Parents*

Chinese parents are strong in their conviction that education is very important for the life-chances of their children. They will vigorously seek entrance for their children to prestigious schools and pay for extra tuition should they consider this necessary. They will insist that their child completes homework meticulously and will complain to the school if their child is not making good progress. After the release of the PIRLS results, and with the knowledge that Hong Kong students perform well in mathematics and science, parents were anxious for an increase in their children's reading skills. Parents also knew that many experts were stressing reading as an essential factor and influence on students' overall academic achievement.

Parents were quite keen for their children to acquire those reading habits that in theory affect reading ability. However, few parents knew what they could do to help. Parents (and *their* parents) had been brought up with the attitude that their part of the parent–teacher unwritten contract is to ensure the child goes to school, completes homework on time, and works hard to revise for examinations. Passing examinations well is, in the eyes of parents, the chief purpose for going to school. Parents do not regard their children reading silently or for leisure as productive or purposeful. Thus, parents seldom buy books for children (other than textbooks) or encourage their children to use libraries. There are few books in the home for their children to read, and parents are loath to discuss with their children the books they are reading (Tse et al., in press). In short, very few homes are good reading environments. It did not seem to surprise parents that girls are more "bookish" than boys are. Nor did this seem to worry parents, since boys seem able to make up the deficit in secondary school.

Many schools sought assistance from the Faculty of Education in changing parental perceptions. The PIRLS research team collaborated with primary and secondary schools and organized more than 10 talks for parents. Over 4,500 parents attended workshops and talks in which they were shown how to set up a good home reading environment, how to develop children's reading ability, how to instill in children positive attitudes about the importance of reading, and how to ensure children acquire good reading habits.

*Promoting Reading Competence with the help of Non-Government Agencies*

Members of the PIRLS survey team were convinced that students' literacy weaknesses were not a recent phenomenon. Nor did they believe that the task of rectifying this deficiency should be left solely to schools and the EMB. The team was convinced that research was needed into the reading and writing process and that the results of this research should be communicated to an audience wider than that of the education sector. The team took their views to the EMB and voiced their concerns to various sections of the Government. They were convinced that a number of non-government organizations could be productively involved in researching how to improve standards of reading in the community and how to help students use reading both as a vehicle for learning and as a source of pleasure.

A number of research initiatives were launched in an effort to identify the most effective way of teaching and learning how to read in Hong Kong. Research into clarifying the processes in teaching and learning reading was conducted. "Developing Students' Independent Learning Capabilities in Secondary Chinese Language Curriculum", a collaboration project with the Curriculum Development Institute, the EMB, and four secondary schools, was organized with the aim of helping students master, monitor, and evaluate their own reading progress and strategies. Information about independent learning strategies was introduced and made known to teachers, parents, and the students themselves. Teachers used students' storybooks as the main teaching materials. Parents were asked to sign an agreement before their children were admitted to the project and also asked to provide a good reading and learning home environment for their children. For example, they were asked to make available a desk, a daily newspaper, possibly a computer, and a quiet environment for silent reading.

Another branch of the EMB the research team contacted was the Hong Kong Education City, a government-owned corporation. The corporation's main duties are to strengthen connections between educators, business and industrial organizations, and government and non-government organizations; to provide information about educational provision for the public; to develop a quality platform for web-based learning and living; and to promote reading habits in the community. Since 2003, the "promotion of reading habits in the community" has been a major objective of Hong Kong Education City. Joint projects with such organizations as Caritas Hong Kong and the Boys and Girls Club Association have been arranged, as have a series of reading activities for the public. These include the Hong Kong Reading City website, "Reading Summer 2003 and 2004", "Let's Read in the Morning— Thousand People's Campaign", "Reading Ambassadors Programme", "Reading Contract", and book festivals.

The principal investigator of the research team was invited to serve as consultant and to evaluate the effectiveness of the "Reading Ambassadors Programme" and the "Reading Contract". Two thousand "reading ambassadors" from 30 secondary schools (including students, teachers, and parents), 10,000 primary students from 70 primary schools, 100 students from two tertiary institutes, and 20 professionals, celebrities, community leaders, and members of non-government organizations and corporate companies participated in the program. Parents and tertiary and secondary school students were trained as reading ambassadors, and then read books and shared the fun of reading with targeted primary school students.

The thrust of these collaborations with non-government organizations was to educate parents about ways to help their children read, using channels quite unconnected with their children's schools. For example, over a thousand parents attended open workshops entitled "Home Reading Strategies", one of the activities of the "Reading Ambassadors Programme". Caritas Hong Kong invited the research team to report the PIRLS results to some 300 parents, teachers, and librarians in Caritas-sponsored kindergarten schools. Caritas Hong Kong also invited the principal investigator to be the consultant of a reading program organized by their Youth and Community Services section to train parents as "reading mothers" and "reading fathers". The aim was to help parents help teachers promote reading in schools and at home. The Boys and Girls Club Association also organized training courses for members of the public interested in promoting reading.

Such has been the interest that the principle investigator has collaborated with a special school for mentally retarded and autistic students organized by the Salvation Army in Hong Kong. This project uses modern methods to help these children learn Chinese characters with the aim of enhancing their reading ability.

### *Impact on Administrative and School Level*

The release of the PIRLS results reminded school principals and teachers alike that the ability to "learn to read" is one of the most important factors affecting students' academic performance, and this prompted great changes in some schools. Using as their reference the rationale and findings of PIRLS 2001, some schools have totally restructured their school-based reading curriculums. Within the schools, there is now an emphasis on teaching reading strategies and on a building up of the reading environment. Students are now encouraged to read more extra-curricular books, parents have been able to attend workshops on the teaching of reading and reading activities for children, and parent-volunteers have been recruited to organize shared-reading activities for students. The research team has spoken at more than 20 seminars organized by schools disseminating the PIRLS 2001 findings.

The concept of "reading to learn" is now one of the major objectives of educational reform in Hong Kong. The PIRLS 2001 findings confirmed that both "learning to read" and "reading to learn" are equally important elements in students' learning. The Government has therefore invested heavily in the teaching and learning of reading. Training courses have been organized for teachers and school librarians in order to publicize the latest reading theories, reading strategies, and classroom reading activities. Resources have been allocated to support reading schemes, and schools now have more funds to buy extra-curricular books for students.

## 7.5    Future Activities

### 7.5.1    Research

Along with the PIRLS findings, the results of a number of studies conducted in Hong Kong since PIRLS 2001 are proving very important for highlighting the strengths and weaknesses of practices in Hong Kong, and for driving future reading-based initiatives. One important study is "Bilingual Reading 2004", conducted during 2003 and 2004. The study's researchers adopted the framework and some research instruments of the PIRLS 2001 survey to investigate the bilingual reading (Chinese and English) ability of Grade 4 students in Hong Kong. This was the first time that the Chinese and English reading standards of Hong Kong students had been simultaneously assessed. The results indicate that only 8% of students in Hong Kong are good at both Chinese and English reading (scores on the tests of 500 or above). The findings of the study have also permitted comparisons with standards in English-speaking countries in the world.

Other examinations either conducted or underway encompass the English reading curricula, English reading teaching strategies, students' English reading habits, attitudes toward English reading, and the home English reading environment in countries where English is a first, second, or additional language.

Further research has been planned, and the research team will participate in PIRLS 2006 and conduct a study in 2006/07 to assess trends in the Chinese reading literacy of Grade 4 students. A follow-up study of Bilingual Reading 2004 will be conducted. We anticipate that the teaching and learning of reading in both languages will have improved.

### 7.5.2    Publications

A series of academic papers dealing with different aspects of teaching and learning of reading (both Chinese and English) is planned.

### 7.5.3    Teacher Training Programs

In order to change the professional training of pre-service and in-service teachers in Hong Kong, the implications of the PIRLS 2001 findings and the Bilingual Reading 2004 analyses have now been included in teacher training programs of the University of Hong Kong.

## 7.6   Concluding Remarks

Participation in the PIRLS exercise has been an experience that has yielded evidence of considerable value for Hong Kong. The findings present a comprehensive picture of the reading performance, habits, and attitudes of students in Hong Kong schools. They also highlight the interface between home and school factors and their influence on students' reading performance. We hope that the efficacy of the measures taken in response to PIRLS 2001 will be shown as successful when they are put to the test in the PIRLS 2006 study.

The PIRLS research findings have certainly had an impact in Hong Kong. For a start, the fact that the relative standing of students' reading is significantly below that of science and mathematics has prompted the Government to review its policies on reading instruction in schools. The emphasis is no longer simply on having every student learn how to read; rather, the accent has moved towards having every student learn how to use reading as a tool for independent learning and for leisure. This has prompted many schools to change their whole approach to the teaching of reading. The idea that a child who can "decode" what a word says will be able to use that word to an educational end has been seriously questioned. Furthermore, the idea that students who extensively practice reading comprehension strategies will be able to apply what they have learnt in any context has been vigorously challenged.

For students to acquire reading as a lifelong learning tool, teachers must start from where each child is at in mastering the complex skill of reading. It may be necessary for teachers to use student-based approaches on occasion, where students apply their reading in small-group and/or whole-class discussions, drama, and when seeking knowledge independently. Teachers of all subject disciplines in schools must accept responsibility by showing students how to read the kinds of text that typify the discipline in question.

Parents must accept the idea of individual students moving at their own pace in class. It is perfectly understandable for parents in Hong Kong to be examination oriented and to believe that the kinds of tedious drill they themselves experienced in their own school days still have a place in today's school world. As noted earlier, parents spend a lot of money paying tutors and buying books containing examination questions that help their children practice the reproduction of model answers. However, these parents must ask themselves whether they inadvertently caused the reading performance of the children taking PIRLS tests to suffer. It is not enough to demand that children work harder and, through their own efforts, master reading. The truth is that Hong Kong students' reading behavior is testimony to the fact that they consider reading a boring activity on the one hand, and an ability they do not always know how to deploy effectively on the other.

The interest shown by parents in the PIRLS findings is evidence of their desire to help their children do well at school. Many parents accept that it is their responsibility to create a good reading environment in the home and to encourage children to read for pleasure. However, very few parents feel that they possess the expertise to help their child use reading as a study aid for learning the various subjects of the curriculum. Quite understandably, they believe that such expertise resides in the schools to which they send their children. They also expect that teachers and schools will respond positively to the PIRLS evidence and that they will reshape practice in order to attend to the weaknesses identified.

This consideration draws attention to the forces that influence classroom practice in schools. In simple terms, the dilemma is whether schools should rely on tried and tested practices that have been demonstrated effective, such as science and mathematics. Alternatively, is there a case for the findings of carefully executed research that has exposed weaknesses to drive classroom practice? The compromise answer is that traditional methods of proven value should be used until we have at hand new approaches emanating from empirical and theoretical research.

It is vital that research of this standing should be communicated to all interested parties in appropriate ways. For this reason, the PIRLS research team has prepared separate publications for the public and for teachers and academics. In addition, materials handed out in PIRLS seminars have been posted on the "Chinese Education Web (Hong Kong)" for the public to access and download. As stated in the introduction to this chapter, there is a strong case for using research into literacy as a catalyst for alerting schools, parents, and society to ways of pooling their efforts and thereby bringing the strength of a combined response to problems.

For academics, an important step has been publication of the findings and implications of the PIRLS study (Tse et al., 2005). It is hoped that these publications will serve as textbooks for the teaching of research methodology in universities. Educators, teachers, and parents who are interested in the PIRLS study may also obtain information from the books. As is always the case, the research exercise itself gives rise to further questions and issues that now need to be addressed. For example, it is essential that a comprehensive picture be obtained about the English as well as the Chinese reading literacy of students in Hong Kong. It is also necessary for the influence of ongoing innovations in educational provision to be taken into account. These include changes to the medium of instruction used in schools, as well as changes to educational practice introduced to accommodate advances in information technology.

## References

Cheung, Y. S. (1992). A preliminary report on the Chinese reading ability of Hong Kong pupils. *International Language Education Journal*, *9*, 35–47.

Curriculum Development Council. (2000). *Learning to learn: The way forward in curriculum development*. Hong Kong: HKSAR Government.

Curriculum Development Institute. (2002). *Reading to learn: The promotion of a reading culture at school*. Hong Kong: Curriculum Development Institute, Education Department, HKSAR Government.

Education Commission. (1996). *Education Commission Report No. 6*. Hong Kong: HKSAR Government.

Education Department. (1997). *Extensive reading scheme*. Hong Kong: HKSAR Government.

The Government of Hong Kong SAR. (2001). *Hong Kong 2000*. Hong Kong: Author.

The Government of Hong Kong SAR. (2003). *Hong Kong 2003*. Hong Kong: Author.

Tse, S. K. (2002). Hong Kong, SAR. In I. V. S. Mullis, M. O. Martin, A. M. Kennedy, & C. L. Flaherty (Eds.), *PIRLS 2001 encyclopedia: A reference guide to reading education in the countries participating in IEA's Progress in International Reading Literacy Study (PIRLS)* (pp. 99–108). Chestnut Hill, MA: Boston College.

Tse, S. K., Lam, W. I. J., Lam, Y. H. R., & Loh, K. Y. E. (2005). *Progress in international reading literacy study: Comparison of Hong Kong and other countries*. Hong Kong: Hong Kong University Press.

Tse, S. K., Lam, W. I. J., Lam, Y. H. R., Loh, K. Y. E., & Westwood, P. (in press). Students' test performance in PIRLS, attitude to reading, and reading self-concept across three ability groups: Data from Hong Kong. *Australian Journal of Learning Disabilities*.

Wong, P. K. (1984). *Collected essays in Chinese language teaching*. Hong Kong: Chinese Language Society of Hong Kong.

## Websites

Census and Statistics Department, HKSAR Government:
http://www.info.gov.hk/censtatd/home.html
Chinese Education Web (Hong Kong): http://www.chineseedu.hku.hk
Education and Manpower Bureau: http://www.emb.gov.hk/
Hong Kong Education City: http://www.hkedcity.net
Hospital Authority: http://www.ha.org.hk/

## Further Reading

Curriculum Development Council. (2000a). *Learning to learn: Chinese key learning area*. Hong Kong: HKSAR Government.

Education Commission. (2000). *Life long learning, whole person development: Education reform*. Hong Kong: HKSAR Government.

Tse, S. K., Chan, W. S., Ho, W. K., Law, N., Lee, T., Shek, C., et al. (1995). *Chinese language education for the 21st century: A Hong Kong perspective.* Hong Kong: Faculty of Education, the University of Hong Kong.

Tse, S. K., & Lai, F. K. (2001). *A study on the promotion and implementation of extensive reading in schools: Report submitted to the Education Department, HKSAR Government*. Hong Kong: Faculty of Education, the University of Hong Kong.

# Chapter 8
# The Impact of PIRLS in Hungary

*Annamária Szabó-Rábai and Péter Vári*

## 8.1 Hungary at a Glance[1]

Hungary lies in the central Danube Basin of Eastern Europe. It borders Slovakia, the Ukraine, Romania, Serbia, Croatia, Slovenia, and Austria. The terrain consists of rolling foothills in the west, a hilly region north of Budapest, and a great variety of landscape in the remainder of the country to the east and south. The highest point is Mount Kekes, at 1,014 meters. The area of the land is approximately 93,030 square kilometers. Hungary has 19 counties, 274 towns, and 2,871 villages. Budapest is the capital and the largest city, with 1.7 million inhabitants.

The total population is approximately 10.1 million (52.3% female). Sixteen percent of the population is under 15 years of age, and 15% of the population is over age 65. Sixty-four per cent of the population lives in urban areas. The population density is 109 people per square kilometer.[2]

The gross domestic product (GDP) per capita in 2003 was $USB82.7.[3] In 2001, 5.19% of GDP was spent on education. In 2002, the figure was 5.57%, and in 2003 it was 5.77%.[4]

## 8.2 Hungary's Education System as Context for PIRLS 2001

Horizontally, administrative responsibility for education is shared between the Ministry of Education and other ministries (primarily the Ministry of Employment and Social Affairs, the Ministry of Finance, and the Ministry of the Interior). Vertically, the administrative control is decentralized, with responsibility shared among the central (national), local (regional), and institutional levels. The local governments administer pre-primary, primary, and secondary education. Most students attend public-sector schools, which are administered and organized by the public authorities, primarily the local governments. In the early 1990s, a great

---

1    This introduction is based on Hungary's country profile in the *PIRLS 2001 Encyclopedia* (Vári & Felvégi, 2002).
2    Retrieved May 10, 2005 from
     http://portal.ksh.hu/portal/page?_pageid=37,111393&_dad=portal&_schema=PORTAL
3    Retrieved May 10, 2005 from
     http://devdata.worldbank.org/external/CPProfile.asp?SelectedCountry=HUN&CCODE=HUN
     &CNAME=Hungary&PTYPE=CP
4    Retrieved April 15, 2005 from http://www.om.hu/letolt/felsoo/stat_felsoo_2003_2004.pdf

number of local governments built new schools, even though the number of children in the Hungarian population was falling.

### 8.2.1   Structure of Hungary's Public Education System

The Hungarian system of public education comprises four main periods: pre-primary, primary, secondary, and tertiary.

Children can attend pre-primary education from three to seven years of age. Participation in pre-primary education (*óvoda*) is optional until age five, after which it is compulsory.

In Hungary, psychologically and physiologically mature children are obliged to attend school in the year in which they are six (at the earliest) or in which they are eight (at the latest). They must not leave school before the end of the year when they are 18.[5] Primary education lasts from Grades 1 through 8. This period of education is further divided into four parts:

1.  Warm-up period, Grades 1 and 2
2.  Starting period, Grades 3 and 4
3.  Establishment period, Grades 5 and 6
4.  Development period, Grades 7 and 8.

Parts 1 and 2 comprise the lower elementary school, and 3 and 4 form the upper elementary school.

Secondary education begins in Grade 9. Students can attend vocational schools until the end of Grade 10 or general secondary schools (which are either comprehensive or vocational) until the end of Grades 12 or 13, at which time they sit a school-leaving examination. Secondary education comprises two parts:

1.  General knowledge period, Grades 9 to 10 or 11
2.  Individual interest-based period, Grades 11 or 12 to 13, in preparation for tertiary studies or entry to the labor market.

In Hungary, the higher education (tertiary) institutions are the public and private denominational universities (*egyetemek*) and colleges (*főiskolák*) accredited and formally recognized by the State. These are specialized and organize courses in their particular field of specialization. The higher education institutions also include non-university institutions (*főiskola*), university-level institutions (*egyetem*), and institutions that provide higher vocational training courses.

Students must have gained the secondary school leaving certificate (*érettségi bizonyítvány*) to enter higher education. Students who successfully complete non-

---

5   The Hungarian Parliament passed legislation relevant to the school age in 1993.

university education courses in the *főiskola* (three or four years' duration) receive the *főiskolai* diploma. Universities and other university-level institutions award the *egyetemi* diploma to students who successfully complete a four- to six-year course. Diplomas have a two-fold function in that they incorporate academic and vocational qualifications.

### 8.2.2 Compulsory Full-time Education

As noted above, education is compulsory from ages five to 18 (see Table 8.1). Students may not commence vocational studies before age 16, up to which time they acquire fundamental (core) education. Legislation imposes the provision of free compulsory education, although private-sector schools may charge fees. A declaration of school readiness is required for admission to primary school. Admission to upper secondary schools is based on the entrance procedures organized by the schools and adherence to guidelines established by the Ministry of Education.

**Table 8.1: Profile of compulsory full-time education in Hungary**

| Type of Education | Age |
| --- | --- |
| *Óvoda* (pre-primary)—one preparatory year, compulsory (ISCED 0) | Ages 5–6 |
| *Általános iskola* (primary—single structure) (ISCED 1 + 2) | Ages 6–14 years (1st cycle: 6–10 years; 2nd: 10–14/16 years) |
| *Gimnázium* (general lower and upper secondary) (ISCED 2 + 3) | Ages 10/12/14–18 |
| *Szakközépiskola*—vocational secondary school (ISCED 3) | Ages 14–18/19 years (4–5 years) |
| *Szakmunkásképző iskola*—apprenticeship school (ISCED 3) | Ages 14–16/17 years (3 years) |
| *Szakiskola*— remedial (ISCED 2) + vocational training school (ISCED 3) | Ages 16–18–20 years (2 + 2 years) |

The school year comprises 185 days of teaching, traditionally starting from the end of August/beginning of September and continuing to 31 August of the following year. As of 2004, there are three (approximately one-week period) school breaks, each of which is approximately one week long. These occur in the autumn, the winter, and in spring. There is also a 10- to 11-week summer break.

An amendment to the law in 1996 set the 185-day school year for all levels. The same amendment determines the maximum number of daily teaching hours. For Grades 1 to 3, this total cannot be more than four lessons, and for Grades 4 to 6, four or five lessons. The weekly average must not exceed 4.5 lessons per day. In Grades 7 and 8, the maximum is five lessons daily. There are five working days every week; each teaching lessons usually lasts 45 minutes. Law stipulates the maximum number of teaching lessons for the various grades.

Regulations also define the maximum number of students per class as 26 (Grades 1–4), 30 (Grades 5–8), and 35 (Grades 9–13). The classes are mixed in terms of ability and are made up of students of the same age. Integrated education has been compulsory since September 2003 in all public educational institutions, and mixed ability groups are set up in all schools.

Students receive formal education lessons in the morning. In the afternoon, the schools offer special classes and accommodate the students for the rest of the day. Schools can also organize extracurricular non-compulsory activities, the time spent on which may not exceed 10% of the total time spent at school in Grades 1 to 3, 25% of the total time spent at school in Grades 4 to 6, and 30% of the time spent in Grades 7 to 8.

### *The National Core Curriculum and the Frame Curriculum*

Since the middle of the 1990s, regulations governing school curricula have doubled. This has had a marked effect on curriculum planning and development. Today, a three-level structure comprising the National Core Curriculum (1995), the Frame Curricula (2000), and local curricula (institutional level) provide a regulatory framework for teachers to develop syllabuses.

The National Core Curriculum (NCC), introduced by the Government in 1995 and launched in academic year 1998/99, and the Frame Curriculum (FC), introduced in 2000, are at the heart of these developments. The Core Curriculum determines detailed requirements for the most relevant educational periods: Grades 1–4, 5–6, 7–8, and 9–12. As long as they adhere to centrally prescribed requirements, teaching staff can adapt curricula to suit their own school-based pedagogical programs (Halász & Lannert, 2003).

The NCC emphasizes the importance of tuition in Hungary's native language from the first grades of primary education onwards, given that skill in it is necessary for effective learning in all subjects. The NCC identifies Hungarian as the basis of social communication, as a medium of cultural and social values, and as the means of self-expression and independent opinion. The main task of native language tuition is to ensure students are able to communicate competently at a level commensurate with their age.

The FC defines the objective of teaching the Hungarian language and literature at Grades 1–4 as "mov[ing] children towards conscious language usage in accordance with their age". Children, the curriculum stresses, should learn to use the language in different communication contexts, be able to express their thoughts, feelings, and opinions in a precise way, and (as a consequence) be able to interact increasingly effectively with children in their age cohort and with adults. The main task of this educational period is to facilitate children's learning by ensuring they can obtain information through reading and proficiency in several written language forms. This is the period when children learn reading and writing techniques and "make friends" with basic reading comprehension and writing texts.

More specifically, the FC for Hungarian language and literature requires children in Grades 1–4 to have the following:

- Adequate skills in reading and writing;
- An understanding of how readers engage with text, so assisting them to interpret texts at an age-appropriate level;
- Ability to construct texts according to their age and in a manner that allows them to begin to use their imagination and to shape their own style;
- Adequate knowledge of grammar and orthography;
- An increasing consciousness of language functions;
- A developing ability to learn; and
- The beginnings of an ability to use and process information.

Under the Hungarian FC, the Grade 4 students surveyed through PIRLS would have been expected to possess the following literacy-based competencies:

- Clear, continuous speech when engaged in everyday communication;
- The ability to use polite forms in everyday spoken language;
- The ability to clearly convey their message;
- Continuous and expressive loud reading after practice;
- The ability to provide a clear understanding (comprehension) of a 15–20 line text appropriate to their age after reading it for themselves; and
- Active participation in a group in order to construct a story, to improvise a story, or to discuss a topic.

PIRLS 1991 surveyed Grade 3 students. A list of literacy-based requirements from the FC for that grade follows:

- Summing up texts with simple structures in a few sentences;
- Creating questions and answers with reference to familiar topics;
- Broad comprehension of half a page of written text about a familiar topic;
- Loud reading of familiar texts after silent practice; and
- Five- to six-sentence composition about a familiar topic.

A comparison of the objectives for Grades 3 and 4 students highlights a crucial difference in children's reading literacy development. Whereas Grade 3 students have only to make statements about texts with simple structures, Grade 4 students must possess the full ability to read and to comprehend what they are reading. The fact that the students assessed by PIRLS 1991 came from Grade 3 and those assessed by PIRLS 2001 came from Grade 4 provides a point of reference when we look, later in this chapter, at Hungarian students' achievements across the two studies (a project known as PIRLS Trend).

### Tuition Tools for Teaching Hungarian Language and Literature in Lower Elementary Classes

Legislation stipulates the number of lessons in Hungarian language and literature lessons that must be taught each year in the lower elementary school. The FC gives this number as 296 lessons in Grades 1, 2, and 3, and 259 lessons in Grade 4. On a weekly basis, these numbers translate into eight lessons in Grades 1 to 3 and seven lessons in Grade 4. Students in the first four grades learn eight subjects altogether, three of which relate to Hungarian language and literature: reading, writing, and composition.

Textbooks on Hungarian language and literature for the lower elementary grades are issued mainly by eight publishers, who tend to produce the books in series covering all four grades. The textbooks focus on reading practice and grammar practice and include students' workbooks and tests. The teacher decides which textbook series to use. The books generally represent one methodological concept of how to teach reading. In 1978, teachers could use every method. The FC changed this system by suggesting teachers use expressive/analyzing/combining methods, and by emphasizing the importance of the preparatory period.

## 8.3   Experience in Large-scale Assessments

In Hungary, the Center for Evaluation Studies has regularly monitored students' reading literacy since 1986. Since 1991, Hungary has conducted regular evaluations of students' abilities in mathematics, reading literacy, science, and information technologies (IT) at the end of each learning period (Grades 4, 6, 8, 10, and 12). It has also conducted national assessments of students' competence in mathematics and reading literacy since 2001 (Grades 6, 8, and 10).

Hungary has participated in IEA reading literacy surveys since 1970/71 (see Table 8.2) and was one of the 32 countries that participated in IEA's Reading Literacy Study 1990/91, which was the antecedent of PIRLS 2001. The survey studied the reading literacy ability of two populations of students (nine-year-olds and 14-year-olds) in three fields: narrative texts, instructional texts, and documentary texts. The study used continuous and non-continuous texts, with tasks presented in multiple-choice format.

**Table 8.2:** **Hungary's participation in international large-scale surveys of educational achievement, 1985–2003**

| Year(s) of data collection | Name of survey | Organization in charge | Target population |
|---|---|---|---|
| 1985–1994 | International Reading Literacy Study (RLS) | IEA | Nine-year-old students and 14-year-old students |
| 1995 | Third International Mathematics and Science Study (TIMSS) | IEA | Thirteen-year-old students (Grades 7 and 8) and three different samples in the final grade of the secondary school |
| 1994–1996 | International Adult Literacy Survey (IALS) | OECD | Ages 16–64 |
| 1998 | Second International Adult Literacy Survey (SIALS) | OECD | Ages 16–65 |
| 1999 | International Mathematics and Science Study-Repeat (TIMSS-R) | IEA | Grade 8 |
| 2000 | Program for International Student Assessment | OECD | Age 15 |
| 2001 | Progress in International Reading Literacy Study 2001 (PIRLS 2001) | IEA | Grade 4 |
| 2003 | Trends in International Mathematics and Science Study 2003 (TIMSS-2003) | IEA | Grades 4 and 8 |

The overall achievement of the nine-year-old Hungarian students in this study set them near the international average on the reading literacy scale. They were best at documents, and they had approximately the same mean scores on the narrative and expository subscales. These results are definitely because the students were about 9.3 years old at the time of the study and in Grade 3. Students from most of the other participating countries were in Grade 4, which, as explained earlier, requires considerably more of students in terms of reading ability than does Grade 3. The performance of the 14-year-old students (attending Grade 8 at the time of the survey) placed them fifth on the international scale. Their mean score of 536 was well above the international average.

Nine countries that had taken part in the 1990/91 survey took part in PIRLS 2001 and so were part of PIRLS Trend (Martin, Mullis, Gonzalez, & Kennedy, 2003). The trend study repeated the 1990/91 survey of nine-year-old students. Students in five of the countries came from Grade 4; those in the other four were from Grade 3. As in PIRLS 1990/91, the Hungarian students came from Grade 3, but their average age was slightly higher (9.7) than that of the 1990/91 cohort (9.3 years of age).

Achievements in reading literacy improved from 1990/91 to 2001 in most of the nine countries. In three of them (Greece, Iceland, and Slovenia), the positive difference between scores was significant. In two countries (Sweden and the USA), students performed at a lower level than in 1990/91. Hungarian students performed better in 2001 than in 1991 (16 points higher on the literacy scale), but the difference, while pleasing, was not significant. Also, Hungary's ranking among the nine repeating countries slipped from eighth place in 1990/91 to ninth place in 2001.

There are several possible reasons for this development. One reason may again relate to the fact that the Hungarian students were in Grade 3. In the nine-year-old age group, a one-year difference within the educational period may be crucial. Another reason may be that in Hungary the emphasis on teaching reading in the lower elementary grades (that is, attainment of correct reading techniques and the development of reading literacy needed for success in later grades) is often not realized, as the results of Hungary's participation in PISA studies have highlighted.

## 8.4     National Results and Impact of PIRLS 2001

### 8.4.1     Results of PIRLS 2001

PIRLS 2001 surveyed students from 35 countries in reading literacy. Sweden was the top-performing country, with an average score of 561 on the international reading literacy scale. Belize, with a score of 327, was at the bottom. Hungary's average of 543 points gave it a ranking on the scale of eighth place. The average performance of the Hungarian students on the reading literacy scale was significantly lower than the achievement of students in three countries (Sweden, the Netherlands, and England), showed no significant difference in relation to seven countries (Bulgaria, Latvia, Canada, Lithuania, USA, Italy, and Germany), and was significantly higher than that of students in 24 countries.

PIRLS 2001 assessed students' ability to comprehend texts representing two major reading purposes: literary and informational. Across the countries, Hungary achieved sixth place on the literary subscale and ninth place on the informational subscale. These results placed Hungary among the group of countries where students were significantly better at comprehending literary texts than informational texts. Hungarian students were significantly less adept than students in Sweden and England at comprehending literary texts and significantly better on this measure than were students in 26 countries. Their performance was on approximately the same level as students in the seven remaining countries. Students in five countries (Sweden, the Netherlands, Bulgaria, Latvia, and England) significantly outperformed Hungarian students in reading for informational purposes.

## 8.4.2 Publication of the PIRLS Results

Publications related to the PIRLS 2001 results focused mainly on the above-average performance of Hungarian students in this study relative to the below-average performance of 15-year-old Hungarian students in the reading test of PISA 2000 (conducted by the OECD). This difference between the two cohorts of students prompted concern in Hungary, and required explanation. One important publication that sought to do this was written by researchers from the Center for Evaluation Studies (see Vári, Balázsi, Bánfi, Szabó, & Szabó, 2003).

Documents presenting the main findings of PIRLS 2001 were printed and distributed to all schools that took part in the study. There were also several official meetings and conferences in connection with the results, and interviews on both national radio and television about the achievement of Hungarian children.

## 8.4.3 Considerations Relating to the Reading Literacy Ability of Hungarian Students in PIRLS 2001 and PISA 2000

The differences between the frameworks of the two surveys provide a possible starting point when discussing the performance of Hungarian students on these studies. The first and most obvious difference is the target population of each study: nine-year-olds for PIRLS 2001 and 15-year-olds for PISA 2000. These are two very different age groups at two very different stages of the educational process. A second difference relates to the focus of the assessment tasks in each study. PIRLS aimed to determine whether children at a certain point in their schooling (the grade in which the majority of students were nine years of age) had acquired reading literacy skills. PISA tried to find out how successfully 15-year-old students could use these skills (last formally taught some five to six years earlier) in everyday life. This difference in approach is evident across all IEA- and OECD-run studies, and it is important to note that Hungarian students have performed above the average in all the IEA studies in which Hungary has participated. The conclusion is clear: Hungarian students perform much better when the survey requires them to exhibit skills or knowledge taught within a specified period of schooling and is conducted at the end of this period than when the survey requires them to apply skills or knowledge acquired some time earlier.

Hungary has had a long and successful tradition of teaching and encouraging reading literacy in the earlier grades of the country's schools. However, it has no similar tradition in the higher grades. Nor does it use the schools to develop a culture encouraging of lifelong reading. Despite efforts by educational decision-makers, researchers, and practitioners to tackle this problem, there have been no changes in the schools.

Another difference concerns the countries that participated in PISA 2000 and PIRLS 2001. PISA assessed 28 OECD countries, whereas PIRLS assessed not only highly developed European countries but also less developed Asian and African countries. Student achievement in the latter group of countries tends to be significantly lower than the international average. The inclusion of this group of countries in PIRLS meant that the achievement rankings of the developed countries for this study were much better than they would have been had the rankings related only to the OECD countries. In short, it is not possible to compare the international average and the international placement scores from the two surveys in an absolute sense. There is greater possibility of valid comparisons when the compared countries are developmentally similar. Figure 8.1 accordingly shows how well the 15 OECD countries that participated in both PIRLS and PISA fared relative to one another.

**Figure 8.1: Relative ranking of the OECD countries that participated in both PIRLS 2001 and PISA 2000**

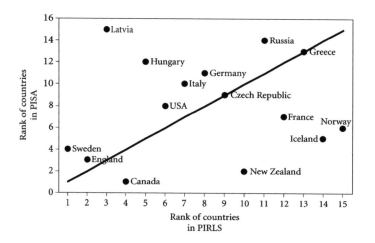

The chart shows that Sweden and England outperformed the other countries in both studies, while Greece had a very low relative achievement in both. Unlike the other countries shown, the Czech Republic, England, and Greece performed at approximately the same level in both studies, strongly suggesting that achievement in these countries did not relate to those periods within children's schooling that focus intensively on developing reading literacy. Certainly, curricula in England maintain a focus on the development of reading literacy and communication skills throughout children's schooling (Mullis, Martin, Kennedy, & Flaherty, 2002). Hungary is included in the group of countries that showed marked changes in performance across the two studies. Latvia was one of the most striking examples from this group. It outperformed most countries in PIRLS yet achieved below the international average in PISA. Conversely, Norway and Iceland performed much better in PISA than they did in PIRLS.

As the comment in relation to England above suggests, explanations for these findings are possible from an examination of the reading curricula of these countries (for full details see Mullis et al., 2002). Latvia, like Hungary, finishes reading education at the end of Grade 4. Iceland and Norway take a different approach. In these countries, the main goal is not to teach material as soon as possible but rather to establish and provide students with a repertoire of oral and written tools that equip them for learning all subjects.

In Iceland, students only play with letters in the first grade; they do not actually begin to identify letters or to learn writing until later. However, 15-year-old Icelandic students experience reading literacy as a standard part of their curricula.

The situation in Norway is worth a closer look still. Here, education is compulsory until the end of Grade 10, and consists of three main periods: Grades 1 to 4, Grades 5 to 7, and Grades 8 to 10. Norwegian children start school in the year in which they turn seven. In Grade 1, they do not begin to learn reading and writing formally, but instead play with sounds, letters, and words as preparation for Grade 2, when formal tuition in reading and writing begins. Development of reading literacy is ongoing throughout the children's schooling; even the curriculum for Grade 10 includes tasks designed to develop reading literacy. Reading literacy objectives differ according to the children's age and the three main periods of schooling. By the end of Grade 4, for example, the expectations are that children should be able to read for fun, which should also inspire them to write, and that their writing ability should be sufficiently proficient to allow them to communicate effectively in this medium.

### 8.4.4  Impact of PIRLS 2001

*Impact on Administrative and School Level*

It is very difficult to discuss the real consequences of the results of the assessment, as these did not have immediate political and educational impacts. The most important visible consequence was the publicity and discussion that surrounded the PIRLS and PISA results. However, government officials did hold several meetings to discuss the assessments. They agreed, as have educationists, that reading literacy is a fundamental skill that students must possess before they can pursue further educational study. They also stressed that this skill is vital for effective participation in a work force that increasingly requires sophisticated training, and in a society that requires its citizens to meet their civic responsibilities. Hungary has therefore begun to revise its National Core Curriculum and Frame Curriculum, and the country is very determined to take part in future literacy assessments.

### Long-term Effects

Much needs doing in Hungary to improve students' basic skills, especially reading literacy. Reading is one of the most important skills students begin to learn in the first grades of school, and it is a skill that needs to be nurtured throughout schooling. Reading literacy is a key competence not only for learning other subjects, for engagement in hobbies and for personal development, but also for enabling young people to become full members of their immediate and wider social environments. It is therefore essential that Hungary solves the structural problems of its education system and revises the content of its curricula. There needs to be a greater emphasis on teaching reading literacy in the higher grades of the education system, and teacher education facilities needs to implement effective changes to how they instruct teachers to teach reading literacy.

## 8.5    Future Activities

Hungarian students start formal writing and reading in Grade 1. By the end of Grade 2, the expectation is that they will be able to read a text aloud after some practice, to know the alphabet, to identify vowels and consonants, and to sound out the difference between short and long sounds in oral and in written forms. They should also be able to write down, using correct orthography, two or three sentences (in copied form) from a text or from dictation.

Until recently, Hungary used the term "reading" mainly for the process involved in putting letters and syllables together to create words. Reading development was seen as learning and adapting techniques. In the last decade, Hungary's approach to reading has changed, but some teachers and the public still tend to interpret reading as the acquisition of a technique. There needs to be a widespread perception that the acquisition of correct reading technique is simply a first step towards mastery of reading literacy. The notion of reading literacy is complex because it includes not only the technique of decoding words, but also the ability to reflect on texts and to use one's own experiences and reading skills in interpreting (drawing meaning from) those texts. School teaching needs to follow this model, with teachers and parents given more information (for example, books, handouts, websites) on how they can assist students achieve reading literacy. Of particular importance is the need for students to practice reading all manner of texts throughout their elementary schooling in order to enhance their reading ability.

## 8.6    Concluding Remarks

The principle of "more, and the sooner the better" that has long governed reading literacy education in Hungary has been strongly discredited by the findings of PISA and PIRLS. Moreover, experience tells us that our ability to communicate effectively in society, to learn new subjects, and to access information relies on being highly proficient in reading and writing literacy. There is therefore an urgent need in Hungary for a new approach to developing children's reading literacy. Our conclusion is that the period in which students receive formal reading tuition must extend beyond the lower elementary school, and that attention must be paid to ensuring that children have opportunity to develop reading and writing literacy throughout their schooling.

## References

Halász, G., & Lannert, J. (2003). *Jelentés a magyar közoktatásról 2003 [Report on public education 2003]*. Budapest: Országos Közoktatási Intézet.

Martin, M. O., Mullis, I. V. S., Gonzalez, E. J., & Kennedy, A. M. (Eds.). (2003). *Trends in children's reading literacy achievement 1991–2001: IEA's repeat in nine countries of the 1991 Reading Literacy Study*. Chestnut Hill, MA: Boston College.

Mullis, I. V. S., Martin, M. O., Kennedy, A. M., & Flaherty, C. L. (Eds.). (2002). *PIRLS encyclopedia: A reference guide to reading education in the countries participating in IEA's Progress in International Reading Literacy Study (PIRLS)*. Chestnut Hill, MA: Boston College.

Vári, P., Balázsi, I., Bánfi, I., Szabó, A., & Szabó, V. L. (2003). Hogyan olvasnak a magyar kilencévesek? A PIRLS 2001 eredményei a PISA-és a PIRLS-vizsgálat összehasonlításának tükrében [How do 9-year-old students read in Hungary?]. *Iskolakultúra, 8*, 118–138.

Vári, P., & Felvégi, E. (2002). Hungary. In I. V. S. Mullis, M. O. Martin, A. M. Kennedy, & C. L. Flaherty (Eds.), *PIRLS 2001 encyclopedia: A reference guide to reading education in the countries participating in IEA's Progress in International Reading Literacy Study (PIRLS)* (pp. 109–114). Chestnut Hill, MA: Boston College.

## Websites

Eurydice European Unit. *Structures of education, vocational training, and adult education systems in Europe: Hungary 2003*.
http://www.eurydice.org/Documents/struct2/en/HUNGARY_EN.pdf

Hungarian Central Statistical Office.
http://portal.ksh.hu/portal/page?_pageid=37,115776&_dad=portal&_schema=PORTAL

Ministry of Education. *Education in Hungary*.
http://www.om.hu/main.php?folderID=137

National Institute for Public Education. *Education in Hungary 2000* (Chapter 3,
    Financing public education).
    http://www.oki.hu/article.php?kod=edu2k-chapter3.html
*The Hungarian educational system.*http://www.sulinet.hu/tart/alkat/ap
The World Bank Group: *ICT at a glance: Hungary.*
    http://www.worldbank.org/data/countrydata/countrydata.html

## Further Reading

Adamikné Jászó, A. (2001). *A magyar olvasástanítás története [History of teaching
    reading].* Budapest: Osiris.
Elley, W. B. (1992). *How in the world do students read?* Hamburg: IEA.
Vári, P. (Ed.). (1997). *National assessment of student performance (Monitor '95).*
    Budapest: Országos Közoktatási Intézet.

# Chapter 9
# The Impact of PIRLS in the Islamic Republic of Iran

*Abdol'azim Karimi and Parvin Daeipour*

## 9.1 Iran at a Glance[1]

The Islamic Republic of Iran, with an area of 1,648,195 square kilometers, is situated in western Asia. It is a mountainous land with three different climatic conditions: humid, mountainous and semi-arid, and desert. The country is bounded by the Caspian Sea and the republics of Azerbaijan, Turkmenistan, Kazakhstan, Armenia, and Russia on the north, Afghanistan and Pakistan on the east, the Oman Sea and Persian Gulf on the south, and Iraq and Turkey on the west.

According to the 2001 census, the population of Iran is about 63 million, with about 66% being of Persian origin, 25% Turkish, 5% Kurdish, and 4% Arab. About 63% of the population are urban dwellers and the rest live in rural areas. Most of the population is Muslim (99.4%), while less than 0.3% are Christians, Jews, Zoroastrians, or members of other religious minorities.

Education in the Islamic Republic of Iran is substantially funded by the Government. The total budget of the Ministry of Education in 1996 was about 3.8% of the Gross National Product.

The country's GDP in 2001 was US$B114.1 and the per capita was $US1,770. Approximately 4% of the total GDP was spent on education in 2001.

## 9.2 Iran's Education System as Context for PIRLS 2001

The formal education system of the Islamic Republic of Iran is organized by the Ministry of Education, which provides for education up to pre-university level. The structure of decision-making in Iran is highly centralized, and this is true also for the Ministry of Education.

Primary education begins at the age of six and lasts for five years. This period is followed by orientation or guidance school (lower secondary), lasting three years. These eight years of education constitute Iran's basic education, which is compulsory for all children. The Government is obliged to provide free education for all learners up to the end of secondary school and free higher education to make the country self-sufficient. Pre-primary education is accessible in most regions and is financed by parents and the Government. Pre-primary education is not compulsory.

---

1   This introduction is based on Iran's country profile in the *PIRLS 2001 Encyclopedia* (Faghihi, 2002).

However, the Ministry of Education intends to expand provision at this level, particularly in bilingual areas and with the co-operation of the private sector. The Ministry also hopes to provide pre-primary education within five years all over the country.

Although educational provision is a government responsibility in Iran, private schools also exist but are managed under the supervision of the Ministry of Education. The curricula, textbooks, and examination regulations of private schools conform to the general rules and criteria of the Ministry of Education. The school year, comprising nine months (about 35 working weeks/200 active days), begins on 23 September each year and ends on 21 June of the subsequent year.

On entering primary school, each student must take part in health tests, which assess students' hearing, eyesight, and mental abilities. If problems are detected, especially in mental ability, students are referred for future examination and, if necessary, they are sent to special school. Every student can repeat a grade three times in order to pass the year successfully. Students can stay in primary school up to the age of 20 in rural regions and 18 in urban regions. All students must pass a final examination at the end of the fifth grade of primary school.

The textbooks used in Iranian schools are unique, and the same books are used across the country. The National Curriculum Council (NCC) uses several general approaches to reading literacy, such as holistic, atomistic, language-experience, and linguistic. Important principles governing the content of textbooks include developing social and life skills, improving thinking processes, encouraging children to read more, instilling moral and ethical values, and cultivating creativity. The primary goals of the reading teaching process are to cultivate in students the ability to read both silently and aloud, respecting the necessary rules when doing so, to read with concentration in order to understand the ideas in the text, and to acquire the ability to interpret these ideas.

## 9.3    Experience in Large-scale Assessments

### 9.3.1   Early Participation

The first large-scale assessment that Iran participated in was IEA's Six Subject Study 1970 (see Table 9.1). This study assessed 10- and 13-year-olds, as well as students in their last year of high school. The results showed that Iranian students, when compared to their counterparts in other countries, not only achieved very poorly in science and reading comprehension but also had the lowest level of academic improvement in the field of reading comprehension.

Because of the social and political changes that took place in Iran in the 1970s and that eventually led to the overthrow of the Shah and the formation of the Islamic

Republic, Iran did not take part in international studies for nearly 20 years. In 1991, Iran became an official member of the IEA, which led to the country participating in three TIMSS studies and one PIRLS study: namely TIMSS 1995, TIMSS 1999-R, TIMSS 2003, and PIRLS 2001.

**Table 9.1: Iran's participation in international large-scale surveys of educational achievement, 1970–2001**

| Year of data collection | Name of survey | Organization in charge | Target population |
|---|---|---|---|
| 1970/71 | Six Subject Study | IEA | Ten-year-old students, 13-year-old students, and students from graduating year of secondary school |
| 1995 | Third International Mathematics and Science Study (TIMSS) | IEA | Ten-year-olds (Grade 4) Thirteen-year-olds (Grade 8) |
| 1999 | Third International Mathematics and Science Study-Repeat (TIMSS-R) | IEA | Ten-year-olds (Grade 4) Thirteen-year-olds (Grade 8) |
| 2001 | Progress in International Reading Literacy Study 2001 (PIRLS 2001) | IEA | Ten-year-olds (Grade 4) |
| 2003 | Trends in International Mathematics and Science Study 2003 (TIMSS 2003) | IEA | Ten-year-olds (Grade 4) Thirteen-year-olds (Grade 8) |

## 9.3.2 Attitudes towards International System-monitoring

For Iranian authorities, the results of TIMSS 1995, especially Iranian students' low ranking on the international achievement scale, was a great shock, and the results were not published for some time. One of the reasons for the shock was the contradiction between the results and the strong performance of Iranian students in world mathematics Olympiad contests. Their success had created the perception that Iranian students were doing well in mathematics. The fact that many Iranian students had obtained prominent positions in credible mathematics and science centers around the world was another reason for this perception.

Resistance from Ministry authorities towards the results of TIMSS 1995 and the resultant distrust in large-scale international system-monitoring studies led to a situation where nothing was done to advance mathematics and science education in Iran. The results of Iran in TIMSS-R were therefore almost the same as the results for TIMSS 1995. By this time, policy-makers in Iran generally held two views in relation to the studies. The first was that Iran should not trust international studies. The second was that the country needed to adopt a logical and reasonable approach towards them. This dichotomy led to uncertainty as to whether Iran should participate in PIRLS 2001, but finally, after a delay of six months, Iran decided to participate.

### 9.3.3   National Large-scale Surveys

Over the past decade, Iran has conducted a number of nationally based large-scale surveys of education-related matters. Table 9.2 lists a selection of these. These studies include those generated by or related to publication of the PIRLS 2001 findings.

One of the large-scale national surveys undertaken by the PIRLS National Center in Iran has involved the preparation of an achievement report card for all schools that participated in PIRLS 2001. In this study, the results of reading tests, along with the results of context factors in the four principal questionnaires, will be provided to each individual school, and they will then be informed about the situation in their own schools.

Although textbooks used in the primary schools were revised nearly three years before PIRLS 2001 to ensure a greater emphasis on developing students' reading and comprehension abilities, such as critical reading and evaluation, dialogue, and questioning, the compilers of these books welcomed suggestions arising out of PIRLS as to how the content of these books might be improved further.

**Table 9.2:   Some of the national large-scale surveys conducted in Iran, 1996–2000**

| Year of data collection | Name of survey | Organization in charge | Target population |
|---|---|---|---|
| 1996 | The study of ability of children for whom Farsi is not the first language | Ministry of Education | Seven-year-old children |
| 1999 | Assessment of basic competencies | UNICEF | Grade 5 students |
| 2000 | National assessment of literacy achievement | Institute for Educational Research | Ten- to 15-year-old students |
| 2000 | Primary and pre-primary students' recognition of basic vocabulary | Research and Educational Planning Organization | Ten- to 12-year-old students |

Publication of the PIRLS results highlighted the importance of pre-primary education for reading achievement, and educationists are now seriously analyzing this issue and developing a plan to gradually include pre-primary education in the compulsory years of education, at least in the country's bilingual/multilingual provinces. About 42% of Iran's students speak more than one language, and for many of them, Farsi, Iran's official language, is not their mother tongue. The largest language group after Farsi is Turkish, but other languages such as Kurdish, Arabic, and Urdu are also common. The Ministry of Education provides a one-month pre-primary course on Farsi for children who do not speak the language.

The PIRLS National Center in Iran has also used the PIRLS results to gain a deeper understanding of factors affecting student performance in reading. One such study compared the background/context information available for the 40 Iranian students who received the highest scores in PIRLS 2001 with the back-ground/context information for the 40 students who received the lowest scores. This analysis indicated that socio-economic factors influenced these students' reading achievement. In another study, students' responses to each reading text used in the survey were separately analyzed in order to identify particular reading-related strengths and weaknesses.

In Iran, the PIRLS results confirmed the need for Iranian teachers to use active and creative methods when teaching children how to read and apply reading skills. As mentioned above, these methods were piloted through curricular reforms involving the revision of school textbooks. Once officials were confident that the changes would have a positive impact on children's reading development, the new textbooks officially replaced the old ones. The Grade 4 students who will participate in PIRLS 2006 will be those taught by these new textbooks. The authorities are therefore particularly interested in comparing the results of PIRLS 2006 with the results of PIRLS 2001, in order to evaluate the effects of curricular change on student achievement within the primary schools.

Another important research-based initiative arising out of the PIRLS results relates to the fact that Iranian students did much better on the tasks associated with the literary texts than those associated with the informational texts. The likely reason for this is that the Iranian curriculum places particular emphasis on literary texts. However, because of the PIRLS findings, educational planners and specialists are seriously trying to provide solutions to redress this problem and to improve the ability of students to acquire and use information.

## 9.4 National Results and Impact of PIRLS 2001

### 9.4.1 Results of PIRLS 2001

Iranian students' average score on the literacy scale of 414 points set their performance significantly below the international average. When ranked against the other 34 participating countries, Iran achieved a placement of 32. As in the other countries, girls outperformed boys. The 27-point difference between the genders was significantly higher than the average international difference of 20 points. On average, Iranian students performed significantly better on the literary subscale than on the informational subscale (a difference of 12 points). Again, girls did significantly better than boys on the tasks for both types of text, but the difference was slightly smaller in relation to the informational tasks (a 24-point difference for informational and a 28-point difference for literary).

Among the points that should be noted when considering Iran's ranking in PIRLS 2001 is that most of the countries that participated in the study (26 out of 35) are countries rated as highly developed by the United Nations Human Development Index. The educational opportunities and facilities available in these countries are not comparable with those in Iran, and are certainly a factor in Iran's poorer performance relative to many of the other participating countries. This point is even more relevant when we remember that Iran has a young population, and therefore a large student population. In 2000, Iran had 18,300,000 students, 8,200,000 of whom were in primary schools. In PIRLS 2001, Iran selected its sample from 1,830,000 fourth graders, a significant number. The schools that these children attend are widely scattered throughout the country, and Iran's centralized system of education means that it is not always easy to ensure a sufficient and equitable distribution of resources to schools, especially those in rural areas.

### 9.4.2   Publication of the PIRLS Results

The PIRLS National Center in Iran has published several articles and reports featuring the PIRLS 2001 national and international results. Most of these works focus on identification of the factors that seem to influence progress in reading literacy in primary education. This information provides parents, teachers, and educational planners with ideas on how to provide better opportunities and conditions for enhancing children's reading literacy.

The specialist journal *Primary Education* also conducted and published an interview with the PIRLS National Research Coordinator (NRC) in Iran. The aim of this interview was to inform primary school teachers about the goals and results of PIRLS and the role of this study in providing trends data about primary school children's progress in reading literacy.

### 9.4.3   Impact of PIRLS 2001

Publication of the results of PIRLS 2001 in Iran produced different reactions and interpretations. The results were disseminated and acted on more quickly than was the case with TIMSS. For policy-makers, the results confirmed that reading literacy is a vital skill and the basis of learning all other subjects. They also realized that ongoing effort must be directed towards sound language learning, especially for children for whom Farsi is not the mother tongue.

### Long-term Effects

Several long-term programs relevant to primary education were developed after authorities had considered the PIRLS 2001 results. Brief descriptions of these follow.

- Revision of the curriculum for reading Farsi that takes into account the findings of PIRLS 2001 relating to content, teaching methods, teachers' professional competence, and reading evaluation methods.
- Revision of the system used to evaluate the learning of reading, with emphasis placed on the deeper layers of this process (that is, comprehension, inference, conclusion, judgment, and evaluation of elements in reading texts).
- Enrichment of school environments in order to provide students with opportunities for mental and social interaction when reading.
- Enhancement of primary-school teachers' knowledge of the processes involved in teaching and learning the four language skills (listening, speaking, reading, and writing).
- Establishment of a scheme that allows students to access books of their own interest.
- Organization of contests (related to the different areas of learning for reading) designed to involve students in book reading.
- Implementation of a program designed to enhance students' reading comprehension by developing their problem-solving, critical-thinking, questioning, evaluation, and judgment skills.
- The holding of meetings of specialists to examine and evaluate reading curricula on a continuous and objective basis and in relation to predetermined aims.
- Preparation of special programs for pre-primary children. Run by the media, these programs are designed to develop a culture of story-telling and consequently to strengthen children's listening, comprehension, and repetition skills, as well as strongly develop their aptitude in Farsi.

Senior government and educational officials are currently engaged in meetings focused on reading curricula policy and planning. The aim of these meetings is to effect revisions in four main areas: reading curricula, the teaching of reading, reading-related resources and equipment, and the culture of book reading.

### Impact on Administrative and School Level

The reason commonly given during deliberations about whether Iran should participate in PIRLS 2001 was that because students in Iran's primary schools are good readers, the results from PIRLS would be better than the results from TIMSS. However, Iranian students did not perform well overall on PIRLS, a situation that again created shockwaves. This time, however, the authorities made particular effort to carefully examine the indices and the results of this study, and to ensure that the PIRLS NRC presented all findings to the education authorities, including the Minister of Education. It is also worth mentioning that from the first stages of the study, the PIRLS National Center in Iran endeavored to familiarize policy-makers with the content of the study and to involve them in the implementation procedures.

After the Government decided that Iran should participate in PIRLS 2006, the Ministry of Education commissioned a group of senior specialists to analyze the PIRLS 2001 results with a view to finding appropriate ways to improve the teaching and learning of reading in primary schools. Also, the PIRLS NRC met with the president of the Academy for Farsi Language and Literature and the head of the Iranology Foundation. During this session, the NRC presented the results of PIRLS 2001 and emphasized that understandings gained from analysis of them should inform programs designed to enhance the learning of Farsi and to improve students' reading abilities.

## 9.5    Future Activities

Iran's low ranking on the PIRLS international literacy scale (32 out of 35) and the weak achievement of Iranian students in reading, specially of informational texts, convinced educationists of the need to change various aspects of the content and teaching methods of reading education. However, before making changes, officials have agreed that other factors likely to be influencing and inhibiting the acquisition of good reading ability need to be identified to ensure that any changes made are effective. As part of this process, researchers are examining complementary, contemporary, and comparative studies, including TIMSS, in order to identify common contextual factors at the national level.

The main questions to which educational planners and policy-makers want answers are these:

- What is the main reason for Iranian students' weak reading performance?
- What factors influence reading literacy, and to what extent does each factor exert an influence?
- What are the reasons for the performance of students in the countries that had high rankings on the international reading literacy scale?

- What changes should Iran make to its education system in order to strengthen students' reading ability?
- How can Iran's educational institutions and organizations help improve children's reading skills?

Researchers are also re-examining the results of national studies on reading literacy and students' ability in comprehension against the findings from PIRLS. Their conclusion thus far is that the quality of teaching and the use of active teaching methods play important roles in enhancing development of children's deeper reading skills.

### 9.5.1 Research

The PIRLS National Center in Iran, with cooperation from psychology and educational specialists and researchers, intends to carry out several studies related to reading literacy. These include:

- Analyzing and comparing the performance of students in Iran's bilingual provinces and students in Iran's monolingual provinces.
- Surveying teachers' knowledge of the reading comprehension process and their capability as teachers of reading.
- Reviewing the status of book reading at home and at school.
- Evaluating the relationship between overall educational achievement and progress in reading literacy.
- Comparing the results of PIRLS 2001 and 2006 to assess the effects of new reading textbooks in Grade 4 on students' progress in reading literacy.
- Inviting interested academic staff and researchers to analyze PIRLS results with the aim of identifying the factors that advance Iranian students' progress in reading literacy.

### 9.5.2 Publications

More than 60 analytical and statistical papers have been prepared in Farsi. A list of these papers was published in a monthly education journal, and readers were advised that they could obtain copies of these upon request. Two books, one presenting the PIRLS results and the other the sample of released stories used in the PIRLS tests, have also been published, and Farsi translations of the released stories provided. Reports have been published (in four different journals) about PIRLS and its goals, content, and results. Finally, three Master's degree students are using the PIRLS results as the basis of their theses. Each is using the results to investigate Iran's educational problems.

### 9.5.3   Programs

The answers given by school-teachers and principals on the PIRLS teacher and school questionnaires revealed that many of these people were not familiar with research findings and innovations related to reading literacy education. Officials therefore decided to organize professional development programs for teachers in this field. As part of this development, the PIRLS National Center in Iran sought agreement from the relevant authorities to facilitate or conduct short- and medium-term courses aimed at familiarizing primary teachers with the main findings from PIRLS, and acquainting them with the methodology of national and international evaluations of educational achievement. So far, the Center has received approval for the following initiatives.

1.   The In-Service General Directorate to provide compulsory training courses for teachers and principals in active teaching methods of reading;
2.   The provision of training courses through the broadcasting education network for primary school teachers; and
3.   The inclusion of information on reading in specialist journals for teachers and principals, and/or the publication of special issues of these journals on this subject.

## 9.6   Concluding Remarks

One of the important and worthy effects of PIRLS 2001 in Iran is that it prompted education policy-makers and planners to review the structure and content of the country's reading literacy program and the system used to evaluate it. Publication of the PIRLS results also accelerated educational reform in Iran. For example, the Organization for Research and Educational Planning, affiliated to the Ministry of Education, has incorporated suggestions arising from analysis of the PIRLS 2001 results within the framework of its future policies and programs. Many educational researchers, especially those interested in the problems that Iran is experiencing in primary education, reading education, and reading literacy, have proposed new research topics aimed at identifying factors likely to advance children's achievement reading literacy. Finally, many provinces have conducted large seminars on reading education, and these have been welcomed by primary teachers and educational specialists.

## Reference

Faghihi, F. (2002). Islamic Republic of Iran. In I. V. S. Mullis, M. O. Martin, A. M. Kennedy, & C. L. Flaherty (Eds.), *PIRLS 2001 encyclopedia: A reference guide to reading education in the countries participating in IEA's Progress in International Reading Literacy Study (PIRLS)* (pp. 125–131). Chestnut Hill, MA: Boston College.

# Chapter 10
# The Impact of PIRLS in Lithuania

*Aistė Elijio*

## 10.1 Lithuania at a Glance[1]

Lithuania, situated in northern Europe, borders the Baltic Sea, Latvia, Poland, Russia, and Belarus. It is the largest of the three Baltic states, with an area of about 65,000 square kilometers. Lithuania is mainly lowland. The highest point, Juozapines Hill, is just 293 meters above sea level. There also are several small, scattered lakes, marshes, and a complex sandy coastline.

About 3.7 million people currently live in Lithuania. The capital is Vilnius, which has a population of 575,000. Although between the world wars Lithuania was regarded as primarily an agricultural country, about 68% of its people now live in urban areas. The population density is 57 persons per square kilometer. Lithuania's ethnic composition is relatively homogeneous: Lithuanians comprise 81% of the population, Russians 8%, and Poles 7%.

About half of the total employment is in services—approximately 30% in industry and 20% in agriculture. Machinery and equipment, mineral products, chemicals, and textiles are the country's major export commodities. The main agricultural products include grain, potatoes, sugar, beets, vegetables, beef, dairy products, and fish. The female labor force represented 48% of the total labor force in 2001. The GNP per capita in 2001 was US$2,640.

In 1998, Lithuania's public expenditure on pre-primary, primary, and secondary education amounted to approximately 28% of its total national budget expenditure.

## 10.2 Lithuania's Education System as Context for PIRLS 2001

The Lithuanian education system has undergone considerable change during the last decade. These changes have included all aspects of education: administration, the curriculum, assessment, and so on. Most of these changes have been implemented, although at the time of the PIRLS 2001 main survey, many were still very much "in transition".

---

1  This introduction is based on Lithuania's country profile in the *PIRLS 2001 Encyclopedia* (Mackeviciute, 2002).

Lithuania's education system is structured as follows:

- *Pre-primary education*: corresponds to International Standard Classification of Education (ISCED) Level 0. It is designed for children ages one to six and is not compulsory. At present, this level consists mainly of public and some private kindergartens, and is not a very popular option, with about half of the relevant age group attending.
- *Primary education*: corresponds to ISCED Level 1. It consists of Grades 1 to 4.
- *Basic education*: corresponds to ISCED Level 2 and consists of Grades 5 to 10.
- *Secondary education*: corresponds to ISCED Level 3 and consists of Grades 11 to 12.

In Lithuania, the students tested in PIRLS 2001 were in Grade 4, which meant their reading literacy skills were measured at the point when they were getting ready to enter basic school. In primary school, students are usually taught by the same teacher, whereas the basic school has subject teachers. The transition from basic to primary school (often in a different school building) can involve substantial changes, which young children can find challenging. However, formal requirements for passing from primary to basic school are virtually non-existent. After-school care used to be widely available in Lithuania, but this is no longer the case because of financial restraints. However, some schools still offer it and others have indicated their intention to resume this service.

Education is compulsory for all students up to the age of 16, with parents able to choose whether their child should begin Grade 1 at age six or seven. The basic school therefore encompasses the bulk of compulsory schooling. Although, theoretically, the suggested age for starting primary education is six, parents increasingly are opting to wait until their children are seven years old before letting them attend school. PIRLS 2001 found no difference in the reading literacy performance of those fourth graders who started their schooling at six and those who started at seven.

Primary and basic schools follow a curriculum that allows for little variation. The curriculum at the primary and basic levels includes mother tongue (generally Lithuanian, but in some schools also Russian, Polish, and Belorussian), mathematics, foreign languages, history, geography, sciences, civil education, music, art, physical training, crafts, informatics, and moral education (either religion or ethics). Reading and writing are taught as part of mother tongue. Schools catering to children from minority language backgrounds also teach Lithuanian, which is the State language.

At the time of PIRLS 2001, Lithuania's official reading policy was reflected in the *General Curriculum for Lithuanian Secondary Schools* (Ministry of Education and Science of the Republic of Lithuania, 1997a) and the *Standards of General*

*Education* (Ministry of Education and Science of the Republic of Lithuania, 1997b). Although the *Standards* were being piloted at the time and so had not been formally approved, they were nevertheless being widely used and constituted probably the most valid indicator of the general education policy regarding the content of subjects taught.

The main goals for primary school language teaching related to reading were set as follows:

1.  Help children develop skills of fluent and conscious reading so that they can use written sources in their lives.
2.  Help children decode the symbolic language used in texts and experience the pleasure of reading.
3.  Acquaint students with research literature, media reports, and other such informational texts that are appropriate for them.
4.  Help students understand that reading opens the way to knowledge of the world and to an active life in society.

The minimum reading standards that primary school children are *required* to meet include:

*   Distinguishing between written and spoken language;
*   Reading with understanding at their own pace;
*   Reading or reciting literary text with the help of a teacher;
*   Reciting, improvising, and playing on the themes of read works;
*   Distinguishing between facts and "artistic expressions";
*   Reading informational texts (for example, textbooks, reference books, children's encyclopedias), identifying and understanding the important elements of these, remembering their content, and understanding the conventional signs, maps, photographs, drawings, and schemas used in them;
*   Reading time schedules, programs, road maps, and the like;
*   Finding needed information with the help of a teacher;
*   Locating parts of a book, such as the title and the author, and locating the key text using the table of contents;
*   Reading entire works of children's literature;
*   Distinguishing in a text those statements that are of most and of lesser importance; and
*   Answering questions about a text (that is, comprehending it), especially in relation to its theme and main idea.

In addition, by the end of primary school, students are expected, although not required, to be able to:

- Read various texts consciously, fluently, and at the right pace;
- Independently find required information in various publications (dictionaries, encyclopedias, books presenting science in popularized form);
- Read children's newspapers and magazines (finding an article on an interesting topic and expressing opinions about it); and
- Locate information relating to all parts of a book (cover, content, text, illustrations, title, author, artist/designer, publishing company, year and place of publication).

At primary and lower secondary school levels, students mainly use textbooks that include children's stories, excerpts from various books, and reading comprehension exercises. Independent reading is also widely practiced in Lithuanian schools. Here, students read children's books of their own choice and are sometimes required to make a presentation (either oral or written) about what they have read. In the higher grades, students are introduced to "readers". These contain excerpts from works of literature and are provided in association with textbooks, which provide information on the authors and theoretical content about the writing. Although the requirements listed above might seem somewhat advanced, there was, until recently, no clear indication of how realistic or attainable these tasks were. It is only through participation in large-scale assessments (both international and national) that Lithuania has had opportunities to evaluate the appropriateness of the *Standards*.

## 10.3  Experience in Large-scale Assessments

Before participating in PIRLS 2001, Lithuania participated in TIMSS 1995 and TIMSS 1999 (see Table 10.1). However, PIRLS was the first large-scale reading literacy study conducted in the country. It was also the first large survey carried out in primary schools. Its implementation was conducted by the National Examinations Center, the institution responsible for the *Matura* and basic school-leaving examinations. At the time of PIRLS 2001, the examination system had just undergone reform, with centralized State examinations introduced at the upper end of the secondary school/university entrance level. A culture of assessment was also developing at this time, with programs put in place to analyze and disseminate the results of the *Matura* examinations, and educationists and researchers sharing ideas about other assessment possibilities (such as diagnostic tests and national evaluations of educational achievement). PIRLS had direct and indirect impacts on this development.

**Table 10.1: Lithuania's participation in international large-scale surveys of educational achievement, 1995–2003**

| Year(s) of data collection | Name of survey | Organization in charge | Target population |
|---|---|---|---|
| 1995 | Third International Mathematics and Science Study (TIMSS) | IEA | Thirteen-year-old students (Grades 7 and 8) |
| 1996/97, 1999/2000 | Civic Education Study (CivEd) | IEA | Grade 8 students |
| 1998/99 | Second Information Technology in Education Study Module 1 (SITES-M1) | IEA | Principals and teachers from primary and secondary schools |
| 1999 | Third International Mathematics and Science Study Repeat (TIMSS-R) | IEA | Thirteen-year-old students (Grades 8 and 9) |
| 2000/01 | Second Information Technology in Education Study Module 2 (SITES-M2) | IEA | Principals and teachers from primary and secondary schools |
| 2001 | Progress in International Reading Literacy Study 2001 (PIRLS 2001) | IEA | Nine-year-old students (Grade 4) |
| 2003 | Trends in Mathematics and Science Study 2003 (TIMSS 2003) | IEA | Grade 4 and Grade 8 students |

# 10.4  National Results and Impact of PIRLS 2001

## 10.4.1  Results of PIRLS 2001

The performance of Lithuanian fourth graders in PIRLS 2001 came as a pleasant surprise to the Lithuanian educational community, especially after the discouraging results of TIMSS in 1995 and 1999, in which student achievement placed Lithuania at the end and mid point of the respective international achievement scales. In PIRLS 2001, Lithuanian students achieved seventh place on the international literacy scale and were statistically significantly outperformed only by Sweden, the Netherlands, and England. These results may have been one reason why the results were widely disseminated, publicized, and heeded in Lithuania. Also, Lithuania found it highly advantageous to have had one of its closest neighbors—Latvia— also participating in PIRLS. This proximity allowed Lithuania to compare its results with those of a very similar country.

Student performance across the two countries was similar in many respects. However, one important difference generated considerable discussion. Lithuanian students achieved statistically significantly higher scores than the Latvian students on the tasks associated with the literary texts, whereas the reverse was true for the tasks associated with the informational texts. Lithuanian primary and mother tongue teachers had a ready explanation for this situation. Lithuanian schools have traditionally concentrated on the teaching of literature, and reading activities therefore usually relate to the reading of literary texts (stories, fairy tales, etc.). In general, reading of informational texts is not considered part of reading instruction. These findings hopefully give impetus for making informational texts an important part of reading instruction.

The PIRLS results also highlighted a strong relationship between students' reading literacy ability and factors associated with their socio-economic background, for example, parents' education. Lithuania was among the group of nations with the highest percentage of parents with a university-level education. As such, it is easy to make a link between the Lithuanian students' good results and the relatively high general level of education in the country. However, the level of parents' education was the same for the students who took part in TIMSS 1995 and TIMSS 1999, and the results of these studies for Lithuania were far from satisfactory. What needs to be remembered, though, is that the students who took part in the two TIMSS surveys were in Grades 7 and 8, not Grade 4, and that TIMSS assessed ability in mathematics and science, while PIRLS assessed reading skills. The question that the Lithuanian educational community naturally enough asked was whether the reason for the difference between the results of TIMSS and PIRLS related to age or subject. They also asked if perhaps teachers were teaching reading much better than they were teaching mathematics and science, or whether problems in basic education, or even primary, had something to do with the situation.

At the time of PIRLS, it was possible only to speculate on what the reasons might be, although there was hope that the TIMSS 2003 results would provide answers. Because this study would assess the mathematics and science skills of both Grade 4 and Grade 8 students, commentators suggested that good results for Grade 4 and poor results for Grade 8 would point to problems within the basic school. If the results for Grade 4 were, however, poor, the problem would appear to lie with the primary school. The suggestion has also been made that Lithuania should participate in the PISA surveys of educational achievement, as this would allow Lithuania to compare its PIRLS results with the reading literacy data collected via PISA for the country's 10- and 15-year-olds. It is the interrelationship and interconnectivity of these different international educational surveys that makes participation in them so useful.

### 10.4.2 Publication of PIRLS Results

The publications and other means whereby Lithuania disseminated the PIRLS results are presented below.

## Ministry of Education and Science

In Lithuania, the main findings of PIRLS 2001 were first officially presented at the Ministry of Education and Science. Officials from the Ministry, media, and other interested groups were present. The presentation aroused interest, and led to further dissemination of the findings.

## Media

The results were next disseminated through the media. Two major educational newspapers published articles about the PIRLS results (one article was concise and the other reasonably extensive). A national Lithuanian newspaper printed a large article on the results, and another large article appeared in a national newspaper in Russian, despite the fact that PIRLS 2001 tested only schools with Lithuanian as a language of instruction. Several local newspapers published articles on PIRLS as well. There were also interviews about the main findings with the PIRLS National Research Coordinator (NRC) on national radio and television programs. This considerable interest from the Lithuanian media was rather unexpected, as previously it had shown little interest in reporting positive news about education.

## National Report and Workshops

After the first flurry of positive attention, interest in the results lessened. It became clear that if the results of the survey were to have a long-term effect, it would not be enough to simply present them to the policy-makers (particularly when the results did not indicate an immediate call for action) and to publicize them in the press or even research journals. Instead, the educational community, teachers in particular, needed to be informed, as they would probably be the people most able to effect change. Plans therefore were made to distribute reports of the national results to all schools in Lithuania. However, because documents sent to schools can end up unread or not reaching their intended recipients, a decision was made to preface the reports with seminars about the PIRLS results and to conduct these in the local districts. Six such seminars were organized.

Representatives from all 60 municipalities were readily able to participate in the seminars, as these took place close to their areas. The invitation list included representatives from local educational offices responsible for primary or Lithuanian language education and members of pedagogical circles/councils of primary education and of the Lithuanian language. The latter usually included the most active teachers in the field in the locality, as it was thought they would most readily be able to carry the message to the teachers in their respective areas. The teachers, their interest in the PIRLS results aroused, would then be more likely to actively read and discuss the national reports.

The seminar format continues to be regarded as the most effective way of disseminating the results from international surveys conducted in Lithuania. For this reason, the structure and content of the PIRLS seminars, which involved half-day workshops, are detailed here.

- *Introduction to the international educational surveys in general*: The aim was to broaden understanding about the procedures and the usefulness of the surveys. Content described and explained the purpose, process, and procedures of the international surveys, how these relate to the national education surveys, and how users can interpret and use the results.
- *PIRLS framework*: The aim was to broaden understanding of reading literacy and how the survey is organized, what it measures, and how the various factors influencing literacy achievement are identified and studied. Content related to goals, aims, definition of reading literacy, purposes and processes of comprehension, survey instruments, etc.
- *Practical assignment*: This required the seminar participants to look through a specimen test booklet, which contained examples of the released literary and informational test items, to try to identify what processes of comprehension certain items measured and what percentage of Lithuanian students would answer them well. Participants were then asked to present and discuss their findings. This process allowed participants to see what the test booklets looked like, the kinds of texts students had to read, and the nature of the items they had to answer. The participants liked the texts very much and were particularly surprised to see the kind of informational text (leaflet) used. The process also gave them more insight into the different processes of reading comprehension, and how various test items can be used to assess these.
- *Results of PIRLS 2001*: Participants heard about the general results, the factors within Lithuania that seem to influence students' reading literacy ability, and "contradictory" or "illogical" conclusions. The latter were included to emphasize the need to be cautious when interpreting survey results.

About 300 teachers and local education officers participated in the seminars. All received copies of national reports and specimen test booklets, and many of them said they would use the booklets to determine how their students would perform. Participants appeared to appreciate the seminars and to come away from them considerably more supportive of the education surveys in general and PIRLS in particular. After the seminars, all remaining national reports and specimen booklets were sent to all schools in Lithuania.

### Research Seminars, Conferences, and Journals

Some of the PIRLS 2001 results were presented as an addition to the presentation "Sample Design Issues in Educational Surveys" made at the international (Baltic and Scandinavian countries) "Workshop on Survey Sampling Theory and Methodology" (28 May–3 June 2003, Palanga, Lithuania). Some of the findings of the first IEA International Research Conference (including secondary analysis of the PIRLS data) were shared at the seminar of the Department of Econometric Analysis at Vilnius University (24 May 2004, Vilnius, Lithuania). A presentation titled the "Impact of Home Factors on Students' Reading Achievements" was made at the XLV Lithuanian Mathematics Association Conference (17–18 June 2004, Kaunas, Lithuania). The idea behind these presentations was to try to draw the interest of mathematics, statistics, and sampling specialists towards education surveys and to look for possibilities for collaboration in conducting more of the secondary analysis.

## 10.4.3 Impact of PIRLS 2001

For individual countries, poor results in international surveys can provoke a tendency to overlook the results or to look for fault in the survey itself rather than to search for ways to improve the situation. However, such results fortunately can also prompt an immediate interest in remedying problems. There are many examples of countries responding to less than satisfactory results by establishing new institutes, amending their educational programs, and paying special attention to certain aspects of teaching or teacher education. There are also excellent examples of countries where these initiatives have improved the performance of students. One example is the Netherlands in relation to the International Reading Literacy Study 1991 and PIRLS 2001.

When countries find their results are good and satisfactory, educational officers are generally pleased to speak about them, and the media happily reports the students' achievements. However, because everything seems well, there is also often a perception that there is no need to take immediate action or to implement changes in the education system. This is what happened with the PIRLS 2001 results in Lithuania. The results were well received and therefore did not prompt a call for changes. Nor did they have immediate political-educational effects, other than an increased determination to participate in international education surveys.

### Long-term Effects

In Lithuania, one of the main long-term effects of the country's participation in PIRLS is the increased interest of the pedagogical and wider community in the benefits of education surveys, particularly in terms of monitoring the quality of education and highlighting factors influencing educational achievement. Long-term positive effects should also flow from the experience of the teachers from all over Lithuania who participated in the PIRLS seminars. Although the results of the study did not call for immediate remedial action, especially as they highlighted the fact that Lithuania has a culture that encourages reading, PIRLS provided teachers with the impetus to gain a greater understanding of the processes influencing the development of reading literacy and of how they can enhance that development. PIRLS has allowed teachers to understand more clearly what is meant by reading literacy, about the importance of learning to read and understand informational (not just literary) texts, about the variety of processes that underpin reading comprehension, and about other related aspects of reading. Lithuania believes that this type of grass-roots movement among teachers ultimately will have a more effective and quicker impact on reading achievement than will implementation by the Ministry of Education of even well-conceived, thoughtful policy decisions.

### *Impact on Administrative and School Level*

The impact of the PIRLS 2001 results on the administrative and school level is presently difficult to assess. As we noted before, the relatively good results of the Lithuanian students did not suggest any immediate reform or changes to the education system, such as to curricula or syllabuses. We expect that the dissemination of results through national reports, specimen test booklets, and workshops for teachers will produce positive changes in the teaching of reading comprehension, especially as it relates to informational texts. However, we have not yet had opportunity to test our expectations.

## 10.5  Future Activities

Lithuania will participate in the PIRLS 2006 as well as in other international education surveys, including IEA TIMSS 2007 and OECD PISA 2006. Although this participation seemed like an impossible dream some years ago, the situation has changed in line with the Ministry of Education's dramatically increased interest in and support for such surveys.

### 10.5.1  Research

In-depth analysis of PIRLS 2001 data is ongoing. The results of the new cycle of PIRLS (PIRLS 2006) will certainly provide more possibilities for the research, particularly in terms of comparisons. Also, data from TIMSS 2003 have provided additional opportunities for even more in-depth analysis of the kind mentioned earlier.

## 10.5.2 Publications

Findings from the ongoing analysis will be publicized in two ways. The first is through educational research journals, and the second is through *Analysis of the PIRLS 2001 Results*, a book that is being written in language easily understood by teachers and educational policy-makers. As occurred with the national reports of the PIRLS results, the book will be widely distributed.

## 10.5.3 Programs

Lithuania presently has no special programs planned in regards to the PIRLS 2001 results or analysis.

# 10.6 Concluding Remarks

In conclusion, we wish to note that the full impact of PIRLS and other surveys of educational achievement is not easily measured. There are effects beyond those determined by the number of immediate articles in the press or research journals, by changes in the curricula, or by new programs in universities. There are certainly impacts that relate to human resource development, such as the skills and qualification enhancement that the numerous training sessions and interaction of researchers from different countries offer those who work on the surveys. There are also impacts related to the increased interest in and understanding of how education systems can use the findings of education surveys to enhance system development and student achievement, to develop the general testing and assessment culture, and to employ the sound practices and procedures of the international surveys within the national ones. These impacts are not easy to pinpoint, but they hold true for Lithuania.

## References

Mackeviciute, A. (2002). Lithuania. In I. V. S. Mullis, M. O. Martin, A. M. Kennedy, & C. L. Flaherty (Eds.), *PIRLS 2001 encyclopedia: A reference guide to reading education in the countries participating in IEA's Progress in International Reading Literacy Study (PIRLS)* (pp. 171–177). Chestnut Hill, MA: Boston College.

Ministry of Education and Science of the Republic of Lithuania. (1997a). *Lietuvos bendrojo lavinimo mokyklos bendrosios programosm 1997 [General curriculum for Lithuanian secondary schools]*. Vilnius: Author.

Ministry of Education and Science of the Republic of Lithuania. (1997b). *Bendrojo išsilavinimo standartai, projektas 1997 [Standards for general education project]*. Vilnius: Author.

**Further Reading**

Elijio, A. (2003). *Progress in International Reading Literacy Study PIRLS 2001: Report*. Vilnius: National Examinations Center.

Elijio, A. (2004). Impact of home factors on students' reading achievement. *Lietuvos matematikos rinkinys*, *44*(Special issue), 441–446.

# Chapter 11
# The Impact of PIRLS in the Republic of Macedonia

*Bojana Naceva and Gorica Mickovska*

## 11.1 Macedonia at a Glance[1]

The Republic of Macedonia is located in the southeastern part of Europe and covers an area of 26,000 square kilometers. It is a landlocked country, with its capital, Skopje, in the center of the Balkan Peninsula. Macedonia borders four countries: Greece, Bulgaria, Serbia, and Albania. The country's highest mountain peak rises to 2,753 meters. Natural lakes cover 2.6% of the country, the largest of which are Ohrid Lake, Prespa Lake, and Dojran Lake.

Of the country's two million inhabitants, 62% live in urban settlements. The average population density is 79 persons per square kilometer. Sixty-six per cent of the population is Macedonian, 23% Albanian, and 10% are Turks, Roma, Serbs, and other minorities.

Macedonia's recent political crises have resulted in a decline in the GDP by about 4% and an increase in the rate of inflation. The GNP per capita is US$1,660.10 Around 300,000 people are employed in agriculture, industry, and services. In 2001, expenditure on education was 3.6% of the GDP.

## 11.2 Macedonia's Education System as Context for PIRLS 2001

### 11.2.1 Structure and Nature of the Education System

The Republic of Macedonia is a small country with a highly centralized education system. However, strong moves towards decentralization have begun in all sectors of society, including education. Education is mandatory from ages six[2] to 15 (or to the end of primary education, for students who reach age 15 before completing this level).

---

1   This introduction is based on Macedonia's country profile in the *PIRLS 2001 Encyclopedia* (Naceva, 2002).
2   Until 2005, mandatory education started at age seven. Since the beginning of school year 2005/2006, children must, under new legislation, begin school at six.

The education system consists of:

- Preschool education (six months to six years of age);
- Primary education, encompassing two elementary school phases (preparatory class and Grades 1 to 4 and 5 to 9) (duration: nine years; ages six to 14);
- Secondary education (duration: two, three, or four years; from ages 14 to 18); and
- Higher and university education (duration: two, four, five, or six years; from age 18).

Education at all levels is free of charge in State educational institutions (except for a small charge for higher and university education). However, parents buy the textbooks and pay for the food provided in kindergartens and primary schools as well as for school excursions. Throughout the education system, education is carried out in both Macedonian and the minority languages (Albanian, Turkish,[3] and Serbian[4]).

In addition to State-founded and State-financed educational institutions, there are several private kindergartens, secondary schools, and universities. Parents pay a large amount of money for private schooling, especially evident when these payments are set against the average salary in Macedonia. The Ministry of Education and Science certifies private educational institutions, but these exercise a high degree of autonomy in determining their curricula. Their work is not under strong Ministry control, as is the case with the State-funded schools.

About 81% of students attend preschool for a one-year minimum before starting primary education. This percentage is almost 100% in urban centers but much lower in small villages and rural areas. Children whose parents are both employed usually attend kindergarten from age one through to enrolment in school. Education in kindergartens is well organized and delivered by professional staff. Children can stay in kindergarten the whole day (maximum nine hours) or half a day (four to six hours). Some kindergartens offer evening care. Unfortunately, during the last 15 years, Macedonia's steadily rising unemployment rate has led to parents not using kindergarten education.

The students tested in PIRLS were at the end of the first phase of primary school, so it was then that these students gained most of their reading knowledge. During this first phase (Grades 1 to 4, ages six to nine), the same teacher teaches the same cohort of students (usually for four years) and that teacher teaches all subjects. During the second phase (Grades 5 to 8, ages 10 to 14), the students have separate teachers for separate subjects.

---

3    In primary and secondary schools.
4    In primary schools.

Primary school students attend 16 to 20 classes (each 45 minutes long) per week (five working days). Most schools offer after-school care for students whose parents require it. Schools organize after-school groups on a mixed-age basis, with one teacher per group responsible for ensuring the children do their homework and for organizing their free time. A small number of schools offer whole-day education (from 7 a.m. to 3 p.m.). However, most school programs require students to attend three to four classes a day, either in the morning or in the afternoon. Because of lack of school space, most schools have two student shifts each day. This system assumes that children will do a substantial amount of their learning at home.

The last 10 years have seen many changes within the first phase of primary education. These include the development of new, more goal-oriented curricula, teachers receiving training in interactive methods of teaching (student-centered teaching), and student-learning-oriented assessment piloted in some schools. This last development is a result of changes to the marking system in the first three years of schooling. Instead of holistic school marks (that is, 1 to 5), analytic descriptive assessment is now used. Another development over the last decade is the publication of several textbooks per subject, with teachers required to choose one text per subject. These innovations have completely changed the processes of teaching and learning in most Macedonian schools. This process has not been easy for some of those teachers strongly oriented towards traditional teaching methods.

There is no reliable empirical evidence of the impact of these changes on students' achievement because Macedonia did not have in place national or any other kind of large-scale assessment before and during the changes. Some evidence has come from the researchers engaged in a project associated with the implementation of interactive learning and teaching in selected schools, which took place during 1995–1998, and from other smaller projects. The former measured and compared the achievement of students in the project classes with the achievement of a sample of students from parallel classes that still employed traditional lecturing. The researchers found students from the interactive classes had higher levels of achievement in mother tongue, mathematics, science, and creative thinking than did students in the traditional classes (Ministry of Education, 1999). However, in interpreting these results, it is important to realize that the schools and teachers who were part of the interactive teaching and learning project volunteered to take part and accordingly received special training and attention. They were therefore enthusiastic and highly motivated. All teachers have now received training in interactive teaching methods. However, there are teachers, as previously mentioned, who prefer traditional methods. As such, it has not been possible to sustain high levels of motivation throughout the teaching community.

In the first three grades of primary school, students can fail a grade because of not having reached minimum achievement standards, but this is very rare, and students are held back to repeat a grade only with the agreement of parents. In Grade 4, students fail the grade if they have three or more F marks. However, the number of students who repeat Grade 4 is very low (less than 0.5%). Because of these trends, students in Grade 4 are of similar age (on average, 10.5 years at the end of the grade).

Students who successfully finish the first four years of primary school move on to the subject-based teaching phase. Most children stay in the same school throughout their primary education. However, some of them find the transition from grade-based teaching to subject-based teaching stressful. Subject teachers have higher expectations of the students, and their teaching style leans more towards the traditional. Changes toward student-centered, problem-solving teaching in the second phase of primary school have only just begun.

### 11.2.2 Reading Policy

Within the mother tongue curriculum (Macedonian, Albanian, Turkish, and Serbian) for primary education, the domain of "reading and literature" is of key importance. The mother tongue curriculum from Grades 1 to 4 stresses that this domain has a central place in teaching and learning the mother tongue and that its objectives are realized through reading and analyzing both popular and informational texts in the arts and sciences.

The Macedonian Government considers reading literacy a key skill for the successful achievement of other subject objectives, as well as a precondition for lifelong learning. Although not specifically stated in the mother tongue curriculum for Grade 1, the expectation is that the largest number of students possible should be able to read independently and correctly by the end of their time in this grade.

### 11.2.3 Reading Curriculum and Standards

Students in Grades 1 to 4 spend 18 to 22 hours per week in school, across a school year that lasts 180 working days. Each teaching lesson lasts 45 minutes. Students experience five lessons per week in mother tongue, which means a total of 180 lessons in this subject per year. One hundred of these lessons are dedicated to reading, which means that this domain is the one most represented in the curriculum. In the Republic of Macedonia, students whose first language is not Macedonian but one of the other officially recognized languages receive tuition from native speakers of that language. However, students still have to learn Macedonian, because it is the country's official language. The curriculum requires students to begin learning Macedonian as a second language in Grade 3, with two lessons per week. Macedonian language teachers teach these lessons.

Formal reading tuition starts at Grade 1, when students are between six and seven years of age (although parents often enroll their children earlier in the school). In Grade 1, the biggest emphasis is on exercises that help students match symbols to sounds and then combine them into words. Students also learn to read sentences and short texts out loud. The reading curriculum objectives for the end of Grade 1 require students to:

- Read aloud 20 to 50 words in a minute;
- Attempt silent reading;
- Read in accordance with the punctuation and to adjust the voice to the nature of each text (for example, glad, funny, sad); and
- Show comprehension of the text by talking about its events, characters, and other characteristics, and by identifying its main idea or theme.

In Grades 2 to 4, greater emphasis is given to developing the children's reading habits, introducing the children to texts for young people written by national and international authors, and increasing the children's ability to interpret texts. By the time children reach the end of Grade 4, the expectation is that they can meet the objectives of one of the following three standards:

- Minimum standard:
  - Recognize the explicit messages of a written text;
  - Recognize and differentiate the patterns and rhythms of written texts;
  - Recognize the structural relationships of a text (that is, how points lead on from one another).
- Sufficient standard:
  - Identify relationships among the content elements of literary texts;
  - Point out the elements of a text (characters, events, places, objects) as they appear in it;
  - Extract information from figures, maps, and tables in informational texts.
- High standard:
  - Identify the common features of the different elements of a text;
  - Interpret (comprehend) part of a text;
  - Identify the main messages of a text and then draw conclusions from that information;
  - Explain the meaning behind the title of a text.

In the primary schools, the objectives for mother tongue are achieved through the domains of reading, grammar, expression, writing, and "medium culture" (the means through which writing is transmitted. Over the last 10 years, curriculum initiatives have emphasized a close integration of these domains. Reading instruction initially focuses on the first three domains, with texts used to facilitate children's oral and written expression. From there, teachers encourage children to develop good reading habits and obtain information from various sources through the domain of medium culture.

### 11.2.4 Materials for Reading Education

Each grade of primary education employs two or three reading books that comprise collections of prose and poetry from national and international authors. Teachers select texts from these books to read and interpret with the students. The books also contain worksheets that allow students to analyze the texts. Each grade of primary education also has available a list of literature works (usually eight to 10) that each student must read and analyze throughout the school year. Students also are encouraged to read magazines for children and books that they can easily find in the school library.

## 11.3  Experience in Large-scale Assessments

Before the transition period (encompassing reform of the education system), large-scale assessment, as a tool for quality control in the education system, was almost unknown. Educational inputs (curriculum, textbooks, teaching methods) were highly centralized and controlled, and this control was thought sufficient to ensure good-quality student achievement. Macedonia's Pedagogical Institute[5] did carry out some large-scale assessment of children's ability in mother tongue and mathematics at the end of primary school, the results of which were used to direct students' entry into secondary schools. However, there were some attempts to use that data to evaluate the performance of education in primary schools.

The first truly large-scale assessment in which Macedonia participated was TIMSS-R (see Table 11.1). The World Bank suggested that Macedonia should participate in TIMSS-R as part of the country's endeavors to reform its education system. The Pedagogical Institute, with support from the Ministry of Education, strongly accepted this idea. The Ministry of Education and the World Bank financed Macedonia's participation in the study, and the Pedagogical Institute was responsible for conducting it.[6]

---

5   Professional institution for supporting education within the jurisdiction of the Ministry of Education (later renamed the Bureau for the Development of Education).

6   The World Bank financed Macedonia's participation in other IEA studies, as did the embassy of the Netherlands in Macedonia. These institutions also financed Macedonia's national assessment studies. The OECD and the Open Society Institute financed participation in PISA. Macedonia's Ministry of Education and Science provided the researchers' salaries and covered office costs.

**Table 11.1: Macedonia's participation in international and national large-scale surveys of educational achievement, 1999–2003**

| Year of data collection | Name of survey | Organization in charge | Target population |
|---|---|---|---|
| 1999 | Third International Mathematics and Science Study-Repeat (TIMSS-R) | IEA | Fourteen-year-old students (Grade 8) |
| 2000 | Program for International Student Assessment (PISA) Plus | OECD | Fifteen-year-old students (mainly first grade of secondary education) |
| 2001 | Progress in International Reading Literacy Study ( PIRLS) | IEA | Ten-year-old students (Grade 4— end of the grade-teaching phase of primary school) |
| 2001 | National Assessment in Macedonian Language, Albanian Language and Mathematics | BDE-AU* | Ten-year-old students (Grade 4— end of the grade-teaching phase of primary school) |
| 2003 | National Assessment in Civic Education (CivEd) | BDE-AU* | Ten-year-old students (Grade 4— end of the grade-teaching phase of primary school) |
| 2003 | Trends in International Mathematics and Science Study 2003 (TIMSS 2003) | IEA | Fourteen-year-old students (Grade 8) |

*BDE-AU: Bureau for Development of Education–Assessment Unit, which is a semi-independent part of the Republic of Macedonia's Ministry of Education and Science.

Macedonian students did not perform well in TIMSS-R. This outcome disappointed educational professionals and the public. They had generally considered Macedonia to have a high level of student achievement in mathematics and the natural sciences, a perception based mainly on the performance of Macedonian students in international competitions. The TIMSS-R results were presented mainly to professionals,[7] and although the data were subject to some analysis and debate, they received little in the way of wider public consideration, possibly because of the social problems confronting Macedonian citizens at the time.

Macedonia also took part in TIMSS 2003, and the main findings were announced at a press conference.[8] The achievement of Macedonian students was again low, lower even than their achievement in TIMSS-R (conducted in 1999). There was, as previously, limited public interest in the results. However, several professionals from teacher faculties for mathematics and science (within universities) began conducting deeper analyses of the results.

---

7   The National Research Center (within the Pedagogical Institute) published reports and sent them to schools and other professional institutions. The Center also organized a round-table symposium for members of the Faculty for Mathematics and Natural Sciences, and arranged regional seminars for mathematics and science teachers.

8   A national report is being prepared.

Given that Macedonia had experienced very little in the way of large-scale assessments before TIMSS-R, one of the main impacts of participation in IEA studies has been raising professional knowledge in this area. IEA technical standards were translated into Macedonian, which allowed the development of standards for national assessment. These developments also helped the Bureau for the Development of Education (the national center now responsible for all international and national assessments) defend the reliability of the TIMSS data.

Another impact was that many educational professionals, having recognized the benefits of access to data from large-scale assessments, became strong supporters of Macedonia's participation in other international studies, among them PIRLS, TIMSS-Trend, and the OECD's PISA. They also began calling for the establishment of national assessment at the end of the grade-based teaching phase of primary education and at the end of primary education.

Macedonia conducted its first indigenous national assessment in 2000. This assessment, carried out by the Assessment Unit[9] of the Bureau for the Development of Education, measured student achievement in mother tongue (Macedonian and Albanian) and mathematics at the end of Grade 4 (the same grade involved in PIRLS). Comparison of the national assessment for mother tongue with the PIRLS assessment shows that the former gave better coverage of the national curriculum for this subject, as it assessed reading, writing, grammar, and vocabulary. The results from the national assessment showed student achievement to be below the expected levels. Particularly disquieting was the significant number of students whose achievement was very low. However, the results were useful in informing the establishment of national standards at three levels: minimum, proficient, and advanced. This differentiation should help teachers more readily identify poorly performing students so they can work with them to remedy deficiencies. The previous practice was to pitch teaching at the level of the "average student", on the premise that this would allow all students to meet learning objectives.

The results of the national assessment also were published and then presented to the public, professionals, and journalists at a national education conference. Workshops on interpreting and using the results were held for school directors, school development support staff (for example, psychologists), and some teachers. Although the results were not as expected, there was little public discussion about the quality of Macedonian education. The main people to make use of the data were educational professionals. They used this information when planning curriculum changes or delivering workshops and seminars for teachers. However, one must

9    The Assessment Unit takes primary responsibility for conducting all large-scale assessments. It receives strong support from the Ministry of Education and Science. Although the Assessment Unit is set within Ministry parameters, its professionals are fully independent of the Ministry in their work, and Ministry officials do not censor the Unit's publications.

keep in mind that because Macedonian society was experiencing a difficult transition period, characterized by many economic and ethnic problems, education was not a priority issue.

In 2003, Macedonia conducted another indigenous national assessment, this time in civic education. This study was also conducted by the Assessment Unit of the Bureau for the Development of Education, and it again tested students at the end of Grade 4 (the "PIRLS grade"). The student achievement results, along with findings about the school and home contexts in which students learn about civics-related matters, were published in a report. Although student achievement was again below what teachers and educational experts expected, this outcome was of little concern, perhaps because the Ministry had introduced civic education-related concepts and content into school programs only four years previously. However, the findings prompted the development of standards for civic education and a revision of the curriculum.

As has been the case in some other countries, a main problem for Macedonia during its participation in the large-scale assessments has been that teachers find it difficult to read and interpret the results in published form. This is because the publications take the form of empirical research reports, a medium that is not familiar to most teachers. Another problem for Macedonia relates to schools receiving only one gratis copy of each assessment-related publication and to not one school ordering additional copies because of not having a budget for professional literature.

To overcome these problems, school advisors[10] organized seminars and workshops that provided teachers with guidance and tuition on interpreting and using the results of the various assessments. As a second step, they delivered (as mentioned earlier in this chapter) seminars and workshops for school principals, school development support staff, and teachers. The purpose of this venue was to acquaint participants with the tests used, the national results and expectations relating to them, the influence of school and home background variables on the results, possible reasons for the achieved results, and the relevance of the data for the participants' work. The schools that participated in the national assessments also received the results for their school, set out in a form that allowed them to compare their students' achievement in each tested domain with the national averages for these domains. They also received some guidance on how their school could use the results to benefit their teaching and learning. However, anecdotal evidence suggests that all this effort has had little real impact on teaching and learning in schools.

---

10  Advisors are subject specialists in the Bureau for the Development of Education. Their main role is to help schools and teachers improve their work.

Macedonia has a long history of basing educational changes on political decisions that are not informed by empirical data. Although some politicians continue to express suspicion about the reliability of the results for Macedonian students who have participated in the international studies, most now accept the findings as reliable. This acceptance is a valuable first step towards politicians and government policy-makers basing their decisions about education on empirical data from large-scale surveys. During the short period in which Macedonia has been conducting large-scale assessments of its students' achievement, efforts to ensure the results benefit education have involved two approaches. The first is to have governmental and educational stakeholders accept empirical data as an important source of information about the quality of the education system. The second is to present data from the studies in accessible form for teachers.

In regard to the first issue, the strong support from and for the international consultants who worked in Macedonia during the period of large-scale assessment has helped familiarize educational policy- and decision-makers with how the data can be used, but this awareness still has to translate into widespread action. However, the efforts being made to address the second issue are a step in the right direction. As the national center for large-scale assessment, the Assessment Unit of the Bureau for the Development of Education is trying to improve how it presents the results to schools and teachers, particularly in terms of providing individual feedback to each school and offering information that can directly influence the practice of principals and teachers. The Unit expects that a new project called "School Development Plans" will enhance this effort, as the project calls on schools to conduct self-evaluation procedures. The Unit anticipates that schools will use understandings gained from the large-scale assessments about student achievement, especially those relating to the influence of home and school background factors on that achievement, to inform their school development plans.

## 11.4  National Results and Impact of PIRLS 2001

### 11.4.1  Results of PIRLS 2001

The average score on the PIRLS literacy scale for students in Macedonia was 442, which was significantly below the international average. Students from 27 countries outperformed Macedonian students. The achievement of students from only six other countries was below that of the Macedonian students. The mean difference between boys and girls in reading in Macedonia was 21 score points, higher than the international difference of 20 score points. There was a significant difference between Macedonian students' average achievement on the literary and informational reading subscales, in favor of informational. Girls significantly outperformed the boys on each purpose, although the difference was smaller for informational (the differences were 22 score points for literary and 17 score points for informational). Macedonia administered the PIRLS literacy tests in two languages, Macedonian and Albanian. The results for the students tested in Macedonian were significantly higher than the results for their Albanian-speaking contemporaries. The average score on the literacy scale was 488 for the Macedonian-speaking students. It was 385 for the Albanian.

The PIRLS results provoked discussion, extending over several days, especially in the public press. The newspapers were full of comments that Macedonian students are not literate, which laypeople interpreted to mean Macedonian students do not know how to read. An immediate important issue therefore was to explain to the public what reading literacy really means. This issue was also important because PIRLS was the first time reading literacy, in the sense that this term is employed in PIRLS, had been tested in Macedonia. Before PIRLS, the country had tested only students' competence in grammar. Almost all newspapers and other media concluded from their reading of the results that the Ministry of Education and Science should make changes to curricula and textbooks and that teaching approaches should be more skill oriented. However, after several days, all discussion stopped.

The other issue arising out of the PIRLS results (one that mainly concerned certain people in the research community) was that students in some countries with social and educational backgrounds similar to those of Macedonia (Slovenia, Bulgaria, Romania, and Slovenia) performed much better than the students in Macedonia. These people concluded that Macedonia needed to improve not only its pre-service teacher training in reading literacy but also its reading curriculum for schools. They argued that this responsibility rested with the Ministry of Education and Science and the Bureau for the Development of Education. The researchers also concluded that Macedonia needed to conduct qualitative comparative studies to identify the main characteristics of teaching and learning approaches in the countries with the highest results in PIRLS, and especially in countries with social and educational backgrounds similar to those of Macedonia.

Discussions among professionals in the Bureau for the Development of Education about what needs to change in the country's reading literacy approaches and how to implement changes are ongoing. However, the one thing that these professionals and other educational administrators are already very clear about is that Macedonia has to establish, as soon as possible, a system of monitoring the quality of its education system, and that this system must include large-scale assessment. This concern became even more important when the results of PISA Plus were published, and Macedonia was faced with the fact that the performance of students in its upper secondary schools was worse than the performance of students in the first phase of its primary schools.

Because there was no reaction about the PIRLS results from teachers and other school staff, the Assessment Unit (which was also the National Center for PIRLS) sent a letter to all primary schools in Macedonia. The letter encouraged teachers to discuss the PIRLS conceptual framework and to consider how they might use what had been learned from the study to enhance their teaching of reading literacy. The letter also asked teachers to inform the Unit, through their professional associations, of the main points of their discussions. The teachers replied that they would like the Bureau for the Development of Education to offer special seminars and workshops about new methods of and strategies for teaching reading. They also said there should be changes to the national reading curriculum and a focus in preschool education on the antecedents of reading literacy.

## 11.4.2 Publication of PIRLS Results

Since the release of the international results, the Bureau for the Development of Education has published a book featuring descriptive results for the representative sample of Macedonian students, and a booklet for teachers containing examples of the texts and items used in the PIRLS tests. There have also been several presentations. The PIRLS National Research Coordinator (NRC) presented the international and national results to the advisors for primary education in the Bureau for the Development of Education. The advisors, in turn, presented the results to teachers at the municipal level.

## 11.4.3 Impact of PIRLS 2001

Without doubt, the results of PIRLS and the other national and international large-scale assessment studies conducted over the past few years in Macedonia have made educational professionals and ordinary people aware that Macedonia's education system is not one of the best in Europe. The studies have also heightened awareness of the need to reform the country's education system and to ensure that reforms take account of the results of the large-scale assessments.

The need to improve the quality of education in Macedonia forced the Ministry of Education to develop a National Program for Educational Development in Macedonia for Years 2005–2015 (Ministry of Education and Science, 2004). The program's objectives include several that should make the teaching of reading in primary schools more efficient. These objectives are embedded in the draft document's chapter titled "Promotion of Intellectual Growth and Learning". This chapter states that the Ministry of Education will take measures to revise the

National Curriculum, will ensure that learning outcomes are based on curriculum-related standards of competencies, and will continue to support and promote the modernization of teaching and learning. One such development is the recently begun implementation (beginning of school year 2005/06) of new syllabuses for all subjects taught during the first phase of primary education, and training programs for teachers at this level.

The finding from PIRLS that early literacy activities are very important for further student performance in reading contributed to the Government's decision to make the school-starting age six instead of seven. This change to the compulsory school starting age does not mean an additional year at the first phase of primary school but rather that children must attend the last year of preschool education. An additional benefit of this law change is that children in rural areas in Macedonia will now have the same opportunity as their urban peers to gain necessary experience in reading, mathematics, and science before they enter Grade 1.

Another main impact of the large-scale assessments, including PIRLS, conducted in Macedonia is that educational policy- and decision-makers are now aware that empirical data provide very important indicators of the quality of education systems and that they can serve as starting points for planning educational interventions and/or reforms. This awareness recently led to the Government establishing a National Center for Assessment and Examinations in Macedonia. The main goal of this institution will be to assist the Ministry of Education and Science establish, monitor, and raise standards in pre-university education by developing systems that employ large-scale assessment and formal examinations.

### Impact on Administrative and School Level

The PIRLS findings have made an important contribution to the creation of new mother tongue syllabuses for the last year of preschool. The new syllabuses contain objectives that require teachers to plan and implement early reading activities. The preparation of new syllabuses for children of younger age in the preschool is presently underway.

Within the Bureau for the Development of Education, a group of experts has begun to analyze the syllabuses of all subjects in primary education, including mother tongue. The experts are using the findings of PIRLS, TIMSS, and the national assessments as well as data from questionnaires they prepared and administered to teachers, parents, and students throughout Macedonia to help them in this task. The aim of the exercise is to determine the strengths and weaknesses of current syllabuses and to effect improvements that will help teachers identify and remedy shortcomings not only in their own teaching practice but also in the teaching and learning process throughout their schools.

The Government recently implemented a nationwide assessment of students' learning outcomes at the end of each phase of primary education (that is, Grades 4 and 8). Each year, two subjects will be assessed, with assessment of each pair of subjects repeated four years later. This cyclical process involves representative samples of schools and students. The first cycle began in 2005. It measured students' achievement in mother tongue at the end of Grade 8 and in science at the end of Grade 4. The main goals of this large-scale assessment are to provide educational authorities and teachers with data about students' achievement that will allow comparison of standards and trends across time, inform the creation of educational policy, and assist measures to improve the quality of teaching and learning in schools.

## 11.5  Future Activities

Macedonia will participate in PIRLS 2006. Assessment Unit staff intend to develop ways of ensuring that teachers can use the PIRLS results and findings to enhance their students' reading literacy skills.

## 11.6  Concluding Remarks

The Republic of Macedonia considers its participation in PIRLS to have been a valuable experience. Educationists and researchers have gained benefit from the process involved in developing and implementing a large-scale assessment of this kind, while educational policy-makers are now far more aware of how Macedonia can use large-scale assessments to monitor the quality of its education system. Government officials, educationists, and members of the public have also gained a more realistic appreciation of the quality of Macedonian education relative to that of other countries. The establishment of a separate unit for assessment within the Bureau for the Development of Education is another important outcome of Macedonia's participation in PIRLS.

More specifically, in relation to reading literacy, PIRLS has provided valuable evidence of the quality of basic reading literacy education in Macedonia. The students' performance within the context of the international comparison and the data on school and home reading factors have given professionals a much clearer picture of the nature and health of Macedonian reading education. The present comparison of Macedonia with countries that outperformed it in reading literacy should further sharpen the picture.

For Macedonia, perhaps the main impact of PIRLS in relation to reading literacy is that the information gained from the study has forced the country to change its conceptualization of and approach to the teaching and learning of reading literacy.

The methodology that PIRLS used to assess reading literacy has had a strong impact on how Macedonia now assesses achievement in mother tongue (Macedonian, Albanian, Serbian, and Turkish), and it has provided direction for revision of the reading curriculum and of teaching practice. Finally, in stressing the importance that home-based and preschool reading activities have for later competency in reading, the PIRLS results directly influenced the Government of Macedonia's decision to change the age at which children must begin school from seven to six.

## References

Ministry of Education. (1999). *Education for all (Report 2000)*. Skopje: Ministry of Education.

Ministry of Education and Science. (2004). *Draft national program for educational development in the Republic of Macedonia 2005–2015*. Skopje: Ministry of Education and Science.

Naceva, B. (2002). Republic of Macedonia. In I. V. S. Mullis, M. O. Martin, A. M. Kennedy, & C. L. Flaherty (Eds.), *PIRLS 2001 encyclopedia: A reference guide to reading education in the countries participating in IEA's Progress in International Reading Literacy Study (PIRLS)* (pp. 179–184). Chestnut Hill, MA: Boston College.

## Further Reading

Mickovska, G., Naceva, B., & Aleksova, A. (2002). *National assessment at the end of the grade teaching phase: Achievement of students in mother tongue and mathematics, 2001*. Skopje: Assessment Unit of the Bureau for the Development of Education.

Naceva, B., & Mickovska, G. (2001). *National assessment at the end of the grade teaching phase: Achievement standards for mother tongue*. Skopje: Assessment Unit of the Bureau for the Development of Education.

Naceva, B., & Mickovska, G. (2003). *PIRLS 2001: Republic of Macedonia: Report of fourth grade students' achievement in reading literacy*. Skopje: Assessment Unit, Bureau for the Development of Education.

# Chapter 12
# The Impact of PIRLS in Romania

*Gabriela Noveanu, Nicoleta Litoiu, and Dragoş Noveanu*

## 12.1 Romania at a Glance[1]

Romania is located in southeastern Central Europe north of the Balkan Peninsula in the Lower Danube basin, bordering the Ukraine, the Republic of Moldova, Bulgaria, Serbia, Hungary, and the Black Sea. Its land area measures 238,391 square kilometers, making it the 12th largest country in Europe. Romania is centered on the Transylvanian Basin, around which the peaks of the Carpathian Mountains and their associated sub-ranges and structural platforms form a series of crescents. The highest point, Peak Moldoveanu, stands 2,544 meters above sea level. Beyond the Carpathian Mountains, the extensive plains of the south and east of the country form a fertile outer-crescent extending to the frontier, their agricultural potential increased by the Danube River and its tributaries.

Romania's population, as of January 2001, was estimated at 22,430,000 inhabitants. The population density is 94 persons per square kilometer. About 57% of the population live in urban areas. Ethnic Romanians comprise 89.5% of the population; Hungarians and Szecklers, 7.1%; Roma and Sinti, 1.8%; and other national groups, such as Germans, Ukrainians, and Turks, 1.7%. Religious beliefs are relatively homogeneous: 70% of the population are Romanian Orthodox, 6% Roman Catholic, 6% Protestant, and 18% unaffiliated.

The country's GDP in 2000 was US$B36.7, and the GNP per capita was US$1,670. Approximately 4% of the GDP was spent on education in 2000.

## 12.2 Romania's Education System as Context for PIRLS 2001

Traditionally, the Romanian education system has been completely centralized. The Government formulates education policy based on the Education Law. Educational policy is implemented by the Ministry of Education and Research as the central authority and by county inspectorates as regional authorities.

Pre-primary education is available to three- to six-year-olds, and is not compulsory. Private and public nursery schools offer various types of programs: normal programs (approximately four or five hours in the morning), long programs

---

1  This introduction is based on Romania's country profile in the *PIRLS 2001 Encyclopedia* (Noveanu & Noveanu, 2002).

(eight to nine hours), and weekly programs (five days per week). The State funds half of the meals and accommodation expenses for the latter two types of programs.

Under the Education Law, all Romanian citizens have been obliged (since school year 2003/04) to receive education for a period of 10 years after preschool education. The obligation to attend school terminates when students are 16 years old or when they have completed lower-secondary school, whichever occurs first.

Primary education includes Grades 1 to 4, usually for six- to 10-year-olds. Parents or legal guardians may request that their child not be enrolled until age seven. Lower secondary education includes Grades 5 to 10 for 11- to 16-year-olds. Upper secondary education for 16- to 19-year-olds is optional, and covers Grades 10 to 12, or 13 for some types of school. Vocational education lasts one to three years for the upper-secondary age group.

According to the National Institute of Statistics, for the school year 2001/02, 13.5% of Romania's population was enrolled in pre-primary (preschool) education, and 22.6% was enrolled in primary education. Of the population in the age group three to six years, 72.3% were enrolled in preschool education. Nearly all children (97.2%) of the population in the age group seven to 10 years were enrolled in primary education.

Romania's official language is Romanian. Languages spoken at home correspond to the various ethnic groups—predominantly Romanian and the various minorities speaking Hungarian, German, Jewish, Gypsy and Slavic dialects, Turkish, Greek, and Armenian. Some of Romania's public schools provide instruction in minority languages, and some private schools provide instruction in English.

In Romania, most children are enrolled in public education. For school year 2001/02, only 5,456 students were enrolled in private preschools and 1,578 in private primary and secondary education institutions. The students tested in PIRLS were at the end of primary education and had been taught by the same teacher for all or almost all subjects and usually for all four years.

Primary school teachers (*învățători*) are trained in upper-secondary teacher-training schools or colleges. College training (special short-term education) lasts for two years for students from an upper-secondary teacher-training school, or three years for those from other types of upper-secondary schools. Since 1999, the Education Law has placed the pre-service education of primary school teachers within university colleges. Generally, within the schools, a single teacher for each class manages the learning process. Specialized teachers may teach foreign languages, religion, physical education, and music. These teachers have a special diploma, and have completed a short- or long-term form of higher education, depending on the subject they are teaching.

During primary education,[2] students have a minimum of 18 to 21 and a maximum of 20 to 23 instructional hours per week. During their time in Grades 1 and 2, students receive seven to nine hours[3] of Romanian language and literature instruction every week. During Grades 3 and 4, they receive five to seven hours weekly.

The 1990s brought many changes to the educational domain in Romania. At the beginning of school year 1998/99, the Government introduced a curriculum framework for compulsory education that allows schools to design timetable schemes more in line with their instructional goals. In general, however, 80% of schools' instructional time is dedicated to the core curriculum and 20% is at the school's disposal.

The aims of primary education in Romania are:

1. Providing basic literacy to all children;
2. Helping the development of a child's personality with respect to his or her individual pace; and
3. Supporting children's knowledge, skills, and attitude acquisition in order to stimulate children's effective and creative approach to their social and natural environment and to make further education possible.

By the end of primary school, Romanian children are expected to have acquired the following:

1. The basics of literacy and numeracy (reading, writing, arithmetic); and
2. Language competency, that is, able to use Romanian, mother tongue, and foreign languages to express themselves in various communication situations.

According to Romania's new National Curriculum,[4] the main reason why children need to study Romanian literature and language in the primary school is to develop elementary competencies in written and oral communication and conversancy with fiction and non-fiction texts appropriate for their age. The curriculum also endeavors to instill in children attitudes and motivations that will encourage them to pursue ongoing study of Romanian language and literature. The requirements of the new curriculum have substantially changed how primary school children study the Romanian language. The previous artificial and arbitrary division of Romanian into three domains—reading, learning content, and communication—has been replaced by an approach (a functional model) that seeks to integrate the

---

2   The information on primary education in this section is drawn from *The New National Curriculum* (Ministry of National Education, 2000).

3   One instructional hour lasts for 50 minutes.

4   The information on studying Romanian language and literature is drawn from *Subject Curricula for Primary Education* (Ministry of National Education, 1998).

development of oral and written communications through inculcation of the following skills: listening, speaking, reading, and writing. Table 12.1 sets out the curriculum standards for Romanian language and literature that students are expected to achieve during the period of compulsory education. It is important to note that the students tested in PIRLS 2001 had not been taught according to the new curriculum.

**Table 12.1: Standards of achievement in Romanian language and literature for compulsory education\***

| Attainment targets | Standards |
|---|---|
| 1. Develop the capacity to understand an oral message | S.1 Understand the overall significance of an oral message and distinguish between essential and irrelevant information |
| | S.2 Identify the meaning of words in relation to the significance of the message |
| 2. Develop the capacity to express oneself orally | S.3 Build an oral message on a given topic |
| | S.4 Orally summarize a narrative text at first sight |
| | S.5 Orally describe the main features of a character in a given text |
| 3. Develop the capacity to understand a written message | S.6 Identify the narrative stages of a given epic work |
| | S.7 Identify narrative, dialog, and description in a story |
| | S.8 Identify, in a given literary work, rhetoric features and elements of literary theory studied |
| | S.9 Understand the significance of a word in its context |
| | S.10 Recognize the expressive values of the morphologic categories and of the syntactic relations in a given text |
| 4. Develop the capacity to express oneself in writing | S.11 Write the summary of a narrative text at first sight |
| | S.12 Describe in writing the main features of a character in a text at first sight |
| | S.13 Describe in writing the main characteristics of an excerpt from a given literary text |
| | S.14 Write functional texts such as application, telegram, invitation, curriculum vitae, etc. |
| | S.15 Observe hyphenation, spelling, and punctuation rules studied |

\* The information on standards in Romanian language and literature for compulsory education is drawn from *The New National Curriculum* (Ministry of National Education, 2000).

## 12.3  Experience in Large-scale Assessments

Although Romania was not involved in large-scale international assessments of educational achievement in reading literacy before PIRLS 2001, it had experienced large-scale assessment through its participation in IEA studies (TIMSS 1995, TIMSS 1999, and CivEd) and in OECD's PISA Plus (see Table 12.2). In Romania, members of the Institute for Educational Sciences in Bucharest carried out the IEA studies. Staff from Romania's National Assessment and Examination Service were responsible for PISA.

**Table 12.2: Romania's participation in international large-scale surveys of educational achievement, 1995–2003**

| Year of data collection | Name of survey | Organization in charge | Target population |
|---|---|---|---|
| 1995 | Third International Mathematics and Science Study 1995 (TIMSS 1995) | IEA | Thirteen-year-old students (Grades 7 and 8) |
| 1999 | Third International Mathematics and Science Study-Repeat (TIMSS-R) | IEA | Thirteen-year-old students (Grade 8) |
| 1999 | Civic Education (CivEd) | IEA | Thirteen-year-old students (Grade 8) |
| 2001 | OECD's Program for International Student Assessment (PISA) Plus | OECD | Fifteen-year-old students (Grades 8 and 9) |
| 2003 | Trends in International Mathematics and Science Study 2003 (TIMSS 2003) | IEA | Grade 8 |

Before TIMSS 1995, large-scale assessment, as a tool for quality control in the education system, was unknown in Romania. People had no facility through which to access data about the achievement levels of large representative samples of students. In the absence of a lack of empirical information about the relative performance of samples of students, Romanians seem to have used the good success of their students in international competitions as a measure of the well-being of the country's education system. The national pride generated by these students' success led to an assumption that all was well. It is not surprising, therefore, that Romanian students' poor performance in TIMSS 1995 was kept quiet, with dissemination of the results limited to a few educational specialists and policy-makers and with no public publicity. When the similarly disappointing results of TIMSS 1999 (TIMSS-R) confirmed beyond doubt the veracity of the 1995 results, Romania had to accept the findings of both studies as a "wake-up call".

TIMSS data subsequently published post 1999 in national reports were used mainly by educational professionals for planning curricula, developing teachers' guides, and writing a new generation of mathematics and science textbooks. The released TIMSS test items were made available to teachers, who were encouraged to use them as a teaching/learning and assessment tool. In some universities, teacher pre-service and in-service training also received a "shake-up" following publication of the results of the IEA assessments. Romania now has new examinations and assessment methods, including surveys of representative samples of students.[5]

In 1995, 1996, 1998, and 2000, Romania assessed the achievement of nationally representative samples of Grade 4 students. The aim was to evaluate basic student skills at the end of primary education in order to provide useful and accurate information for educational stakeholders, such as decision-makers, teachers, students, parents, inspectors, researchers, curriculum developers, textbook authors, and the public at large. Since 2000, the National Assessment and Examination Service has carried out a major nationwide assessment program called the National Program for the Assessment of Educational Progress. This has three major aims:

1.  To identify, over time, the main changes in student academic achievement and progress;
2.  To gather reliable data pertaining to the impact of new curricula, textbooks, and other important changes, in particular, and of the education system, in general; and
3.  To provide reliable measures of the degrees and levels of students' functional literacy, as well as their mathematical and science literacy at the end of primary education.

In 2000, evaluation instruments were generated, for the first time, for the new curriculum and the new assessment system. Based on band descriptors, these were implemented starting with school year 1998/99. Students were tested in three subjects: Romanian language, mathematics, and science. (This was the first time that student achievement (knowledge and skills) had been investigated in science.) The findings of these national assessments are now linked to the assessment techniques primary school teachers are encouraged to use in the classroom.[6]

Romania has designed and used only a few primary-school-based standardized reading, mathematics, and science tests. Those that are available were elaborated by the National Assessment and Examination Service (NAES) for national assessments and students' "high-stake contests". Most teachers still use their own experience and knowledge to monitor students' abilities. The educational professionals who have been involved with the standardized tests have immediately recognized the benefits of large-scale assessment data and have encouraged Romania's ongoing participation in TIMSS, PIRLS, and PISA.

---

5   The information on assessment and evaluation in this section is drawn from *Four Position Papers on Learning Assessment* (National Institute for Education Measurements (Netherlands)/National Assessment and Examination Service (Romania), 2001).
6   The information on evaluation instruments and techniques is drawn from *School-based Assessment and Examination: Guide for Teachers* (Litoiu, 2001).

## 12.4 National Results and Impact of PIRLS 2001

### 12.4.1 Results of PIRLS 2001[7]

Romanian students' average score of 512 on the PIRLS 2001 literacy scale placed Romania 22nd among the countries that participated in the study. Girls were better readers than were boys of both the literary and the informational texts. The score difference of 12 points between boys and girls put Romania at eighth place on the international ranking. The students' across-country placement for the literary subscale was 22. It was 21 for the informational subscale. Of the former communist countries that participated in PIRLS 2001, namely Bulgaria, Hungary, Latvia, Lithuania, Czech Republic, Slovak Republic, Slovenia, Moldova, and Macedonia, the first six countries outranked Romania.

Eleven per cent of Romanian students performed in the top 10% of the international sample, 27% in the upper quarter, 54% in the median, and 81% in the lower quarter.[8] If we consider only the students performing in the top 10% of the international sample, Romania attained a ranking of 16. Of the former communist countries, Romania was outranked only by Bulgaria, Hungary, Latvia, and Lithuania. This ranking and the placement for Romania of 22 overall clearly shows that the 19% of Romanian students who were the lowest achievers on the Romanian literacy scale had very low scores indeed. These figures made obvious the need to provide special reading literacy assistance for at least one-fifth of Romania's Grade 4 students.

Scrutiny of the data gathered during PIRLS 2001 on school and home background factors highlighted the following as exerting a strong influence on Romanian student achievement:

- Specific literacy-related activities engaged in at home with family members during early childhood;
- The language spoken at home;
- Available educational resources in the home and at school;
- Number of years spent in the kindergarten;
- Community type (urban, rural, suburban);
- School "climate";

---

7   The information in this section is drawn from *Learning to Read: PIRLS National Report* (Noveanu, Noveanu, Tudor, & Pescaru, 2003).

8   The International Study Center for PIRLS identified four points on the scale as international benchmarks: top 10%, defined as the 90th percentile and corresponding to a scale score of 615; the upper quarter benchmark, defined as the 75th percentile and corresponding to a scale score of 570; the median benchmark, defined as the 50th percentile and corresponding to a scale score of 510; and the lower quarter benchmark, defined as the 25th percentile and coresponding to a scale score of 435.

- Students' attitude towards reading; and
- Students' self-concept.

Several findings in particular captured our attention and are worth mentioning here. Students whose parents owned a small business achieved the highest average score (540). The reason for this may be that these parents were more able than other parents to pay for extra tuition (outside of school hours) for their children. The students in the next highest achieving group, with an average score of 530, had at least one parent with a university qualification. The lowest average score of 486 was for students whose fathers were not in paid employment. The second lowest average score (498) was for the group of students whose mothers were in the "skilled" category (paid workforce). Students whose mothers were not in paid employment achieved a higher average score (516), suggesting that at-home mothers are more readily able to oversee the learning of their children for all or at least a part of the time the children are in primary school. This finding emphasizes a problem that is well recognized in Romania, that of the parallel instruction system. It also raises questions about the quality and efficiency of official class instruction.

Eighty-five per cent of the students assessed in PIRLS 2001 belonged to schools where the principals reported a special focus on reading activities relative to other curricular areas. This fact, along with the number of supplemental hours dedicated to study of language and literature,[9] raises questions about the efficiency of the intended curriculum. A rather unexpected finding was that classes with more than 31 students had the best achievement scores. This finding has its roots in a local distribution phenomenon wherein classes that have either a small or very small number of students—fewer than 10—are over-represented in the rural communities, while classes with large numbers of students are over-represented in the urban communities, especially in schools located in the centre of the cities. Schools in urban areas (city centers in particular) attract the better teachers.

Almost half of the Romanian students reported having never participated in project activities related to a text after they had read it. Those students who had never participated in these activities achieved higher scores, undermining the common conception among educators that these activities offer remedial teaching and learning.

In Romania, students are not used to reading informational texts, as both the intended and the implemented curriculum focus on literary reading. This finding and the fact that 68% of students (both boys and girls) reported a preference for reading

---

9    Many of the hours of instruction set aside under the National Curriculum for science, music, art and crafts, and physical education were actually being spent in classrooms on literature and language study.

informational texts highlight the need to revise the curriculum to include informational texts, a strategy that should improve students' motivation to read.

## 12.4.2 Publication of PIRLS Results

The findings of a survey of educational achievement, such as PIRLS 2001, are most likely to have a strong local impact if they are widely disseminated to policy-makers, schools, and teachers. The publication of an authoritative report that sets out the results in a clear and concise manner so that readers can easily judge and understand the importance of the findings is a vital part of this process. Although Romania distributed a national report of the PIRLS 2001 findings to policy-makers and certain educational professionals, it did not send a report to schools and teachers, even though it had provided these audiences with a report of the earlier TIMSS results. Schools and teachers did not receive a PIRLS report because money was not available to do this. Despite this situation, furnishing schools and teachers with a report of the PIRLS results remains a top priority.

## 12.4.3 Impact of PIRLS 2001

### *Impact on Administrative and School Level*

The PIRLS findings for Romania attracted limited attention when they were released mainly because the Ministerial team, unpleasantly surprised at Romania's 22nd placement on the international ranking, did not allow a press conference. However, the PIRLS National Research Coordinator (NRC) did, in time, present the findings at several official meetings with educational professionals throughout the country, and to members of local television and radio stations. The relationships between student achievement and various contextual factors and associated problems did raise considerable interest and appreciation among these audiences, partly because they had not been aware of them.

In Romania, empirical data on educational achievement have traditionally not informed educational policies. Romania's experience of large-scale assessment of education is, of course, relatively recent and limited to the aforementioned IEA studies and OECD's PISA Plus. Also, published information has been limited to TIMSS and PIRLS, although the PIRLS material is minimal relative to that for TIMSS. However, the National Council for Curriculum did refer to the national report on PIRLS when revising the curricula for Grades 3 and 4. The report has also informed various research activities developed by the Institute for Educational Sciences. Romania's experience with TIMSS-related publications strongly suggests that publishing the released PIRLS texts and items would also have a very useful impact. Teachers could use them in class, and as a model for item construction and text selection for further practice.

Overall, our experience with both TIMSS and PIRLS tells us that the findings of such studies are most likely to facilitate educational change when they are employed in two ways. The first involves a top–down approach, where the information is used in the design and implementation of new and revised curricula. The second is a bottom–up approach that involves teachers, students, and parents.

### Long-term Effects

For several Romanian educational experts, the PIRLS results confirmed their suspicion that the reading literacy achievement of Romanian students needs remedial attention. However, schools, educational administrators, and members of the public generally remain unconvinced that anything is wrong. As long as politicians and opinion-makers perpetuate the myth that Romanian students generally achieve well and that the country has a high-quality education system, the extent to which PIRLS and other such studies can influence opinion in the direction of educational reform is difficult to gauge. In short, the question of long-term effects remains an open one.

## 12.5   Future Activities

Romanian researchers are conducting secondary analyses of the PIRLS data in order to gain maximum benefit from this rich source of information. These analyses are helping us identify the specific factors that contribute to students' reading performance and providing us with direction for improving reading curricula and pedagogy. This secondary research is also acquainting policy-makers with the need for Romania to refer to large-scale assessment data when planning the future of education in Romania. Romania's decision to participate in PIRLS 2006 is part of this recognition. Moreover, the trend data provided from this study will allow Romania to assess the influence of the new curriculum on students' reading literacy ability.

## 12.6   Concluding Remarks

Although the findings of PIRLS 2001 have had a disappointingly limited impact on public perception and educational policy- and decision-making in Romania, the history of our country over the last 15 years reminds us that change takes time. The PIRLS 2001 results accordingly remain relevant for everyone in the country: the poor performance of Romanian students in reading literacy is too serious to ignore or take lightly. Although national agencies have brought in some changes to how reading literacy is taught in schools, political will is needed to ensure that the changes that are made have long-standing positive outcomes.

## References

Litoiu, N. (2001). Assessment methods and instruments. In A. Stoica (Ed.), *School-based assessment and examinations: Guide for teachers* (pp. 48–70). Bucharest: Prognosis.

Ministry of National Education. (1998). *Subject curricula for primary education.* Bucharest: Corint.

Ministry of National Education. (2000). *The new national curriculum.* Bucharest: Imprimeriile Media Pro Brasov.

National Institute for Education Measurements (Netherlands)/National Assessment and Examination Service (Romania). (2001). *Four position papers on learning assessment.* Bucharest: Ed. Prognosis.

Noveanu, G., & Noveanu, D. (2002). Romania. In I. V. S. Mullis, M. O. Martin, A. M. Kennedy & C. L. Flaherty (Eds*.), PIRLS 2001 encyclopedia: A reference guide to reading education in the countries participating in IEA's Progress in International Reading Literacy Study (PIRLS)* (pp. 227–232). Chestnut Hill, MA: Boston College.

Noveanu, G., Noveanu, D., Tudor, V., & Pescaru, A. (2003). *Learning to read: PIRLS national report.* Bucharest: Institute for Educational Sciences.

# Chapter 13
# The Impact of PIRLS in the Slovak Republic

*Zuzana Lukačková and Oľga Zápotočná*

## 13.1 Slovakia at a Glance[1]

The Slovak Republic, or Slovakia, is situated in the middle of Central Europe. It borders the Czech Republic to the west, Poland to the north, Austria and Hungary to the south, and the Ukraine to the east. Bratislava, the capital of Slovakia, lies on the Danube River. The area of the country is 49,035 square kilometers. The landscape of the Slovak Republic is hilly in the central and northern parts, with plains in the south.

According to the 2001 census, the population is five million inhabitants. The population density is 112 persons per square kilometer and is highest in southwestern and eastern Slovakia. The largest city is Bratislava with almost 428,672 inhabitants. Approximately 57% of the population lives in urban areas.

Slovakia is a member of the United Nations, the Council of Europe, UNESCO, and the Organization for Economic Cooperation and Development (OECD), and strives to join the European Union and the North Atlantic Treaty Organization. The GDP per capita in 2001 was US$3,770. Since the fall of the communist regime in 1989, the centrally controlled economy has been transforming into a market economy. In 2000, Slovak public expenditure on education was 4.17% of its total GNP.

## 13.2 Slovakia's Education System as Context for PIRLS 2001

### 13.2.1 Overview

Education in Slovakia comprises preschool, primary, and secondary schools, and higher education. Compulsory education in Slovakia lasts for 10 years, from ages six to 16. It is completed at primary school (*Základná škola*), which has nine grades, and in the first year of a secondary school. The Ministry of Education approves the nationwide curricula documents that govern what is taught in the primary and secondary schools.

---

1   This introduction is based on Slovakia's country profile in the *PIRLS 2001 Encyclopedia* (Lukačková, 2002).

## Preschool Education

Preschool education (kindergarten) is considered the first level of the education system in the Slovak Republic, yet attendance is voluntary. Preschool provides education for children two to six years of age and prepares them for compulsory school attendance. It is comparable with ISCED Level 0.

## Primary Education

Primary school has two stages. The first stage (Grades 1 to 4) is comparable with ISCED Level 1, and the second stage (Grades 5 to 9) is comparable with ISCED Level 2. The upper primary stage is comparable with lower secondary education. Primary education in the State schools is free and offered in the State language as well as in the language of national minorities (for example, Hungarian, Ukrainian). Public primary schools are established by municipalities or local administration bodies, but may also be established by churches, private persons, and legal entities. They must follow the regulations of the Ministry of Education. After completing primary school, students apply for a secondary school of their choice. Some students apply to enter the eight-year *gymnázium* (a type of secondary education) after completing the fourth year of primary school and passing an entrance examination.

## Secondary Education

Slovakia currently offers secondary education at three types of schools: *gymnázium* (grammar school), secondary specialized schools, and secondary vocational schools. Admission to secondary schools is conditional on passing entrance examinations. The secondary schools provide education gratis, although the church and private schools may charge fees. Secondary schools fall within the jurisdiction of the Ministry of Education, but their legal status is that of a semi-autonomous entity. This means that their principals, in association with school and regional school boards, can make decisions about the administration, resourcing, and pedagogical direction of their schools.

The *gymnázium* (comparable with ISCED Level 3A) offers general education and prepares students primarily for study at universities and in higher education institutions. The *gymnázium* has leeway to modify school curricula and study plans according to the interests and skills of students, to provide additional optional subjects, and to provide classes in other subject areas. Study is directed towards the school-leaving examination, the *maturitná skúška*. The Slovak Government implemented a revised form of this examination in school year 2004/05, after trialing it over several years.

Secondary specialized schools (comparable with ISCED Level 3B) equip students with the skills necessary to enter industrial and technical employment or to work in many other spheres of society on leaving secondary school. They also prepare students for study in tertiary-level education. Secondary specialized schools also offer post-secondary education in one, two, or three-year courses (higher vocational education, ISCED Level 4).

Secondary vocational schools (comparable with ISCED Level 3C) prepare graduates for qualified performance in trades-related occupations. Education and training comprises general and vocational tuition, and involves apprenticeships. Courses last for two or three years, at the end of which students sit a final examination. If they pass, they receive a certificate approving their professional skills.

### Higher Education

This sector of the education system provides higher education courses at three levels: a three- to four-year program of study leading to a Bachelor's degree at the first level; a five- to six-year program of study leading to a Master's degree at the second level; and PhD study programs at the third level.

### 13.2.2 Literacy Education

Literacy education in Slovakia starts with formal reading and writing instruction in Grade 1 of the primary school, and it is mainly during the primary period (Grades 1 to 4) that children receive the majority of their literacy education. The development of children's literacy skills is considered one of the most important goals at this level. Slovakia has long employed a "basal-reader" approach to reading instruction. This "traditional" approach is based on a teaching method that has been used since the 19th century, and it has accordingly developed strengths and weaknesses over time.

In Slovakia, the so-called "phoneme/analytic/synthetic" method of beginning reading is built on the phonemic analysis and blending of 38 sounds corresponding to 38 letters, an approach that is easy to apply thanks to the phonemic regularity of the Slovak language. Reading instruction in Grade 1 (ages six to seven) is devoted to ensuring children acquire basal reading skill. The procedure follows a prescribed letter-by-letter sequence and lasts about eight to 10 months on average. At the same time, children have to learn four different letter shapes (upper and lower case letters, each in printed and handwritten form), and the performance criteria for these are very high. The requirement for children to meet formal criteria of accuracy in reading and writing has always taken precedence over children extracting meaning from and making use of written language. Slovak children consequently experience considerable training and practice in reading and sounding out words and sentences and engaging in repetitive writing exercises (mechanical copying, dictation, etc). The aim of the next two or three years of schooling is to improve and reinforce children's "reading technique" (skill). A common assumption is that children will acquire the ability to comprehend what they read as a natural outcome of having perfected their reading skill.

These attitudes and related teaching activities occur to the detriment of more important tasks that encourage children to draw meaning from context—that is, to understand what they are reading and to use that understanding to develop their thinking skills. Teachers in Slovak schools often neglect important reading comprehension tools and strategies such as guessing, predicting, negotiating, group discussions, social interactions, and transaction. The importance of children engaging in meaningful writing activities involving personal expression is equally underestimated during the first two or three years of schooling. It is perhaps not surprising, then, that most children seem to have poorly developed reading habits and interests.

With formal reading instruction more or less accomplished at primary level, the expectation is that children by age 10 should be able to "read to learn" efficiently and to cope with further educational goals and requirements independently. Today, reasonable doubt exists as to whether they really can. Despite critiques and professional disputes relating to literacy education appearing in published form, and some efforts to introduce change, the traditional method of teaching reading literacy seems entrenched. One of the reasons for this resistance might be the fact that until Slovakia took part in PIRLS 2001, it had no strong empirical evidence, drawn from a large-scale nationwide assessment, of how well the country's students were performing in the area of literacy. Nor did the country have evidence of how well Slovak students were performing in reading relative to their peers in other countries. PIRLS 2001 and the release of the results of PISA 2003 changed this situation.

## 13.3  Experience in Large-scale Assessments

Before taking part in PIRLS 2001, the only involvement the Slovak Republic had with large-scale international studies of educational achievement was TIMSS 1995 (see Table 13.1).

**Table 13.1: Slovakia's participation in international large-scale surveys of educational achievement, 1995–2006**

| Year of data collection | Name of survey | Organization in charge | Target population |
|---|---|---|---|
| 1995 | Third International Mathematics and Science Study (TIMSS) | IEA | Thirteen-year-old students (Grades 7–8); sample size: 7,101 students from 290 schools |
| 1999 | Third International Mathematics and Science Study-Repeat (TIMSS-R) | IEA | Thirteen-year-old students (Grades 7–8 ); sample size: 3,497 students from 154 schools |
| 2001 | Progress in Reading Literacy Study (PIRLS) | IEA | Ten-year-old students; sample size: 3,807 students from 150 schools |
| 2002 | Civic Education Study (CivEd) | IEA | Fourteen-year-old students; sample size: 3,463 students from 145 schools |
| 2003 | Trends in Mathematics and Science Study 2003 (TIMSS 2003) | IEA | Fourteen-year-old students (Grade 8); sample size: 4,428 students from 180 schools |
| 2003 | Program for International Student Assessment (PISA) | OECD | Fifteen-year-old students; sample size: 7,346 students from 281 schools |
| 2006 | Progress in Reading Literacy Study (PIRLS) | IEA | Ten-year-old students; sample size: 6,256 students from 174 schools |

The country had no parallel experience in the area of reading literacy other than its unsuccessful attempt to join the IEA Reading Literacy Study of 1990/91. Slovakia also had no previous history of assessing students' reading literacy at national level. Soon after PIRLS 2001, Slovakia implemented, in 2002 and with assistance from the French Ministry of Education, national monitoring at the beginning of primary education. This study, which involved a sample of 2,772 students, concentrated primarily on mother tongue and mathematics achievement, and its results showed that Slovak primary school children tended to have poor reading comprehension skills. The experience gained from participation in PIRLS 2001 was very useful and relevant in regard to the evaluation, with methodological input and strategies proving particularly helpful and inspiring. This study was to have been repeated every four years at the beginning of primary education. However, and probably for financial reasons, a decision was made instead to test all students (primarily in mother tongue and mathematics) every year (from 2003) at the end of the second stage of primary school. This means that all children finishing primary school are subject to compulsory testing in these subject areas.

At present, the only reading literacy assessment instrument available to primary school teachers focuses mainly on reading performance measures. However, teachers are not obliged to use it. If teachers encounter students with serious reading difficulties, they can recommend them to educational/psychological counseling service centers. Here, specialists assess each child's reading abilities, specify the difficulties, and offer intervention and other treatment. Teachers' monitoring of approximately 95% of children not seen as requiring remedial help tends to be based on experience and knowledge, which is often vague and intuitive. There is also no officially declared need or effort to individualize (adapt) teaching according to children's individual needs and abilities. The curriculum is directed at what authorities expect a child of average ability to achieve, with the level of achievement set at "zero" for all children on their entry to school, regardless of any reading abilities they may have acquired beforehand. In short, the same starting point and standards apply to all, and the consequences are obvious.

Given these restraints, Slovakia's National Institute for Education found participation in the large international projects PIRLS 2001 and PISA 2003 very challenging. However, the Institute managed to run and complete both evaluation projects with great success, which was very much due to the efforts of the few (and devoted) staff within the Institute responsible for conducting them. The data collected are proving of enormous value, especially in terms of validating (or otherwise) the attitudes and beliefs about reading literacy held by the many people involved in literacy promotion and development at all levels of the education system. The data have also been a boon for researchers and teacher educators and it is hoped that they will, in time, receive equal scrutiny from educational policy- and decision-makers at the levels of State and local government, and from members of the general public.

## 13.4  National Results and Impact of PIRLS 2001

### 13.4.1  Results of PIRLS 2001

Although the literacy performance of students in Slovakia registered as above average on the international scale (518 score points), we cannot consider the result satisfactory when comparing it with the results for students in most of the other post-communist countries that participated in PIRLS 2001. This was especially the case with those countries with cultural and educational backgrounds similar to Slovakia's. Children from Bulgaria, the Czech Republic, Hungary, Latvia, Lithuania, and Russia outperformed their Slovak peers to a considerable degree on the literacy scale (by 10 to 32 score points, on average). The distribution among the four reading levels shows that only 7% of Slovak children reached the top 10% benchmark of reading literacy (in comparison to 21% from Bulgaria, 13% from Hungary and Lithuania, 12% from Latvia, and 11, 10, and 8% respectively from Romania, the Czech Republic, and Russia). Twelve per cent of Slovak students fell within the lower quarter benchmark (in comparison with 4 to 9% from the other identified countries).

The difference in performance between the Slovak students and their peers in these other countries may partly be because the education systems of some of those countries had experienced reform by the time of PIRLS 2001 or because their educational institutions are more flexible and open than are Slovak institutions to positive influence from other parts of the world. Most of these countries had also participated in previous IEA and PISA reading literacy evaluations, which suggests that these countries tend to pay more (and appropriate) attention to literacy matters than does Slovakia. The results from PIRLS also confirmed the assumption that teaching reading in Slovakia supports more the "lower-level" processes of reading (such as retrieving explicit information) than the "upper-level" processes (connected with critical evaluation and interpretation). These findings, along with the many others that have come out of PIRLS, support the argument that Slovakia needs to change its reading instruction approach, and to set this approach within a new and clearly articulated reading policy that applies nationwide. Certainly, given the advantage of the easy Slovak orthography, Slovak children, in comparison with many other language-users, should have achieved much better results.

Although this cross-country analysis presents a discouraging picture of the Slovak results, there are also encouraging data. For example, the performance of the students, and especially the boys, when reading informational texts was better than expected, as reading lessons in Slovak schools are mostly limited to literary genres. It appears that Slovak children, during their independent attempts to "read to learn", are used to reading, like to read, and/or are able to read for informational purposes as well as literary. They possess a skill that schools should build on and support, rather than ignore or leave the children to cope with on their own. Teaching strategic reading and developing students' meta-cognitive processes in reading (that is, supporting the key skills of reading) are among the weakest aspects of our teaching practice.

Other findings worth mentioning are those showing the strong relationship between reading success and early literacy support in the home environment and between reading success and motivation to read/positive attitudes to reading. The data on demographic and regional differences also highlight important factors influencing reading achievement. These, along with further and deeper analyses, which have yet to be completed, suggest many straightforward inferences and instructional implications not only for the different levels of formal schooling but also for preschool education. Reference to the data gained from the PIRLS study (and subsequently PISA) makes obvious the changes the Slovak Republic must inevitably make to its system of reading literacy education.

### 13.4.2 Publication of PIRLS Results

*Public Release and Reactions*

The National Institute of Education (ŠPÚ), as the National Center for PIRLS, began publicizing the PIRLS project before data collection began in spring 2001. The Institute wanted to ensure educational stakeholders (and not just those directly involved in PIRLS) and the public readily understood the immense importance of this study. After the first release of the PIRLS international data, the ŠPÚ held a press conference for representatives from the various media (May 2003) at the Ministry of Education. The Institute provided press kits presenting the issues from various points of view. Although some articles and reports subsequently appeared in the daily press and on radio stations, and information was presented at conferences of non-governmental organizations dealing with reading (for example, the Orava Association), the results and related issues attracted only limited public attention and no widespread or ongoing debate. The public seemed generally satisfied with the performance of Slovak children relative to their international peers, while policy-makers, as a group, seemed indifferent. Within the context of other "hot" issues in education, notably financial problems (underestimated budgets, schools balancing on the edge of survival) and the reform of school-leaving examinations, the concerns arising out of the PIRLS 2001 (and PISA) data have not rated highly. However, the more detailed interpretations and secondary analyses that have yet to be completed may raise the profile of these concerns.

The ŠPÚ sent a summary of the results and other specific information about the study directly to the schools that participated in both the PIRLS pilot and the main studies. The results sent to each school showed how well that school's students had performed on the test compared to the performance of the students in the other participating schools. One reason why the Institute is mindful of keeping schools informed is that its staff consider that schools need to be aware of what participation in similar studies offers them. The Institute is aware that school principals and teachers need to have a much greater appreciation of large-scale measurement of educational achievement, as this practice is still relatively new in the Slovak Republic, and even more so in relation to reading literacy comprehension. Although the team responsible for PIRLS in Slovakia is small, it has gained much experience from the study, particularly in terms of being able to apply the methodology and procedures in other national surveys of educational achievement presently underway.

The ŠPÚ, aware that, despite all effort, PIRLS needed more intensive and constant promotion to attract the attention needed to effect change, set up a website (www.statpedu.sk) to publicize the PIRLS data and associated issues. The Institute regularly updates this website by providing the results of new analyses and other information about PIRLS.

Although the response to PIRLS from some quarters has been disappointing, the study has received considerable appreciation and interest from the academic community, researchers, and a few progressive teachers. These people tend to be well aware of the crucial importance of literacy issues in the contemporary world and in our culture. They acknowledge the shortcomings of literacy education in Slovakia and are willing to join collaborative effort for its improvement and change. Direction on just how they might help achieve this should come from further and deeper analyses of the PIRLS and PISA data.

An important current area of analysis concerns the relationships between children's reading literacy performance and the other factors assessed in PIRLS. Those aspects of the teaching and family environments associated with the better results in the participating countries are of particular interest. In related vein, researchers are completing case study analyses of the schools or countries where "literacy thrives", an approach that should also provide valuable leads for Slovakia.

### *Specific Publications*

Several articles, written by Institute members, have been published in research journals and the media, with the latter directed at a wide audience. The Institute has also published and distributed (at various occasions) leaflets setting out the most important PIRLS 2001 results. PIRLS was brought to the attention of the media during the second meeting of the PIRLS National Research Coordinators (NRCs) in Bratislava in March 2004. This effort led to feature articles in the press and a radio program on the national channel that explored the issue of reading literacy and conducted interviews with the Boston College-based directors of the PIRLS International Steering Committee. The Institute also launched the aforementioned website at this time.

The national report presenting the PIRLS 2001 results was published in 2004. Prepared by the team of authors from the ŠPÚ, it was sent to schools and local bodies responsible for educational administration bodies, where it attracted only mild interest. The ŠPÚ has also continued to disseminate the PIRLS results and ideas at conferences and seminars for teachers and to researchers at universities and teacher education colleges.

### 13.4.3 Impact of PIRLS 2001

Before the announcement of the results of PISA 2003 in 2004, the Slovak Republic had seen no reason to be concerned about its students' reading abilities. The release of the results of both PISA and PIRLS in 2004 changed that view. People were shocked to discover that the performance of the Slovak students in PIRLS 2001 was average and in PISA 2003 was the worst of the participating European Union countries. Suddenly, reading literacy became a very urgent concern in Slovakia.

In addition to being shocked by the below-average reading scores of 15-year-old Slovak students in PISA 2003, educational stakeholders and the public were awoken to the vital importance of using large-scale assessments of educational achievement to monitor the quality of educational provision. Many articles about the results appeared in newspapers, discussions took place in the electronic media, and teachers and local administrative bodies met to consider the implications of the results.

The traditional knowledge-based (rather than competence-based) focus of Slovakia's school system is now under threat with the acknowledgment that reforms to the content and delivery of the school curriculum are inevitable. It is particularly clear that the aims and principles of reading tuition need to be redefined and transformed, and that a much stronger emphasis needs to be placed on competence development, especially in the teaching and learning of languages.

Although much needs doing in terms of educational reform, some relevant initiatives are underway in the Slovak Republic. With reference to Council of Europe policy, the Slovak Ministry of Education and the National Institute for Education are involved in several projects relating to curricular reform. Allied with this initiative is a desire to bring an integrated approach to the subjects that make up the National Curriculum. The desire here is to set all school subjects within a philosophy that incorporates up-to-date global thinking on education. This philosophy would embrace the necessity to strengthen students' personal and social skills and their ability to act and learn with autonomy. Notions such as lifelong learning and learning for life would be natural consequences of such a philosophy.

With time, the results of large-scale international studies such as PIRLS and PISA have attracted more attention to the quality of educational provision in the Slovak Republic. The public is finally becoming aware that the way the country chooses to teach children and young people, the form in which it imposes knowledge on them, and the skills students learn at school have a marked impact on their future lives and careers. Unless Slovakia transforms its whole concept of education toward the needs of modern society, certain groups of our people will be unable to compete in the global marketplace. We must equip our students and future workers with the skills they need so that they will not be disadvantaged. One of the most important of these skills is reading literacy. Without good reading literacy ability, students have difficulty learning and gaining educational qualifications. Without educational qualifications, they have difficulty procuring employment and meeting the skills needs of our workforce and society. PIRLS and PISA have shown us that we need to create conditions more advantageous for the development of this vital skill.

### 13.4.4  Impact on Administrative and School Level

We anticipate that completion of the above-mentioned projects will give educational administrators and the schools themselves the tools and resources to give greater attention to developing students' reading literacy as it is specified in the PIRLS framework.

### 13.4.5  Long-term Effects

Although, as previously mentioned, Slovakia still has much to do in terms of future developments, several initiatives have already been implemented that are likely to have long-term benefit. These relate mainly to pre-service teacher education courses in the universities for preschool and primary school teachers. In collaboration with the ŠPÚ, and informed by the understandings gained from PIRLS, the universities have in place newly accredited study programs that allocate more courses, time, and credits to literacy issues than was previously the case. The difference is not only quantitative, but also qualitative. Students are also being encouraged to gain a deeper insight into contemporary approaches to and experiences with literacy education from all over the world. The universities do differ, however, in the extent to which they have embedded these components in their pre-service courses.

Of course, revision of teacher education programs will not ensure change at the level of school practice unless in-service teachers accept it. In-service teachers represent the most important target audience for further education, and it is they, in particular, who need to be firmly acquainted with the reports from both PISA and PIRLS. There is no guarantee that teacher journals and articles will achieve this objective. What is needed is the cooperation and collaboration of all educational bodies, whether State (and including the universities and teacher training colleges), non-governmental, civic, or professional association.

Some of these organizations have already initiated networking activities in the field of research. For example, the Association of Teachers of the Slovak Language recently submitted a proposal for a research project (undertaken as a joint venture of various institutions) to the Cultural and Educational Grant Agency. The objectives of the project are to seek out policies and successful strategies that other countries have applied in relation to the advancement of literacy education. The data obtained will be used to conceptualize a new curriculum for Slovak language and literature, in which language education will be strongly linked into (integrated with) the content areas of other school subjects. Another initiative centers on the complexities of reading comprehension at the different levels defined in the PIRLS and PISA frameworks. The Slovak Reading Association (a member of the International Reading Association) and the Orava Association (see www.zdruzenieorava.sk) have also signaled their wish to collaborate on reading literacy initiatives, including teacher-training projects. The ŠPÚ, of course, is presently conducting a number of research tasks aimed at developing a coherent reading literacy strategy. At the time of writing (2005), the Institute was also preparing manuals for teachers that provide a theoretical introduction to reading literacy and specific examples of reading tasks.

A brief account of other areas where the PISA/PIRLS data could contribute to meaningful future developments follows.

- *Preschool education*: The question of how to ensure all children receive an optimal start to their literacy learning is being widely discussed in Slovakia. Some experts and teachers still hold the traditional view that the ideal time for children to start learning to read and write is in the first year of compulsory schooling at the age of six. They think children are not mature enough to start formal instruction until this age. As a result, most kindergartens still concentrate on stimulating children's fine psychomotor skills and their oral speech and pay very little or no attention to facilitating their early literacy development. The opponents of this idea claim that children's reading/writing development does not start abruptly but evolves gradually, emerging in small steps and involving both cognitive and social development. They see oral and written language development as complementary and mutually supportive. They contend that kindergartens should stimulate a large measure of children's literacy skills and that the preschool curriculum needs revising in line with this aim. To support their argument, they point to the strong relationship found in PIRLS between high literacy achievement in later life and early literacy stimulation in the preschool years.

- *Minorities*: The PIRLS data corroborated the severity of the difficulties, including literacy acquisition, that children from language and cultural minorities tend to experience during their schooling. For example, PIRLS showed that, in Slovakia, the schools from regions with a high number of Romany children tended to have low achievement scores. It is likely that this problem will become even greater in the near future as Slovakia experiences growing cultural and linguistic diversity.

- *Beginning of reading instruction*: An important issue that has attracted animated discussion in Slovakia is that of teaching to each child's individual literacy needs during the early stage of reading instruction. While educationists and teachers generally accept this idea, teachers do not have the tools to put it into practice. They do not have modern and flexible teaching and reading materials, and they do not have instruments for testing each child's level of literacy achievement and literacy needs. However, interdependent projects aimed at addressing these deficits is underway, and needed reading and assessment resources are nearly ready for implementation, although some administrative concerns will need to be addressed before this happens.

- *Changes in attitude*: The PIRLS data, as a whole, and the distribution data in particular (for example, the relatively low proportion of students in the top levels of reading literacy), confirm that using the same teaching approach for all children is no longer tenable. The crucial importance of assessing students' educational achievement—the main message to come out of all IEA evaluations—is an idea that has yet to gain widespread acceptance in the Slovak Republic. Hopefully, the lessons learned from the participation of Slovak schools in PIRLS 2001 and 2006 and PISA 2003 will see an overall positive change in the country's attitudes towards the assessment and evaluation of educational achievement.

## 13.5  Future Activities

We have already mentioned some of Slovakia's future reading-literacy activities and plans. However, the country also needs to consider and establish some other long-term goals. First is the necessity to provide more information on reading literacy for teachers, inspectors, educational policy-makers, and parents. Second is the need to make the public more familiar with contemporary educational approaches and trends. We are aware that the provision of more study materials and professional literature on the theoretical background of reading literacy is essential. So, too, are practical handouts for teachers. These need to provide new pedagogical ideas and techniques, along with examples of efficient teaching strategies and activities to employ in everyday classroom practice. Third, we need to provide pre- and in-service teachers with professional development (workshops and the like) in reading literacy. And last, but not least, we need to create a network of the various institutions and experts in the field of reading literacy. In this regard, we need to plan and hold more national as well as international conferences and workshops. Such opportunities will allow professionals and literacy experts to communicate and share their knowledge and experience, so bringing a unified approach to reading literacy development across the different levels of the educational and research communities.

### 13.5.1 Research

The ŠPÚ plans to conduct further research in collaboration with researchers from the universities. Our aim is to continue our comparative studies and secondary analyses of the PIRLS and PISA data. In particular, we hope, among other considerations, to find explanations for achievement differences (for example, between boys and girls), to consider the influence of the home on literacy acquisition, to sift out the school and home preconditions of the best and worst achievers, to determine the influence of curriculum and instruction issues, and to consider issues of equity.

### 13.5.2 Publications

Plans are underway to publish a series of short reports dealing with certain aspects of the study outcomes already mentioned.

### 13.5.3 Programs

We have in mind some modified professional development courses on reading literacy targeted at practicing teachers. However, we have yet to specify the content and format of these courses. This work will require the close cooperation of various bodies (universities, teacher training colleges, methodological centers, research institutes, teachers' associations, non-governmental organizations, etc.). Although this work will take time, we consider it vitally important for ensuring improvements in reading literacy.

## 13.6  Concluding Remarks

This chapter provides only a brief review of the most important results and impacts of Slovakia's participation in PIRLS 2001. What we have said here covers only the most pressing topics and issues raised by the PIRLS data. We are well aware that we are far from fully exploiting the enormously rich source of information the PIRLS data provide. Further analyses are inevitable. We also wish to stress our awareness that some of the "impacts" we mention are just preliminary impressions and perspectives and that the country's responses to these to date are far from final. We believe that the real impact of Slovakia's participation in PIRLS, that is, positive and useful changes in literacy education visible at the level of our national curriculum and at the level of our schools and their everyday practice, will come in the very near future. However, getting ourselves to this point will require ongoing hard work and the dedicated participation of more experts in the research.

## Reference

Lukačková, Z. (2002). The Slovak Republic. In C. L. Flaherty (Ed.), *PIRLS 2001 encyclopedia: A reference guide to reading education in the countries participating in IEA's Progress in International Reading Literacy Study (PIRLS)* (pp. 261–269). Chestnut Hill, MA: Boston College.

## Further Reading

Gavora, P., & Zápotočná, O. (Eds.). (2000). Unity and diversity in literacy development. In *Proceedings of papers from the Central European Conference on Reading* (p. 239). Bratislava: SRA a SLJS.

Hobsbaum, A. (2001). *Early Literacy Assessment Project (Comenius—Socrates, 2.1, Ref. 94314-CP-1-2001-1-UK)*. London: Institute of Education, University of London.

Mancova, M., Kollarik, K., & Marusincova, E. (2002). *Záverecná správa z overovania experimentálnej ucebnice šlabikár pre 1. roc. ZŠ [The final report from experimental verification of the new basal reader for the first grade of primary school]*. Bratislava: National Institute for Education.

Obrancová, E., Heldová, D., Lukačková, Z., & Sklenárová, I. (2004). *Citatelská gramotnost žiakov 4. rocníka ZŠ Výsledky medzinárodnej štúdie PIRLS 2001 [Reading literacy of 4th grade students: The results from the international PIRLS 2001 study]*. Bratislava: Štátny pedagogický ústav.

Stefeková, K., & Culková, R. (2001). *Šlabikár pre 1. rocník základných škôl [The new basal reader for the first grade of primary school]*. Bratislava: Orbis Pictus Istropolitana.

Zápotočná, O., & Gavora, P. (2001). Débats actuels sur la littératie [Current debates on literacy]. *Caracteres, 5*(3), 25–26.

Zápotočná, O., & Lukačková, Z. (2001). Citatelská gramotnost žiakov 1. stupna ZŠ v medzinárodnom kontexte: Informácia o projekte PIRLS. *Ucitelské Noviny, 11*, p. 5.

# Chapter 14
# The Impact of PIRLS in Slovenia

*Marjeta Doupona Horvat*

## 14.1 Slovenia at a Glance[1]

One of the new European countries since the collapse of communism, Slovenia borders Italy, Austria, Hungary, Croatia, and the Adriatic (part of the Mediterranean) Sea. The total area of the country is 20,273 square kilometers. Slovenia has a diverse landscape: alpine, karst, coastal, and Pannonian plain. More than half of Slovenia is covered by forest. The country also has a considerable amount of water, approximately four times the European average.

The population of Slovenia is two million, with a population density of 97 persons per square kilometer. Ljubljana, the capital, is the largest city with 300,000 inhabitants. Some 30% of the population lives in towns with more than 10,000 inhabitants.

The GNP per capita in 2000 was US$9,105. The strongest economic sectors are manufacturing (automobile, chemical, pharmaceutical), real estate, retail, wholesale, transport, storage, and communications. Slovenia spends 6% of its GNP (13% of total public expenditure) on education.

## 14.2 Slovenia's Education System as Context for PIRLS 2001

### 14.2.1 The School System in Slovenia

Over the past few years, Slovenia has implemented reforms in its elementary schools. One of the most obvious changes is the extension of compulsory schooling from eight to nine years. Elementary education still ends at the age of 15, but children enter elementary school one year younger than before. PIRLS 2001 was conducted at just the right time, as it allowed evaluation of the last generation of students entirely in the old system. Thus, most children at the PIRLS target grade (Grade 3 for Slovenia) had entered school at age seven.[2]

---

1  This introduction is based on Slovenia's country profile in the *PIRLS 2001 Encyclopedia* (Doupona Horvat, 2002).
2  The previous legislation relating to elementary school required children to enter Grade 1 in the autumn (September 1) of the year in which they had their seventh birthday.

## *From Kindergarten to University*

One aspect of Slovenia's education system that is well organized relative to other countries in Europe and elsewhere is its kindergartens. The great majority of these are public kindergartens that care for children from age 11 months[3] until they enter elementary school (that is, at six years of age). Almost half of all parents with preschool children take advantage of public kindergartens.[4] Kindergartens offer not only care for children but also a prescribed curriculum. Parents pay only a portion of the fees; the Government provides the remainder. The sum individual parents pay depends on family income, number of family members, and other indices. A child can stay at the kindergarten up to nine hours daily and get at least three meals. In Slovenia, kindergarten teachers must have, at the least, a degree from a faculty of pedagogy (teachers' college). (The degree is one step below a university degree.)

Children attend elementary school for nine years. If, after Grade 9, children do not want or are unable to go to "middle" school (see below), they may complete a Grade 10 class. All elementary schools have to provide after school care for students up to Grade 4 level.[5]

The next step after the elementary school is the middle school (that is, high schools in most countries), which offers two-, three- (vocational schools), or four-year programs (technical, non-technical schools, and *gymnasiums*). Only four-year programs lead to university, but students have to pass the *Matura* examination to enter. Elementary school is officially gratis, but parents provide schoolbooks, textbooks, and all the material needed for work (pencils, workbooks, etc.). Schools have to provide certain excursions according to the requirements of both the curriculum and what are termed school-year working plans, but parents finance these. All schools provide snacks and almost all of them provide warm meals, but again parents pay for these.[6]

---

3   One of the parents (usually the mother) is entitled to stay at home for one year after the birth of a child. She (or he) receives almost the full salary and all benefits (except promotion) as if on the job.

4   One of the reasons for introducing the nine-year-elementary school was that only 50% of Slovenian preschool children go to kindergarten. Children who do not attend tend to be those from lower socio-economic strata, and are often doubly disadvantaged compared to those children who do attend. This is because they rarely receive the same early educational advantage that a stimulating environment, such as that found in the kindergartens, offers.

5   The PIRLS 2001 data showed that not all schools provide care for children either before or after official school hours. We did not examine this further, but it is possible that at some schools (especially in rural areas) parents are not interested in day care.

6   Schools and social services help children and families that are below defined income limits. However, as one teacher explained: "They [people from the Ministry for Education and Sport] cannot imagine how it is when half of the students in the class have parents who lost their jobs in the same day. School excursions? We can't afford to ask parents even to pay for a cinema ticket!"

One of the most important things in Slovenian schools is grades/marks. In the first three years of schooling, grades are descriptive. During the ensuing years (the fourth to ninth years of schooling), grades are assigned with numbers from 1 (not passed) to 5 (excellent). The problem is that a grading of 5 is almost the norm. After PIRLS 2001, schools were asked to provide data on children's grades. Another study found that almost half (45%) of the students who participated in PIRLS[7] attained grade 5 as the final grade of the year. Thirty-one per cent of the students achieved a grade of 4 and 17%, a grade of 3. If we plot these grades on a bell curve, we can see a distinct skew to the distribution of final grades for the Slovenian Grade 3 students who participated in PIRLS.

The reason for this situation is that Slovenian children (or is it their parents?) are intent on entering the coveted middle school, and only children with good grades can do so. There is therefore intense pressure on schools to award children good grades. Children collect points after they complete elementary education. They acquire half of these points from the grades they achieve through their three final years of elementary school and half from external examinations that they sit at the end of the final year of elementary school. Insufficient points create a "direct-line" effect. Children who do not enter middle school are less likely to go to university and so are less likely to enter the higher paying professions. Essentially, lower grades limit work and lifestyle choices.

Entry to university also rests on the acquisition of points, but this time from the middle school, and in almost the same manner as at the elementary school. The final examination of the middle school is the *Matura*, and students can choose to sit it or a concluding examination. However, if they wish to go to university, they must sit and pass the *Matura*.

### Variety despite Centralization

The Slovenian school system is a centralized one. All decisions are top–down and made by the Ministry for Education and Sports or various councils at the State level. There are 450 elementary schools, governed by principals, and many of these have dislocated units. These are buildings apart from the main school building, sometimes by as much as several kilometers, but still part of the school. The principal and the essential services (for example, the library) of such a school reside in the main building. All elementary schools (except one) are public. The only private school is a Rudolf Steiner school, and it receives almost 100% of its funding from the Government.

---

7    PIRLS 2001 students were from Grade 3 and did not get descriptive grades because they were schooled within the old eight-year elementary school.

Slovenia is diverse not only in its topography but also in its languages. Slovenian is the official language throughout the country, with Italian and Hungarian spoken in a few areas. However, what we need to emphasize is that the Slovenian language has as many as 36 separate dialects. To confuse matters further, the Government is situated in the capital, which is the biggest urban area (300,000 inhabitants). The distance from the capital (in the middle of the country) to the most distant town is 250 kilometers. The dialect there is totally different from that in the capital and is not understood by many of the people who live in the capital. The capital sets "the norm" for the rest of the country, which means that government bodies and officials often seem unaware of what is happening beyond the city's boundaries. However, centralization does not mean the same knowledge standards, as the discussion relating to PIRLS 2001 below will show.

### *Literacy/Reading Education*

The reforms in the elementary schools include new principles of teaching reading. The change to nine years of elementary schooling means that there is now one year extra at the beginning of compulsory education in which to implement literacy instruction. Also, the curriculum for the Slovenian language now explicitly defines the basic standards in reading and writing for each of the three cycles of elementary school (that is, at the end of Grades 3, 6, and 9) and for each grade within the three cycles.

The first year of schooling aims to *prepare* children for learning how to read and write. Therefore, at the very beginning of their schooling, children are introduced to a variety of written materials. They also:

- Learn the "technical" basics of writing (for example, holding pencils, practicing drawing from left to right);
- Learn and respect the basic principles of polite communication;
- Do presentations related to texts (they do this in front of other students in the class and are required to describe what happens to the characters in the story and what is going on in the pictures accompanying the text);
- Read pictograms and write familiar pictograms;
- Compare fictional persons to themselves;
- Compare fictional experiences with their own experiences;
- Recognize fairy tales;
- Watch theatre shows;
- Describe cartoons and children's movies; and
- Recite poems.

The *Curriculum for Slovenian Language Classes* defines the standards for reading and writing. Because literacy is complex, schools are advised that every teacher, including school librarians and the teacher-aides who look after children attending the after-school care programs, should be involved in teaching it.

By the end of Grade 3 (the end of the first cycle), the expectation is that children will be able to:

- Comprehend texts that they have read silently on their own (what the topic is, what happened and when, who the characters in the text are, why something happened);
- Identify themselves with one character from the text and describe that character from different perspectives;
- Understand the motives behind the behavior of characters in the text (i.e., give reasons and tell what happens next);
- Write a story, change the components of the story around, and combine two stories into one; and
- Know basic grammar and orthographic rules.

In terms of literacy, the aim of the whole first cycle of the elementary school is to ensure children reach basic levels of skill in reading and writing. The more elaborate literacy program begins in the second cycle (from Grade 4). A major problem with the literacy programs in Slovenian schools is that the rules for teaching how to read and write for every grade/level are so extensive and detailed that they do not leave enough room for teachers' creativity.

## 14.3  Experience in Large-scale Assessments

### 14.3.1 National Large-Scale Assessments

The National Examination Center prepares and conducts all national examinations for the elementary and middle schools (including *Matura*).Under the previous eight-year system of elementary schooling, students sat final examinations at the end of Grade 8. The new nine-year system requires student achievement to be externally assessed at the end of each three-year cycle (that is, at the end of Grades 3, 6, and 9). However, only the examination at the end of Grade 9 is compulsory. Those for the other two cycles are optional.

The past 30 years in Slovenia have seen the school system changed several times. Until 1985, the middle schools (*gymnasium*, technical schools, and general middle schools) finished with *Matura*. In 1985, the *Matura* was suspended until 1995. In that period, even the *gymnasium* was suspended in favor of so-called science-mathematical middle schools and linguistic-humanistic middle schools.[8] In 1995, the gymnasiums and *Matura* returned, and final examinations were introduced for students not wanting to go to university. At that time (1985–1995), students did not have to collect points to enter university. However, a few faculties had admission examinations in instances where the number of candidate students exceeded the number of study places available.

### 14.3.2 International Large-scale Assessments

Slovenia has quite a tradition of participation in IEA studies. It includes Pre-Primary, SITES, TIMSS, TIMSS-R, Reading Literacy, PIRLS 2001, and TIMSS 2003 (see Table 14.1).

**Table 14.1: Slovenia's participation in international large-scale surveys of educational achievement, 1991–2003**

| Year(s) of data collection | Name of survey | Organization in charge | Target population |
|---|---|---|---|
| 1991 | Reading Literacy | IEA | Grade 3 and Grade 7 |
| 1994–1996 | International Adult Literacy Survey (IALS) | OECD | Ages 16–64 |
| 1995 | Third International Mathematics and Science Study (TIMSS) | IEA | Nine-year-old students (Grades 3 and 4), 13-year-old students (Grades 7 and 8), and students in the final grade of the secondary school |
| 1999 | Second Information Technology in Education Study (SITES) | IEA | Grade 8 |
| 1999 | Third International Mathematics and Science Study Repeat (TIMSS-R) | IEA | Grade 8 and final year of high school |
| 2001 | Progress in Reading Literacy Survey 2001 (PIRLS 2001) and PIRLS Trend Study 1991–2001 | IEA | Grade 3 for both surveys |
| 2003 | Trends in International Mathematics and Science Study 2003 (TIMSS 2003) | IEA | Grades 3–8, 4–9 and 7–9, 8–9 |

Slovenia is currently participating in TIMSS 2003 and PIRLS 2006, and will probably take part in TIMSS 2007. In 2000, Slovenia also participated in the

---

8   The years from 1985 to 1995 were years of great social change in Slovenia. The country's first democatic elections occurred in 1990, and in that year people decided, through a referendum, to make Slovenia an independent country. Until 1991, Slovenia was part of Yugoslavia. Independence was declared on 25 June 1991.

OECD's International Adult Literacy Survey (IALS), the results of which were disastrous for Slovenia. Slovenia is also participating in another OECD survey, PISA.[9] Slovenia's Educational Research Institute is responsible for overseeing and conducting this study within Slovenia. The Institute has also assumed the same responsibility for Slovenia's participation in the IEA studies.

### Secondary Analysis Studies

The Ministry of Education has financed two secondary analysis studies of the PIRLS 2001 data. Other studies focusing on the PIRLS data are also underway, and several researchers are looking at various aspects of reading. The first study comprised two parts. One part explored the prognostic value of reading achievement results, namely, determining how students from different levels perform at school. The other involved a linguistic survey in which the researchers used linguistic pragmatics[10] tools to analyze the literacy-based skills and processes underpinning the students' answers to the open-ended questions. Another study involved 10 schools that performed well and 10 schools that did not perform well on PIRLS 2001. The distinction between the two sets of schools rested on the students' reading literacy scores and their socio-economic status (SES) (determined according to such parameters as family income, parents' education, parents' self-perception, and the like). If a school's achievement was much higher or much lower than expected based on the SES of its students, then the researchers singled the school out, conducted structured interviews with its principals, teachers, and librarians, and asked these people to complete written questionnaires. The goal was to find a pattern differentiating "good" and "bad" schools, assuming the existence of such a pattern.[11]

### Feedback System

In every IEA study conducted in Slovenia, good co-operation has marked the relationship between the participating schools and the IEA National Center. Nearly all schools selected for participation have agreed to participate because they want feedback on their performance. From 2006, schools participating in IEA studies will gain a much clearer indication of their students' achievement because two classes per school will be sampled.

---

9   The decision to participate was a political one rather than the result of deliberate educational policy. In Europe, the decision is dictated by the pressure to join "at any cost".

10  Linguistic pragmatics is a sub-field in linguistics. It deals with language used in contextualized communication and the principles associated with it.

11  The results of the study were presented at the European Conference on Educational Research in Dublin, Ireland, September 2005.

After release of the national results, the participating schools received details of the achievement of their students. However, they were not given details about how well Slovenian students fared relative to students in the other countries that participated in PIRLS. More effort is need to ensure schools receive this type of information. There was also a long lag time between administration of the survey and announcement of the results. Some of the participating schools had changed their principals and school advisory staff in this period. If the PIRLS contact person had changed or left a school, staff sometimes had no idea what the results were all about. Essentially, insufficient effort went into promoting PIRLS 2001. Although the schools where problems of this kind arose were relatively few, they are important, because many of them face the high probability of being sampled during the next round of PIRLS (or TIMSS). Schools that have had poor experience of one large-scale assessment may not be willing to participate in another. One third of all schools (150 out of 450) in Slovenia are sampled in each IEA survey (even more than a third, if the field test schools are included).

The schools did receive indirect information about the international results, and this was through the National Agency for Education,[12] which has a network of school advisors throughout Slovenia. The advisors work with schools on different matters, but meet together once a month. The advisors received information about the "workings" of PIRLS and details of the international results during a lecture convened expressly to inform this group. The advisors were very accepting of the lecture and did an excellent job of passing on PIRLS information to their schools. The success of this process led to the advisors being recruited to help on future large-scale assessment surveys and studies.

The PIRLS 2001 results were also presented and discussed at various national conferences for specialist school staff. These groups included psychologists (employed at schools as counseling staff) and librarians (all elementary schools[13] have school libraries and professional librarians). Various other lectures were held throughout the country at schools, professional meetings, and the like.

---

12   The National Agency for Education (*Zavod za šolstvo*) is sometimes translated as the National Institute for Education, which leads to the false assumption that there are two educational institutes, when there is only one.

13   The notion of "all schools" can be explained in different ways. Here, the term means schools with school principals. One school may consist of a main school building and several dislocated units. All schools are headed by the same school principal. Dislocated units are sometimes very small; some of them have combined classes with two or more grades in a single class. An extreme example is a school sampled in the field trial for PIRLS 2006 that had four grades in one class and yet only 10 students in the class. State policy is that schools must be provided in remote areas, even those areas where only a few children are present to attend them.

## 14.4  National Results and Impact of PIRLS 2001

### 14.4.1  Results of PIRLS 2001

Slovenian students achieved an average score of 502 points on the reading literacy scale, which set them at the international average. The girls outperformed the boys, and students from wealthier families outperformed students from poorer families. The gender difference attracted much attention, but this was not the case for the difference between the students from the poorer and wealthier families. However, researchers are trying to raise public awareness of this latter finding. Slovenia is a former socialist country with only a rudimentary capitalist system, and the giant wealth distribution gap that has recently appeared is primarily because of some people acquiring wealth through the privatization of properties that were previously within the public domain, while another sector of society remains very poor and powerless. Although a large majority of the population falls in the middle of the wealth distribution, the gap between considerable wealth and little or no wealth is substantial. In Slovenia, people seem to take this gap for granted, perhaps because the mass media rarely challenges it. It is no surprise, then, that people seem to find achievement differences between students from wealthy and non-wealthy backgrounds acceptable.

One might think that because Slovenia is a small country with a small population and a centralized school system, the country should be able to ensure all Grade 3 students across all schools achieve a standardized and acceptable level of reading. But this is not the case. PIRLS highlighted huge achievement differences between schools. The average reading literacy achievement score of the Grade 3 students in the best-performing school among the sampled schools was 570 points. The children in the worst-performing school had an average score of 430 points. To put it bluntly, these children could barely read or write. Their score fell beneath the lower quarter benchmark. To complicate the picture further, the "best" school was not a school with children from high SES families, although the children from the "worst" school did come from low SES families. Nonetheless, across the country, SES did help explain the big differences.

*Considerations Relating to Target Grade*

The question of which grade to test in PIRLS 2001 was a concern at both national and international levels. The PIRLS 2001 framework defines the target population as "the upper of the two adjacent grades with the most 9 years old . . . In most countries this is the fourth grade" (Campbell, Kelly, Mullis, Martin, & Sainsbury, 2001, p. 7). However, this grade level meant the average age of the international students participating in PIRLS was 10.3 years, but in Slovenia it was 9.8 years. Those of us in Slovenia associated with conducting the study had two choices. We could sample Grade 4, in which case our children would be half a year older (10.8 years) than the average child in PIRLS 2001, or we could sample Grade 3. The first option meant the children would be half a year older than the international average, but this seemed a little too old. Although the second option meant risking lower achievement, we chose it. As it turned out, the Slovenian third graders were found to be reading at the level of the international average, although they were 20 points behind the Swedish third graders, who were the same age.

The decision to sample at Grade 3 meant that the grade tested was the same as that tested for the IEA International Reading Literacy Study in 1991, which allowed Slovenia to participate in the PIRLS Trend Study. It also means that Slovenia will be able to participate in the trend study for PIRLS 2006, even though the students being tested in Slovenia during this most recent cycle will comprise approximately 50% from Grade 3 and 50% from Grade 4 (of the new, nine-year elementary school). However, there will be a sufficient number of Grade 3 students to allow direct comparison between the PIRLS 2001 and PIRLS 2006 populations and thus allow evaluation of the recent school reforms. By the time of the next PIRLS cycle, all children in all elementary schools (see Table 14.2) will have been part of the new nine-year elementary system. They will have had an extra year of schooling and the benefit of the new Grade 1, where the children mostly listen, talk, and learn social skills. Under the old system, Grade 1 was where children actually learned how to read and write. They will now do this in Grade 2.

**Table 14.2: Number of eight-year and nine-year elementary schools by school year in Slovenia**

| School year | Eight-year elementary school (number of schools) | Nine-year elementary school (number of schools) |
| --- | --- | --- |
| 1999/2000 | 406 | 42 |
| 2000/2001 | 349 | 99 |
| 2001/2002 | 293 | 151 |
| 2002/2003 | 196 | 252 |
| 2003/2004 | 0 | 448 |

### 14.4.2  Publication of PIRLS Results

The first public release of the PIRLS 2001 results in Slovenia occurred on the same day (even the same time) as the international press conference (8 April 2003, 4 p. m.). The time of day was unusual for a Slovenian press conference, but we (the PIRLS team) chose it deliberately. If we had waited until the next day, journalists could have accessed the results through Internet (as they did with TIMSS 1999) and published them in the media, which could have been to our disadvantage. While not wishing to discredit journalists (some are very familiar with the international surveys and the subject of reading literacy), we wanted to ensure the results were fairly presented and interpreted. We also wanted to include some secondary analyses of the factors influencing the students' performance.

Our main focus when reporting and interpreting the results was the PIRLS Trend Study. Because interpretation is never neutral—there is always more than one way to look at research findings—we knew that tables of figures would mean little to most people, but trend data would. In PIRLS 2001, Slovenian students were at the international average, and of the countries participating in PIRLS Trend, only one had a lower average score on the literacy scale. However, overall, the results for Slovenian students in PIRLS 2001 were considerably better than their results for Reading Literacy 1991. Only one other country had as big a leap forward in achievement over the 10-year period, and that was Greece. However, the Greek students who participated in the 2001 survey were much older than their 1991 counterparts. Slovenian students were the same age in both surveys. The trend data also threw up some particularly interesting findings to which we wanted to draw attention. These included the aforementioned wealth-related gap and the fact that, despite fewer children appearing in the highest category of "number of books at home" in the 2001 survey than in the 1991 survey, the overall level of literacy in Slovenia had risen.

We presented the results this way not because we wanted to "cover up" what many saw as poor results but because we wanted to present them in a way that was useful and would attract public attention. At the time of the release of the PIRLS findings, public opinion[14] was concentrated on issues other than literacy, and we considered poor literacy results would be expected in any case, which also explains our decision to present the results in a way likely to attract interest. Fortunately, the topic of adult literacy was being widely covered in Slovenia's media when we released the PIRLS results (the topic is still being debated today), and this had heightened people's interest in children's literacy abilities.

Despite this apparent interest in literacy, the public was and continues to be more interested in the issue of so-called burnt-out students at elementary school and the place of religion in public schools. Another problem in Slovenia (as is probably the case in many ex-socialist/communist countries) is that the country tends to compare itself with "the developed West", and so perhaps sets unrealistic standards

---

14  Public opinion at the time can best be captured by reading the collection of newspaper articles (in Slovene) available on the National Agency for Education website: http://www. dosegplus.si/main.php

for itself as it strives to move from a socialist to a capitalist state. It sees itself as easily "written off" by those nations—and by most eastern European countries as well. Under this atmosphere, it is easy for people to look for someone to blame, and teachers frequently are the target. The perception is that schools (and by implication, the country) are not doing well because teachers are "not competent", "do not like their jobs", "only strike for salaries", "have two months free in the summer", "what else do they want?" and so on. In addition, concern over children's rights is constantly intensifying. These rights are not wrong per se, of course, but sometimes parents advocating for their children against teachers has the opposite effect. Teachers feel pressured, uncomfortable, and undermined, all of which limits their ability to work well with and for children. Also, teachers' rights are very limited. In general, the mood within many schools is not conducive to sound education for children.

The release of the results did produce a reasonable number of press articles and radio talk shows and interviews. National television showed little interest, other than reporting on prime-time news on 8 April that watching television is not negatively correlated with reading achievement. There were also some misunderstandings in the press and among members of the public, one of which was that there is not a positive relationship between high levels of parental engagement in children's reading and high reading achievement scores (when in fact, there is). In general, the issues that we endeavored to bring to light, such as rising poverty, and its probable effects on educational achievement, tend not to be topics that sell magazines and newspapers. However, as mentioned previously, we are making greater effort to raise public awareness of these concerns.

Finally, lack of funding has meant publication of only one national report of the results so far (see also Future Activities below). However, interested persons can access the results on the web pages of the Educational Research Institute (http://www.pei.si).

### 14.4.3 Impact of PIRLS 2001

***Impact on Administrative and School Level***

Impact is a matter of perspective. At the time of writing the first draft of this chapter (2005), only two years had passed since publication of the PIRLS 2001 international results. These two years saw many attempts in Slovenia to situate the PIRLS survey within the context of reliable and resourceful studies of educational achievement. This is not to say that the survey itself is open to question but rather that its value remains relatively unknown to the wider public. Because the results provided mixed messages (poor on the one hand; encouraging on the other), much effort went into explaining the nature of the survey. Although PIRLS does not yet have the profile in Slovenia that we would like it to, it does have a good image, not only in terms of what it has found out but also in how it is conducted.[15]

Even though PIRLS itself may not have a strong public profile, we can certainly say that the public's awareness of the topic of reading literacy has increased markedly. Before PIRLS, many people would not even have known what the term "reading literacy" meant. Increasingly, schools are eager to participate in future PIRLS studies. More and more are asking for PIRLS-related materials (especially after being sent the released passages), want to learn more about PIRLS, and are using the released items for their own assessments. We are capitalizing on this growing interest by holding seminars for schools about PIRLS 2006.

Elsewhere, scholars and other professional staff are expressing interest in the implications of the results and looking forward to the findings of the next survey. Researchers have presented papers featuring or related to the PIRLS findings at numerous national conferences (pedagogical, psychological, librarian, reading association). These and publications in research journals have been very well received, not only in terms of the high quality of the work but also in terms of the relevance of the chosen topics. Among these topics are ones not previously covered and that PIRLS has made possible. These include a study looking at the influence of language dialects on reading literacy achievement and an exploration of why some schools within low socio-economic communities went against the common pattern by having high reading achievement.

Soon after the data collection phase of PIRLS 2001, the Ministry for Education established the State Commission for Literacy. The members of the Commission are also the researchers who took part in PIRLS. The Commission has met regularly to develop a document that will direct the future development of reading literacy in Slovenia. The implementation of reforms to the curriculum, the implications of these for the education of teachers, the establishment of reading standards for schools, children and adults, and the place and nature of assessments are among the topics that will feature in the document. Suggestions arising out of the PIRLS findings are naturally finding their way into the document, and no doubt more will have done so by the time the Commission finishes this work.

---

15 An example of this relates to the previously mentioned dislocated units found within Slovenia's elementary school system. To ensure the reliability of the PIRLS sample, these units were included in the sampling plan, and many units had to be sampled to make one regular pseudo-class. In the field trial of 2005, there was an instance of only one child being tested from within a dislocated unit. Although there were six children in the particular unit, only two were in the test grade, and one of them did not have parental permission to take part in PIRLS. It is very expensive to locate and test only one student. However, such examples raise the credibility of the survey (in Slovenia), and predispose teachers to taking an interest in the work of the Educational Research Institute and to participating in future studies.

### Long-term Effects

The long-term effects should become more obvious with the completion of secondary analysis studies. These studies are more nationally oriented in that they focus on specific problems regarding literacy and education at the level of central government. The recent changes to school curricula take into account the fact that children have reading and writing difficulties not only in relation to the Slovenian language but also in relation to other courses. The PIRLS findings offer particularly useful direction because the study focuses on linguistic pragmatics (that is, how to use language) and so includes all aspects of reading. Under the previous system of education, the only people who taught reading were specialists in the Slovenian language, and they tended to have little understanding of the broader use of the language. The PIRLS findings confirmed that Slovenian students were not being encouraged to find the meaning of the text by themselves but more or less to summarize someone else's thoughts. (What else can we think about the reading capacity of children who, when asked to say something about the character of the main person as it appears in the story, simply present a summary?) The PIRLS data and secondary analysis studies are informing (and should continue to inform) the ongoing debate in Slovenia about the importance of reading.

## 14.5  Future Activities

The PIRLS team in Slovenia intends to do more to promote PIRLS. The team consequently is planning endeavors that will place the study more in the public eye and is increasing its level of contact with universities and schools.

### 14.5.1  Research

Only a few studies on reading have been conducted in Slovenia. Two of them (one is already finished) are based on the PIRLS data. Two studies are not enough, of course, but we plan to do more. Among the subjects we intend to cover are these:

- How poverty and/or SES influence the acquisition of reading skills (a related consideration is that of supplying free textbooks for all school children, something that is not presently done in Slovenia);
- Case studies of schools where children had good reading literacy achievement scores;
- The extent to which being a native speaker of Slovenian or a second language speaker (thus immigrant children and the children and grandchildren of immigrant parents/grandparents) influences the acquisition of reading skills;

- The extent to which being a member of other minority and/or underprivileged groups (for example, children with disabilities) influences the acquisition of reading skills;
- Factors relating to teaching the Slovenian language; and
- Reading techniques.

### 14.5.2 Publications

Funding also has finally been procured for publishing details about PIRLS 2001 and 2006. Four such publications are currently underway. The first is a newsletter about PIRLS for all primary schools in Slovenia. The first issue appeared in May 2006. The second publication presents the PIRLS results for teachers and researchers of reading. The third is a booklet containing the released items from PIRLS 2001 and from the PIRLS 2001 field test, together with instructions for coding and evaluating open-ended items. This publication also provides examples of the answers actually given by the children tested in PIRLS 2001. The fourth publication sets out the PIRLS 2006 frameworks.

### 14.5.3 Programs

The lag between the conducting of research and government-led changes to school practice is proving to be considerable in Slovenia. It is unlikely that school curricula will be changed to the extent needed simply because the country has participated in an international survey. A program of national evaluation surveys and reference to international data are likely to be much more powerful catalysts.

As mentioned above, the PIRLS team is increasing its contacts with universities and students. These contacts include seminars for student-teachers that give them guidelines on interpreting data from international studies and then using that knowledge to influence their teaching practice. We would welcome more IEA seminars. We certainly put to good use the information on survey methodology, data management, and related matters that we and other practitioners and researchers gain first hand from knowledgeable presenters. However, we think IEA could offer more in this direction, especially for economically deprived and emerging countries, and for countries without a tradition of teaching data analysis at their teacher education faculties and colleges.

## 14.6 Concluding Remarks

Self-evident and trivial assertions are often the toughest to explain and justify. The importance of reading is one such example. In Slovenia, elementary schools urge their students to *read well*. Yet it is difficult to explain, in our multimedia era, why it is so important to do so. Surveys like PIRLS give teachers a powerful tool with which to explain such basics. Reference to the definitions of reading literacy used in PIRLS 2001 and PIRLS 2006 is a good starting point when endeavoring to do this. The definitions encapsulate the importance of understanding, interpreting, and independent thinking. We can encourage even those children for whom reading is not fun to learn to read—not for the sake of good grades or even enjoyment but because of the need to make sense of the world around them. In Slovenia, reading was simply, for many years, a matter of conducting classes in the Slovenian language, and so failed to provide a powerful tool for explaining the world. The automatization of reading was important. Understanding—in the sense used in PIRLS and seen in the study's results—was not so important.

PIRLS 2001 also showed that children at the ages of nine and 10 in Slovenia do not read well when compared to many of their peers in the rest of the world. While their reading improved over the 10 years between 1991 and 2001, the improvement was insufficient to lift their achievement level on the international reading literacy scale. Another major concern is that despite the centralized school system and the small size of the country, the PIRLS data highlighted huge differences between schools in relation to their students' reading achievement. (As we emphasized earlier, this concern is an important focus of our secondary analyses of the PIRLS data.) The Slovenian Government still seems relatively unaware of the situation regarding reading literacy in Slovenia's schools, and we think changes will come from other directions—from the schools and from the teachers, especially. This is why the PIRLS team is so intent on continuing its contacts and maintaining support for PIRLS at this level.

## References

Campbell, J. R., Kelly, D. L., Mullis, I. V. S., Martin, M. O., & Sainsbury, M. (2001). *Framework and specifications for PIRLS assessment 2001* (2nd ed.). Chestnut Hill, MA: Boston College.

Doupona Horvat, M. (2002). Slovenia. In I. V. S. Mullis, M. O. Martin, A. M. Kennedy, & C. L. Flaherty (Eds.), *PIRLS 2001 encyclopedia: A reference guide to reading education in the countries participating in IEA's Progress in International Reading Literacy Study (PIRLS)* (pp. 271–278). Chestnut Hill, MA: Boston College.

## Further Reading

Doupona Horvat, M. (2003). *Prejudices or wrong expectations? Third graders in Slovenian elementary schools who are good readers but not good students.*

Paper presented at the European Conference on Educational Research, 17–20 September 2003, University of Hamburg.

Doupona Horvat, M. (2004). *Errors in argumentation of Slovenian students in PIRLS 2001.* Paper presented at the European Conference on Educational Research, 22–25 September 2004, University of Cyprus, Nicosia.

Doupona Horvat, M. (2004). Reading achievement and school performance. In C. Papanastasiou (Ed.), *Proceedings of the 1st IEA International Research Conference, Lefkosia, Cyprus, May 2004* (pp. 224–239). Nicosia: Department of Education, University of Cyprus.

Doupona Horvat, M., Brecko, B. N., Cucek, M., Straus, M., Japelj Pavesic, B., Krevh, A., & Kocis, K. (2004). *Analiza pogojev za razvoj razumevanja pripovedovalnih in razlagalnih besedil: konkurencnost Slovenije 2001–2006: zakljucno porocilo o rezultatih opravljenega raziskovalnega dela na projektu ciljnega raziskovalnega programa/nosilka projekta [Analysis of children's understanding of written texts: Reports on the findings of the research].* Ljubljana: Pedagoški inštitut.

Gradišar, A., & Lapajne, Z. (1998). *Kako berejo otroci po svetu in pri nas? [How children read at home and across the world].* Nova Gorica: Educa.

Justin, J., Doupona Horvat, M., Gril, A, Pecjak, S., Straus, M., & Cucek, M. (2004). *Mednarodna raziskava bralne pismenosti PIRLS 2001 (1999–2003). Porocilo o raziskavi [PIRLS 2001: Report on the findings of the research].* Ljubljana: ISH fakulteta za podiplomski humanisticni študij.

Ministry of Education and Sports. (1995). *White paper on education in the Republic of Slovenia.* Ljubljana: Ministry of Education and Sports.

Peklaj, C., & Pecjak, S. (2004). *Dimensions of reading motivation and reading achievement in 3rd- and 7th-grade students.* Paper presented at the Third International Biennial SELF Research Conference, Berlin, Germany, July 4–7, 2004.

# Chapter 15
# The Impact of PIRLS in Sweden

*Monica Rosén and Jan-Eric Gustafsson*

## 15.1 Sweden at a Glance[1]

Sweden is located in northern Europe, with land frontiers with Finland (586 kilometers) to the east and Norway (1,619 kilometers) to the west, and is linked to Denmark in the southwest via the Öresund Bridge. The Baltic Sea separates the country from Finland, Russia, the Baltic states, Poland, and Germany. Europe's fifth largest country in geographic size, Sweden has a total area of 449,964 square kilometers, of which 410,934 square kilometers is land and the rest is water.

In just a few decades, Sweden has changed from a largely monolingual and ethnically homogeneous society into a multilingual society with a large number of groups with different linguistic, religious, and cultural backgrounds. The population totals nearly nine million with a population density of 19.7 persons per square kilometer. At the end of 1997, there were about 522,000 foreign nationals living in Sweden. In addition, about 690,550 immigrants have become naturalized Swedish citizens. About 50% of all foreign nationals in Sweden are from the other Nordic countries (Denmark, Finland, Iceland, and Norway). About one-fifth of the total population is immigrants or people with at least one foreign-born parent. This estimate includes persons from other Nordic countries. Immigration has accounted for over 40% of the country's population growth.

Once one of the richest countries in the world in terms of production value, Sweden is highly industrialized and still has a GDP per capita of €27,800 (US$24,800). Public and household expenditures on education represent 5.13% of the GDP, not including infrastructure (buildings, etc.) and privately funded company-internal education.

## 15.2 Sweden's Education System as Context for PIRLS 2001

From the 1960s onward, the Swedish education system has been transformed through a series of reforms. One goal, which was most clearly pronounced up to the early 1990s, was to reduce social differences in society. Since then, efficiency goals have been more prominent.

---

1   This introduction is based on Sweden's country profile in the *PIRLS 2001 Encyclopedia.* (Lansfjord, 2002).

The education system in Sweden is organized for lifelong and recurrent education from the age of one until retirement. After preschool, education is, as a rule, free of charge. The nine-year-long compulsory school, which normally starts at age seven, is a comprehensive school without any organizational differentiation. School lunch is free of charge, as are most schoolbooks. Upper secondary school offers a variety of programs and continues for three or sometimes four years. It is formally non-compulsory but almost everyone in the age bracket 16 to 19 attends. Universities and university colleges are thereafter available for anyone meeting the various requirements for enrolment, and close to 50% of the younger cohorts go to university. Sweden also has a well-developed system of adult education.

### 15.2.1 Preschool, the Primary Grades, and Compulsory Education

The municipalities offer public child care for children from age one until age 12. Child care is financed partly by taxes and partly by parental fees. One aim of child care is to make it possible for parents to work or study; another aim is to support children's development and learning. The child care for children up to five years of age usually takes place in preschools, which are typically located in the neighborhood of the caretakers' homes. A recent decision requires municipalities to offer 15 hours of preschool per week free of charge to all children from the age of four. Currently 96% of all four-year-olds attend preschool.

Preschool ends at the age of six, which is when children enter the so-called "preschool class" (or "Grade 0"). Building upon similar previous activities, Sweden formally established the preschool class on 1 January 1998. The aim of this class is to prepare children for school, but not to actually teach school subjects. Even though the preschool class is not compulsory, the municipalities have an obligation to provide these classes, and virtually all children six years of age attend. The preschool classes are usually located within the compulsory schools and collaborate with the first grades.

Leisure-time centers are available for children before and after school, from preschool class (age six) until Grade 6 (ages 12 to 13). These centers are intended as a supplement to schooling; they aim to facilitate the children's development by providing them with meaningful leisure-time activities. Childcare services staff are generally well trained, and many complete a three-year pedagogical training program at university.

The nine-year compulsory school normally starts with Grade 1 in the autumn of the year when the children reach age seven, and finishes at the end of the spring of the year they reach age 16. However, any child may start school one year earlier at the age of six, if that is the parents' wish.

The National Agency for Education (hereafter referred to as the National Agency) is the central administrative authority for the school system for children, young people, and adults, as well as for preschool activities and childcare for school-children. Steering documents, such as the nationally approved course syllabi and the criteria for grading criteria, constitute the Agency's main responsibilities. The National Agency is also responsible for Sweden's participation in the international studies of student achievement, and for national evaluation.

### 15.2.2 Organizational Changes

In the years between Sweden's participation in the IEA International Reading Literacy Study (RLS) (1991) and its participation in the first round of PIRLS (2001), the country experienced major changes. From the early 1990s, Sweden transformed its highly centralized school system into a decentralized and deregulated system with power and responsibility transferred to municipalities, schools, teachers, and parents. In addition, free school choice was introduced in 1992, together with a voucher plan, which rests on the premise that "funds follow the child". Schools thus are funded in strict proportion to enrolment (Skolverket, 2003; West, 1997). These reforms have, among other societal changes, resulted in a growing number of independent schools, that is, schools that are run privately but are publicly funded (Skolverket, 2000, 2003; Richardson, 2004). Independent schools must be approved by the National Agency. An independent school must also follow the general regulations for compulsory schools, that is, have the same basic objectives, but it may have a profile that distinguishes it from the public school.

The National Curriculum also has changed. The new National Curriculum for Compulsory Education (Lpo 94/Lpf 94, 1994) stipulates goals and expected results, and leaves it up to the municipalities and local schools to decide how they will reach the goals. Previous curricula were not only goal-oriented but also, to a certain degree, rule-oriented, since they explicitly touched upon possible content and methodology for the teaching of various subjects in addition to stated achievement goals.

The current curriculum and its syllabi reject the idea that children's cognitive and social development is age related. This standpoint makes it difficult to specify achievement goals for certain grades, and the label "grade" for Grade 1, Grade 2, and so on has been replaced with "year", so that each year in school is now labeled Year 1, Year 2, and so forth up to Year 9. The general idea is that children develop differently, and perhaps unevenly, across school subjects, which makes it necessary to individualize teaching. Achievement goals for different subjects are defined for two occasions only: the goals that students should attain by the end of their fifth year in school, and the goals they should attain by the end of their ninth year in compulsory school.

### 15.2.3 The Teaching of Reading

The school subject primarily responsible for the development of reading literacy skills is Swedish. The subject of Swedish provides students with opportunities to use and develop their ability to speak, listen, see, read, and write, as well as experience and learn from literature, film, and the theatre. The reading achievement goals that students should have attained by Year 5 are the ability to:

1. Read with fluency, both aloud and to themselves, and to understand events and meanings in books and non-fiction written for children and young persons, and to discuss their experiences from reading, as well as reflect on the content of texts;
2. Produce texts for different purposes as tools for learning and communication; and
3. Apply the most common rules of the written language and the most common rules of spelling, as well as to use dictionaries.

No school marks or grades are awarded until Year 8 (ages 14 to 15), and there are no national tests of school achievement until Year 5 (ages 11 to 12). National tests are only available for the subjects of Swedish, Swedish as a second language, English, and mathematics, and these are set at the end of the final year of compulsory school for the purposes of checking goal attainment and supporting final grading. Examinations to assess student progress in these four subjects are also available at the end of Year 5 (ages 11 to 12), although schools are not mandated to use them. None of these national tests is designed to be comparable across time.

## 15.3  Experience in Large-scale Assessments

The lack of regularly collected nationally representative data of student achievement that allow comparisons over time makes it difficult to detect changes in the levels of student performance. While there are national tests in Swedish, mathematics, and English in Years 5 and 9, these are for diagnostic and grading purposes only, and not constructed to allow investigations of changes in level of achievement over time. Studies like PIRLS therefore take on a special importance for assessing and improving the Swedish school system.

Sweden has taken part in large-scale comparative assessments of education ever since these studies were launched in the early 1960s, when the recently formed IEA organization conducted the first pilot study under the sponsorship of UNESCO. The pilot study was managed from Hamburg, and comprised measures of educational achievement for some 10,000 13-year-olds in 12 countries in mathematics, reading comprehension, geography, science, and non-verbal ability (Foshay, Thorndike, Hotyat, Pidgeon, & Walker, 1962). The success of this study led to the establishment of the IEA. One of the IEA "founding fathers" was Torsten Husén from Stockholm. He was also chair of IEA during these early days (Härnqvist, 1975). The first IEA Bureau was located in Sweden at the Department of International Education, Stockholm University, from the early 1970s until the mid-1980s.

Sweden has participated in 11 IEA studies since the first pilot study, starting with the First International Mathematics Study (FIMS) in 1964, which compared the mathematics achievement of 13-year-olds in 12 countries (Husén, 1967). Next, Sweden participated in the Six Subject Study (1970/71), which compared achievement at three levels: 10-year-olds, 14-year-olds, and students in the last year of full-time secondary education. The subjects were science, reading comprehension, literature, French and English as foreign languages, and civic education. The number of countries that participated varied across subjects from 10 (in literature) to 19 (in science), as did the levels of the various education systems involved in each subject (Walker, 1976).

During the 1980s, Sweden participated in the Second International Mathematics Study (SIMS) in 1980, in the Second International Science Study (SISS) in 1983, and in the IEA Written Composition Study in 1986 (Löfqvist, 1990; Purves, 1992) . According to the National Agency (Skolverket, 2004), the first two of these studies have been quite influential on Swedish educational policy, but the latter has received very little attention. The study has not gone unnoticed, however, since its national report is labeled "course literature" at our university library.

Up to 1991, the Swedish National Board of Education was the authority responsible for compulsory and secondary education, and also responsible for Sweden's participation in international studies. When the Swedish school system was decentralized, the National Board of Education closed down and was replaced with the National Agency for Education. During the 1990s, Sweden participated in three IEA studies: the IEA International Reading Literacy Study (RLS) in 1991, the Third International Mathematics and Science Study (TIMSS) in 1995, and the IEA Civic Education Study (CivEd) in 1999/2000. Sweden also participated in two OECD studies (the International Adult Literacy Survey (IALS), 1994–1996, and the Program for International Student Assessment (PISA), 2000), and in a European comparative study of English as a second language at the end of compulsory school (conducted by The European Network of Policy Makers of the Evaluation of Education Systems, 1996).

Besides PIRLS, the most recent international studies in which Sweden has participated are a replication study of the above-mentioned European Study of English as a Second Language (2002), the IEA Trends in Mathematics and Science Study (2003), and OECD's PISA (2003). Table 15.1 presents an overview of the international studies in which Sweden has participated, and the populations that were tested in each.

The potential value of the comparative studies of educational achievement received early recognition from educational policy-makers and educational researchers (Härnqvist, 1975; Marklund, 1983). For example, the results of FIMS and the Six Subject Study played an important role in the work of improving the Swedish education system during the late 1970s. In an article reviewing the state of educational research in Europe in the mid-1970s, de Landsheere (1975) drew the following conclusion about Sweden and the role of educational research:

> Only when democracy has become a way of life and an accepted national philosophy does research play a vital and functional role in the functioning of education. Sweden and to a somewhat lesser extent Great Britain provide examples of such a high level of development. (pp. 110–111)

The same author also noted that the role of the Swedish research funding agencies during this time was not limited to funding; they also had to make sure that the research results were taken into account in the educational planning and decision-making processes.

Educational research in Sweden is traditionally financed—and thus controlled by—national agencies. However, as in Germany, an important principle has been to ensure independence in the comparative evaluations of the education system by contracting researchers within university research departments to manage the studies and analyze the data. The contracting agency, The National Agency for Education (or previously The National Board of Education) has always been involved in the studies in different ways. During the 1970s, the National Board of Education made a considerable effort to suggest analyses, reporting formats, and other improvements that would allow policy-makers and practitioners to gain maximum benefit from the studies (see, for example, Marklund, 1983). The researchers in charge of the studies also have been engaged in improving the studies, although primarily from a research perspective. The researchers' focus of concern has been methodology (that is, the validity and reliability of measurement), data collection, data management, and analysis, and the connection to theory and to previous and contemporary research. Both researchers and the National Board of Education were eager to point out that IEA studies were not intended to provide an "Olympic Games" in the area of school achievement (Härnqvist, 1975; Marklund, 1983).

**Table 15.1: Sweden's participation in international large-scale surveys of educational achievement, 1964–2003**

| Year(s) of data collection | Name of survey | Organization in charge | Target population |
|---|---|---|---|
| 1959–1962 | The Pilot Twelve-Country Study | UNESCO/IEA | Thirteen-year-olds |
| 1964 | The First International Mathematics Study (FIMS) | IEA | Thirteen-year-olds and graduate year of secondary school |
| 1970/71 | The Six Subject Study, including the First International Science Study (FISS) | IEA | Ten-year-olds, 13-year-olds, and graduate year of secondary school |
| 1980 | Second International Mathematics Study (SIMS) | IEA | Thirteen-year-olds and graduate year of secondary school |
| 1983 | Second International Science Study (SISS) | IEA | Ten-year-olds, 14-year-olds, and graduate year of science-oriented programs at secondary school |
| 1985 | The Written Composition Study | IEA | Students near the end of primary schooling, students near the end of compulsory schooling, and students near the end of academic secondary schooling |
| 1991 | The International Reading Literacy Study (RLS) | IEA | Nine-year olds and 14-year-olds |
| 1994–1996 | International Adult Literacy Survey (IALS) | OECD | Ages 16–64 |
| 1995 | Third International Mathematics and Science Study (TIMSS) | IEA | Thirteen-year-old students (Grades 7 and 8) and three different samples in the final grade of the secondary school |
| 1996 | Assessment of English as a Second Language | European Network* | Students in the final semester of the final year in compulsory school (15-year-olds) |
| 1999/2000 | Civic Education Study (CivEd) | IEA | Fourteen-year-old students, and students in the 3rd grade of academic secondary school |
| 2000 | Program for International Student Assessment (reading comprehension) (PISA 2000) | OECD | Fifteen-year-olds |
| 2001 | Progress in Reading Literacy Study 2001 (PIRLS 2001), including the Ten-Year Trend Study | IEA | Students in Grade 3 (9-year-olds), and students in Grade 4 (10-year-olds) |
| 2002 | Assessment of English as a Second Language (a repeat of the 1996 study) | European Network* | Students in the final semester of the final year in compulsory school (15-year-olds) |
| 2003 | Program for International Student Assessment (mathematics) (PISA 2003) | OECD | Fifteen-year-olds |
| 2003 | Trends in International Mathematics and Science Study (TIMSS 2003) | IEA | Students in Grade 8 (14-year-olds) |

* The European Network of Policy Makers for the Evaluation of Education Systems.

In a recent overview of 40 years of international studies (Skolverket, 2004), the National Agency expressed a somewhat changed attitude towards comparative studies. While the report initially mentions the importance for Sweden of participating in comparative studies, it mainly concentrates on problems associated with such studies. It notes that comparative studies are expensive and complicated, that the data produced are useful but not perfect, since they are difficult to handle, and that there is a cultural bias favoring Anglo-Saxon cultures. Very little space is devoted to the actual and/or potential contributions to knowledge from these studies, and no space at all to possible improvements to support the development of the education system.

## 15.4  National Results and Impact of PIRLS 2001

The National Agency contracted a project group at Gothenburg University to work on PIRLS from late 1999 until the end of 2002. The Agency and the PIRLS project group subsequently collaborated closely to develop the PIRLS design for Sweden.

### 15.4.1  Results of PIRLS 2001

Sweden took an ambitious approach to its participation in PIRLS 2001, as it also elected to engage in the PIRLS "10-Year Trend Study" (or the Trend Study, for short) and to extend the basic international design in a number of different ways. We first describe these extensions.

### *The Swedish PIRLS Design*

The most important extension related to the fact that Sweden was the only country that participated at both Grade 3 and Grade 4. The decision to participate with two grades was due to uncertainty about which grade would actually best fit the population definition for PIRLS. Sweden participated in the International Reading Literacy Study (RLS) of 1991 with students in Grade 3, so it was obvious that Grade 3 should be selected to participate in the Trend Study. The fact that the initially proposed population definition for PIRLS (nine- to 10-year-olds) agreed with the population definition for RLS 1991 also made it natural to select Grade 3 for participation in PIRLS. However, as the international planning of the PIRLS project evolved, the population definition changed into a grade-based definition, namely Grade 4.

The Swedish project team and the National Agency were, for several reasons, hesitant to switch from Grade 3 to Grade 4. One reason was that we wanted to make comparisons between the Trend and PIRLS projects, which would be impossible if the two did not include the same grades. Another reason was that because school in

Sweden usually starts at age seven, Swedish students are older than are students in a given grade in most other countries. Furthermore, since most of the students eventually to be included in the study would have had the opportunity to attend "Grade 0", it could be argued that Grade 4 in Sweden corresponds to Grade 5 in some other countries (for example, Norway). It could thus also be argued that selecting Grade 4 students to participate in the Swedish PIRLS sample would result in a sample containing students older than students in most other countries, and who had experienced one year more of schooling than had students in many countries. Since good reasons were evident for selecting from both Grades 3 and 4, the project group argued in favor of the solution to include both grades rather than to select one grade, and the National Agency decided to provide the financial support needed for this extension.

Another extension was a broadening of the matrix sampling design employed in PIRLS to include the Trend instruments as well. This development made it possible to investigate the measurement properties of the two sets of assessment tasks. Each PIRLS student accordingly was assigned one of the two booklets included in the Trend Study. These booklets were given out about a week after the regular PIRLS data collection.

Yet another extension was that every class in the sampled schools was included in the design. The main reason for this was to make it possible to separate class and school as sources of variance in achievement, which was judged to be of particular interest in the Trend Study, given the organizational changes to the Swedish school system during the 1990s.

The sampling of schools was, furthermore, done in such a way that independent schools were over-represented, to allow comparisons between public and independent schools.

### The Swedish Results

The pattern of results that emerged from the analyses of the Trend and PIRLS 2001 data was most interesting. The Swedish Grade 4 students had the highest achievement of all participating countries. However, while the Swedish Grade 3 students had been amongst the three highest performing countries in RLS 1991, the performance of the Grade 3 students in PIRLS 2001 was close to the international mean, and more than half of the participating countries had a higher level of performance. Even though a somewhat different set of countries participated in RLS 1991 than in PIRLS 2001, the Swedish Grade 3 results suggested a decline in level of reading performance between 1991 and 2001.

The results from the Trend Study supported this conclusion. The 2001 results were lower than the 1991 results. Among the nine participating countries in the

Trend Study, Sweden held sixth highest place in 2001 whereas it had the top position in 1991. Two independent studies with completely different assessment instruments thus showed a decline in the level of performance of Grade 3 students, while at the same time the Swedish Grade 4 students had the highest level of performance of all countries.

### 15.4.2 Publication of the PIRLS Results

Our intention when reporting the Swedish results was to include one national report for the Trend Study and one national report for PIRLS, along with a short, popular, summary report written by a journalist. The international report, prepared by the International Steering Committee for PIRLS, would present only the Swedish Grade 4 results, with a limited reporting of the Grade 3 results in an appendix. Thus, one major aim of the national PIRLS report was to give a full account of the results, including those based on the questionnaires, for both Grades 3 and 4.

We presented these results to the National Agency in early 2003. The findings met a range of reactions, from deep concern to dismissal, because they seemed contradictory and difficult to understand. We delivered the preliminary manuscripts for the two reports in late February, and a group within the National Agency read and commented on them. However, this group agreed to release only the positive results for Grade 4, and demanded that we strike out all the negative results pertaining to Grade 3. We refused to edit the reports as demanded, which meant that there were no Swedish reports at the time of the international release of the PIRLS results (see Gustafsson & Rosén, 2004b, for a more detailed account; see also Gustafsson & Rosén, 2004a; Lundh, Ramstedt, & Wester, 2004).

The National Agency did hold a national press conference, which coincided with the release of the PIRLS international results. A photocopy of a preliminary summary report was available, along with a short press release describing selected results. Articles appeared in some of the daily newspapers, and there was a news report on national television.

It should be mentioned that the other school authority in Sweden, the Swedish National Agency for School Improvement, later decided to publish the national report for the Trend Study (Gustafsson & Rosén, 2005), and the national report for PIRLS (Rosén, Myrberg, & Gustafsson, 2005). These are now available as web publications (on http://www.skolutveckling.se/publikationer/).

### 15.4.3 Impact of PIRLS 2001

Because the national reports were not published, the Swedish results for PIRLS 2001 attracted little attention. The National Agency and other stakeholders have made only a few comments on the results. However, even though the impact of PIRLS on Swedish educational policy and debate has been very limited, it has been possible to do some research with the PIRLS data. The Swedish Research Council has funded this work through a grant to Monica Rosén. We briefly summarize some of this work below.

Gustafsson and Rosén (in press) applied confirmatory factor analysis to analyze the dimensional structure of the assessment tasks used in PIRLS and RLS. These analyses took advantage of the extended matrix sampling design, which included both the PIRLS and the RLS booklets. The results showed that the two sets of tasks share a large common core, but that each of them also represents unique sources of variance. In the RLS instrument, reading speed is one such component, and performance on tasks from the documents domain is another. In the PIRLS tasks, the requirement to produce constructed responses is a unique source of variance.

Gustafsson and Rosén (in press) tried to account for the decline in reading performance in Sweden between 1991 and 2001 through statistical models in which different hypothesized explanatory factors were introduced as mediating variables. The results showed that the decline could be accounted for by increased use of computers out of school and a decrease in reading activities. While the results from these analyses cannot prove causality, they do indicate that it may be necessary to look for explanations both out of school and in school.

Gustafsson and Rosén (2004b) re-analyzed the data from the nine countries participating in the Trend Study, using multivariate methods. The researchers fitted a three-factor latent-variable model to the reading tasks. One factor was a reading comprehension factor, another was interpreted as a speed factor, and the third factor reflected performance on documents texts. Differences in the latent variable means for the countries were then investigated. The most important finding was that the speed factor identified in the latent variable model affected the estimates of the changes in level of reading comprehension over time, as well as the estimated differences between countries.

Hansen, Rosén, and Gustafsson (2004) investigated if the effect of the students' social background on reading performance had changed between 1991 and 2001 in Sweden. They analyzed the Trend Study data using two-level structural equation modeling, which allowed measurement of socio-economic status (SES) at both school level and individual level. The results indicated that the relationship between school-level SES and achievement was higher in 2001 than in 1991. The researchers explained this finding in terms of the segregating effects of free school choice.

Myrberg and Rosén (2004) investigated the influence of teacher competence on Grade 3 students' reading achievement in public and independent schools in Sweden. Regression analysis was employed to explore the relative effects of several indicators of teacher quality. Teacher certification for teaching had a strong effect on students' mean reading test score. This effect was as strong in independent schools as in public schools. Students in independent schools achieved better on the reading test than did students in public schools. When parents' education was kept under control, the school-type effect on achievement disappeared. While school type had no influence of itself, it was a mediating factor for parents' education and teachers' education, meaning that the factors worked in opposite directions. Myrberg and Rosén (in press) also show that the performance advantage of students in independent schools can be accounted for in terms of differences in the social selection into independent and public schools. We can conclude from this that students in independent schools have better-educated parents, and that students in public schools have better-educated teachers.

Hansen, Rosén, and Gust (in press) used latent variable modeling techniques to identify constructs of self-reported reading resources, attitudes, and activities based on items in the PIRLS student and parent questionnaires. The researchers then computed individual factor scores for the different constructs, which related to reading achievement. Comparisons between the factor scores and the indices used in the international report to capture similar constructs showed that the factor scores had better measurement properties and higher correlations with achievement.

Currently, several studies are underway. One study is extending the analysis of changes in level of reading performance in Sweden 30 years back in time by including the Six Subject Study reading data from 1970. Another study is analyzing differences in performance between Grade 3 and Grade 4 within the same schools, and relating the differences to school factors.

Thus, even though the impact of the PIRLS 2001 results has been very limited at the administrative and school level, we do hope that the research based on the PIRLS 2001 data will generate long-term effects.

## 15.5  Future Activities

A month after the release of the international report, the Swedish PIRLS project was formally closed down, and the National Agency decided that Sweden will not participate in PIRLS 2006. The Ministry of Education, however, did not accept this decision, and provided some funding to allow continued participation. While this is a positive development, there are two reasons for concern.

The first is that the National Agency has decided to conduct the study itself rather than contracting the work to a university. The main argument for this is the high overhead costs required by the universities, along with the judgment that participation in the PIRLS study mainly involves work of an "administrative and logistical" kind because the International Steering Committee at Boston College "makes all the decisions". While such a conception of the nature of the work involved in conducting a comparative study of reading literacy may seem natural from the point of view of an administrative body such as the National Agency, it does not agree with our experiences. These strongly indicate that planning and conducting a study like PIRLS is a collaborative effort in which the contributions from the participating countries are very important indeed. The fact that the National Agency from now on intends to conduct the international studies without the involvement of the universities may thus be the end of a long tradition of independent research involvement from Sweden in the IEA studies.

The other reason for concern is that the study will be limited to Grade 4. As we have shown above, this implies that Sweden participates with students who not only are older than students from many other countries, but who also have one more year of schooling through the Grade 0 year. This reduces the possibilities of getting useful information about the Swedish school system from the study, and it limits the possibilities of making comparisons with other countries. In Norway, for example, school starts with Grade 1 at age six, and has a curriculum for Grade 1 that is close to the Grade 0 curriculum in Sweden.

## 15.6  Concluding Remarks

In Sweden, the attitude and influence of the funding agencies has important ramifications for the impact and practical use of comparative studies like PIRLS. The closing down of the National Board of Education and the changed tasks and responsibilities for the National Agency for Education seem to be associated with a changed attitude towards comparative studies and the results of educational research.

So far, PIRLS 2001 has had limited impact on educational policy and debate in Sweden. This is not because the study lacks important and relevant findings, but because the reports have not been published and because the policy implications of the results have not been discussed. It may be hypothesized that the decision not to publish the negative results were taken because the National Agency feared the PIRLS results would have a strong impact on discussion about the effectiveness of Swedish schools.

This raises a general question about the division of responsibility in Sweden for creating knowledge about the school system. To what extent should this responsibility rest with the universities and to what extent should it lie with the State? In Sweden, the State has this responsibility through the National Agency, and while the universities may be involved in the work, the National Agency publishes the reports. This division of responsibility is different from that in many other countries. Schwippert (this volume, Chapter 6) describes the German system in which funding institutions cannot influence the type and content of research-based publications. This is because professors of universities in Germany are, for historical reasons, able to conduct their research and teaching independently of State organizations.

## References

de Landsheere, G. (1975). Educational research and development in Europe. *Review of Research in Education, 3*, 110–133.

Foshay, A. W., Thorndike, R. L., Hotyat, F., Pidgeon, D. A., & Walker, D. A. (1962). *Educational achievements of thirteen-year-olds in twelve countries: Results of an international research project, 1959–61*. Hamburg: UNESCO Institute for Education.

Gustafsson, J.-E., & Rosén, M. (in press). The dimensional structure of reading assessment tasks in the IEA Reading Literacy Study 1991 and the Progress in International Reading Literacy Study 2001. Accepted for publication in *Educational Research and Evaluation*.

Gustafsson, J.-E., & Rosén, M. (2004a). Kommentar till Skolverkets svar på artikeln "Makt och etik i Skolverkets utvärdering av den svenska skolan. Erfarenheter från PIRLS-projektet" [A commentary on the Swedish National Agency for Education's rejoinder on the article "Power and ethics in the Swedish National Agency for Education's evaluation of the Swedish school: Experiences from the PIRLS project"]. *Pedagogisk Forskning i Sverige [Journal of Swedish Educational Research], 9*(3), 220–223.

Gustafsson, J.-E., & Rosén, M. (2004b). Makt och etik i Skolverkets utvärdering av den svenska skolan. Erfarenheter från PIRLS-projektet. [Power and ethics in the Swedish National Agency for Education's evaluation of the Swedish school: Experiences from the PIRLS-project]. *Pedagogisk Forskning i Sverige [Journal of Swedish Educational Research], 9*(1), 58–70.

Gustafsson, J.-E., & Rosén, M. (2005). Förändringar i läskompetens 1991–2001. En jämförelse över tid och länder. [Trends in reading literacy 1991–2001: A comparison across time and countries]. In *Forskning i Fokus nr 22 [Research in Focus no 22]*. Stockholm: Myndigheten för Skolutveckling.

Hansen, K. J., Rosén, M., & Gustafsson, J.-E. (in press). Measures of self-reported reading resources, attitudes and activities based on latent variable modeling. Accepted for publication in the *International Journal of Research and Method in Education*.

Hansen, K. J., Rosén, M., & Gustafsson, J.-E. (2004). *Effects of socio-economic status on reading achievement at collective and individual levels in Sweden in 1991 and 2001*. Paper presented at the 1st IEA International Research Conference, Lefkosia, Cyprus, May 11–13, 2004.

Härnqvist, K. (1975). The international study of educational achievement. *Review of Research in Education, 3*, 85–109.

Husén, T. (Ed.). (1967). *A comparison of twelve countries: International study of achievement in mathematics (Vols. 1–2)*. Stockholm: Almquist & Wiksell.

Lansfjord, M. (2002). Sweden. In I. V. S. Mullis, M. O. Martin, A. M. Kennedy, & C. L. Flaherty (Eds.), *PIRLS 2001 encyclopedia: A reference guide to reading education in the countries participating in IEA's Progress in International Reading Literacy Study (PIRLS)* (pp. 279–288). Chestnut Hill, MA: Boston College.

Löfqvist, G. (1990). *The IEA study of written composition in Sweden.* Lund: Studentlitteratur.

Lpo 94/Lpf 94. (1994). *Läroplan för det obligatoriska skolväsendet, förskoleklassen och fritidshemmet, Lpo94 [Curriculum for the compulsory school system: The pre-school class and the leisure-time center, Lpo 94].* Stockholm: Utbildningsdepartementet.

Lundh, S., Ramstedt, K., & Wester, A. (2004). Om PIRLS-projektet: Svar på Jan-Eric Gustafsson och Monica Roséns inlägg [About the PIRLS project: A rejoinder to Jan-Eric Gustafsson and Monica Rosén's contribution]. *Pedagogisk Forskning i Sverige [Journal of Swedish Educational Research], 9*(3), 216–219.

Marklund, S. (1983). *The IEA Project: An unfinished audit.* The Yellow Report Series, 64. Stockholm: The Institute of International Education, Stockholm University.

Myrberg, E., & Rosén, M. (in press). Social selection into independent schools in Sweden: Results from IEA PIRLS 2001. *Scandinavian Journal of Educational Research.*

Myrberg, E., & Rosén, M. (2004). *The impact of teacher competence in public and independent schools in Sweden.* Paper presented at the 1st IEA International Research Conference, Lefkosia, Cyprus, May 11–13, 2004.

Purves, A. C. (Ed.). (1992). *The IEA study of written composition II: Education and performance in fourteen countries.* Oxford: Pergamon Press.

Richardson, G. (2004). *Svensk utbildningshistoria: skola och samhälle förr och nu [Swedish educational history: School and society past and present].* Lund: Studentlitteratur.

Rosén, M., Myrberg, E., & Gustafsson, J.-E. (2005). PIRLS 2001: Läskompetens i skolår 3 och 4–en jämförelse mellan 35 länder. [PIRLS 2001: Reading literacy in school-year 3 and 4–a comparison of 35 countries]. *Forskning i Fokusnr, 21 [Research in Focus, no 21].* Stockholm: Myndigheten för Skolutveckling.

Skolverket. (2000). *Kartläggning av elever i fristående skolor [Mapping of students in independent schools]. (Dnr 2000: 686).* Stockholm: Skolverket.

Skolverket. (2003). *Valfrihet och dess effekter inom skolområdet. [Freedom of choice and its effects with respect to school and education]* (Rapport 230). Stockholm: Skolverket.

Skolverket. (2004). *Internationella studier under 40 år: Svenska resultat och erfarenheter [Forty years of international studies: Swedish results and experiences].* Stockholm: Skolverket.

Walker, D. A. (1976). *The IEA Six Subjects Survey: An empirical study of education in twenty-one countries.* New York: John Wiley & Sons.

West, E. G. (1997). Educational vouchers in principle and practice: A survey. *The World Bank Research Observer, 12*(1), 83–103.

**Website**

*Skolverket, Swedish National Agency for Education*: http://www.skolverket.se

**Further Reading**

Egidius, H. (2001). *Skola och utbildning i historiskt och internationellt perspektiv [School and education in historic and international perspective]*. Borås: Natur och Kultur.

Rosén, M., & Gustafsson, J.-E. (2003). *Changes in levels of reading literacy between 1991 and 2001: A trend study of 9-year olds in Sweden*. Paper presented at the EARLI 10th Biennial Conference, Padova, Italy, August 26–30, 2003.

# Chapter 16
# Comparative Synthesis

*Isabell van Ackeren*

## 16.1  Structure of the Comparative Analysis

The first step in the Impact of PIRLS Study comprised preparation of the 13 individual country reports and the juxtaposition of information on specific issues in accordance with the framework presented at the beginning of this publication. The emphasis was on the report writers' expertise and their inside perspectives of the countries in relation to the individual thematic areas. The reports were based on the common analytical framework, but the authors were allowed a certain degree of freedom in how they interpreted that framework. This was deemed necessary in order to preserve the specific underlying conditions and national characteristics. However, the limited information base underlying the country reports means that no guarantee can be given that the reports document all the particularities of the respective education systems.

The second step, presented in this chapter, includes the comparative synthesis based on a comparative methodology. This means that the following commentary focuses on comparable aspects and statements drawn from the country reports. The option of using additional sources was declined due to lack of comparability. As an exception, general knowledge about context data (for example, information on basic policy and economy issues) was included in some parts of the following comparative analysis to ensure completeness.

As described earlier, the criteria for comparison derived from the specific research interests underlying this project. These criteria also provide the structure for the comparative analysis, the elements of which are detailed in Table 16.1. While this comparative synthesis can offer only a first glance at how the 13 countries have received the findings of PIRLS 2001, it is possible to gain general ideas concerning the impact of the study's findings by clarifying common features across the countries and, from there, deducing differences between those features.

**Table 16.1: Adjusted framework for the comparison of the country reports**

| Topics | Suggested aspects to be covered |
|---|---|
| General Context Data: Countries at a Glance | • *Geography, demography, and policy aspects*<br>• *Economic facts* |
| Countries' Education Systems as Context for PIRLS | • *Governance of the school system*<br>• *Structure of the school system (primary and lower secondary education)*<br>• *Pre-primary education, school enrolment, afternoon care and language policy* |
| Experience in Large-scale Assessments | • *International surveys*<br>• *National surveys and final examinations*<br>• *Feedback systems and quality agencies* |
| National PIRLS Results at a Glance | • *Average reading performance and reading achievement for different reading purposes*<br>• *Gender differences, achievement of different language groups, and reading attitudes*<br>• *Comparisons with former student assessments and to other countries* |
| Reporting of PIRLS Results and their National Impact | • *Publications, media interest, and data feedback to schools*<br>• *Data as a source of policy decision-making*<br>• *Impact on schools' context and input qualities*<br>• *Impact on process and output-oriented strategies*<br>• *Impact on further research schemes* |
| Final Conclusions | |

## 16.2  General Context Data: Countries at a Glance

The following section reviews key aspects, namely geography, demography, policy aspects and economic facts, and tracings, in particular, trends in political and economic developments over the past two decades. This section utilizes not only the country information provided in this book, but also includes general data on political and economic conditions.[1]

## 16.2.1 Geography, Demography, and Policy Aspects

The 13 countries that have taken part in the PIRLS Impact Study are distributed over three continents. America is represented by Canada (Ontario), Asia by Iran and Hong Kong (SAR), and the remaining countries are European. Together, these countries represent a breadth of geographical coverage and a wide spread of economic wealth.

Canada is a federation of 10 provinces with three territories in North America, and is the second largest country after Russia from an area point of view. In contrast, Iran is a Middle Eastern country located in Southwest Asia. The Middle East comprises the lands around the southern and eastern parts of the Mediterranean Sea. This region is at the center of world affairs and is an economically, politically, and culturally sensitive area. Hong Kong is a special administrative region of the People's Republic of China and enjoys a high degree of autonomy from the mainland. However, most of the countries looked at in this study belong to Europe.

Geographically, Europe is a collection of connected peninsulas ("mainland" Europe and Scandinavia, Iberia, Italy and the Balkans; to the east, Europe spreads as far as the boundary with Asia). In practice, the borders of Europe are often drawn with greater regard to political, economic, and other cultural considerations. This has led to several different "Europes" that include or exclude countries according to the definition of Europe applied. Europe is increasingly being used as a short form for the European Union (EU) and its members (such as England, France, and Germany, along with new member states like Hungary, Slovenia, and Lithuania). A number of other European countries are in membership negotiations (for example, Romania), and several more are expected to enter into negotiations in the future.

On the map, Northern Europe encompasses the Nordic countries (Norway, *Sweden*,[2] Finland, Iceland, and Denmark) and the Baltic States (Estonia, Latvia, and *Lithuania*). Southern Europe includes the Iberian Peninsula (Spain, Portugal), the Italian Peninsula, Monaco, and the Balkan Peninsula (Albania, Bosnia and Herzegovina, Bulgaria, Croatia, Greece, the *Republic of Macedonia*, *Romania*, Serbia, and Montenegro).

Western Europe is always assumed to include Great Britain (*England*, Scotland, and Wales), Ireland, *France*, and Benelux, and usually also includes *Germany*. Similar to the term Western Europe, the term Eastern Europe may be used in

---

1    This is mainly done with reference to official websites of national ministries and the *CIA World Factbook* (Central Intelligence Agency, 2005).

2    The countries included in the comparison are highlighted in italics.

different ways. During the Cold War, the eastern bloc communist states (Czech Republic, *Hungary*, Baltic States, Poland, etc.) were referred to as Eastern Europe. In a broader economic and political context, Eastern Europe may also encompass Poland, the Czech Republic, *Slovakia*, *Hungary*, and the Balkans (the *Republic of Macedonia*, *Romania*).

Until relatively recently, Eastern Europe was seen as an area that was falling behind the rest of Europe economically due to the domination of the region by communism and more specifically by the Soviet Union after the Second World War. The communist reign ended in the late 1980s, and this subsequently impacted on those countries included in the comparison. The *Republic of Macedonia* renamed itself in 1991 and peacefully seceded from Yugoslavia. It is recognized by most states and international organizations as the Former Yugoslav Republic of Macedonia (FYROM). *Slovenia* was part of Yugoslavia from 1945 until it gained independence in 1991. In 1989, the end of communist rule in Czechoslovakia (after the peaceful revolution) was followed once again by the country's dissolution. *Slovakia* and the Czech Republic went their separate ways after January 1993. Slovakia became a member of the European Union in May 2004. Communist rule ended after the advent of *glasnost*, and *Lithuania* proclaimed its renewed independence in 1990.

There are some more significant differences between the countries compared, namely with respect to their sizes, their populations, and their population densities (see Table 16.2). Canada is the second-largest country with respect to surface area, but the 2001 census only recorded about 30 million people concentrated in a few urban centers. In the context of this study, the populations range from two million inhabitants in Slovenia and Macedonia (two of the smallest European countries according to area), and about 50 million inhabitants in England, 60 million in France, 63 million in Iran, and 82 million in Germany. England and Germany are among the most densely populated countries in Europe, whereas Hong Kong is one of the most densely populated areas in the world. On the other hand, Sweden has quite a low population density in all but its metropolitan areas. Given this diversity, a comparison of urban or rural areas could be of special interest in the analysis of the PIRLS data in the various countries. In this context, France resorts to single-class-learning in some rural areas, which involves grouping together all children of different ages and achievement levels. Here, achievement differences could lead to further analysis.

**Table 16.2: Population and population density of the 13 countries participating in the Impact of PIRLS Study**

| Country | Total population in 2001 (in millions, rounded) | Population density in 2001 (Residents per square kilometer, rounded) |
|---|---|---|
| Canada | 31 | 3 |
| England | 50 | 381 |
| France | 60 (in 2000) | 108 (in 2000) |
| Germany | 82 | 145 |
| Hong Kong, SAR | 7 | 6,320 |
| Hungary | 10 | 109 |
| Iran, Islamic Rep. of | 63 | 41 |
| Lithuania | 4 | 57 |
| Macedonia, Rep. of | 2 | 79 |
| Romania | 22 | 94 |
| Slovak Republic | 5 | 112 |
| Slovenia | 2 | 97 |
| Sweden | 9 | 20 |

Source: Country reports from the Impact of PIRLS Study and national census data (France).

Essentially, the cultural and political contexts in particular of the countries vary considerably due to differing historical traditions. Against this background, we can assume that these contextual features influence the impact of large-scale assessments such as PIRLS in different ways. For example, transitions in the political situation of a country will probably increase the need for comparative data to assess the effectiveness of the education system. In this sense, educational success also serves as a criterion for the economic success of a country.

The following passage deals with the current economic context of the countries and deepens the comparative analysis of this section.

## 16.2.2 Economic Facts

Countries like Canada, England, France, Germany, and Sweden belong to the world's leading industrialized countries, which have large economies measured by gross domestic product. They rank among the top nations in relation to the well-being of their inhabitants and enjoy high living standards. Hong Kong is one of the main financial centers of Asia. Nevertheless, its *entrepôt* economy is highly dependent on international trade.

The newest members of the European Union demonstrate strong economic growth. Hungarians will probably be able to approach the economic level of their western neighbors in the coming years. Slovenia also has a high-income economy. In Lithuania, growing domestic consumption and increased investment have similarly advanced recovery. In all these countries, trade has been increasingly oriented towards the West. In this context, the Slovenian report emphasizes the problem of one small part of the population striking it rich while the remainder remains "poor" and "powerless". The results of PIRLS reflect the interrelation between students' socio-economic backgrounds and the results achieved.

Macedonia's economy has also suffered from the same problems faced by other former socialist East European countries, and the weak economy continues to be a challenge for the country. Romania was left with an obsolete industrial base after the communist regime was overthrown in late 1989, which led to several years of recession. Nowadays, the country's unstable economy has been transformed into an economy with macroeconomic stability, high growth, and low unemployment. Slovakia has also developed from being a centrally controlled economy to a market economy and has mastered much of this difficult transition.

Iran is one of the world's largest oil producers and has one of the largest natural gas reserves. Most economic activity is controlled by the State. However, Iran has recently been pursuing some privatization.

Thus, there are varying moves across the participating countries in accordance with wider trends, such as democratization, technological change, demographic factors, and/or the globalization process. These developments are connected to the countries' efforts to adapt their education systems to cater for the needs of changing economies and societies. The extent to which education, seen as human capital, contributes to economic growth and social well-being is an important issue for politicians and researchers. In general, research shows that increased investment in health, skills, and knowledge provides future returns to the economy through increases in labor productivity. Against this background, education itself is part of a larger economic system and is influenced by the patterns of supply and demand. As society shifts from an industrial age, in which people got along with basic literacy and mathematical skills, to an information age, which requires the ability to analyze and use information for decision-making, the competencies needed to succeed in the workplace are changing. The Hong Kong country report, for example, describes concern "about whether the performance bodes well for a society with ambitions to be a central figure in the global economy".

These elements constitute the broad context within which student performance measures provide outcome data for planning at all levels of the respective education systems. The quality and quantity of data needed for this kind of evidence-based planning can differ within different cultural contexts. Moreover, the feedback gained through analysis of the data can be the impulse for data-based decision-making, as pointed out in the concluding chapter of this book.

# 16.3 Countries' Education Systems in the Context of PIRLS

The following description focuses on the kind of education-system-related information given in the country reports that might help explain the different impacts that PIRLS had in the participating countries.

## 16.3.1 Governance of the School System

The school systems of different countries differ in how they are administered. Some are more or less centrally organized for ease of regulation and organization and to ensure same learning conditions and opportunities. Others are more decentralized and deregulated in order to raise the level of competitiveness or to adapt institutions to local conditions. Countries accordingly have diverse existing information needs and different recipients and so vary in how they perceive and distribute data. While this consideration provides a reason for collecting information in relation to administration, it is not possible to derive cause-and-effect chains from the reports.

Canada and Germany, which both comprise a number of self-governing regions united by a central government, are federally administered. In Canada, each of the 10 provinces and three territories is responsible for its own policies for the context conditions of the school system. A coordinative board, the Council of Ministers of Education, has a solely consultative function. Although there are a great many similarities in the 13 education systems across Canada, each system reflects the diversity of its own regional history, culture, and geography. Germany's school system also is organized by the federal states (*Länder*), with the Standing Conference of the Ministers of Education and Cultural Affairs responsible for ensuring comparability. Within the boundaries of each *Länder*, the degree of centralization or decentralization may differ.

Some country reports point to the central organization of the country's school system. The Iranian commentators describe a "highly centralized" school system, which is under the jurisdiction of the Ministry of Education and Training. So do the authors from Romania and Slovenia, where educational policy and educational administration are also highly centralized. France is a prime example of the planning-oriented centralist model, with a heavy concentration of responsibilities in the national ministry.

In other country reports, we find descriptions of both tendencies. There is a central body that regulates and organizes, and, at the same time, governments abolish selected regulations. The share of administrative control between the central, local, and institutional levels is brought up in the English, Hungarian, and Macedonian chapters.

Lithuania and Sweden describe a strong shift from centrally administered responsibilities to the institutional level of each single school, which has led to increased school autonomy. This seems to be a key mechanism in nearly all the reference countries, but it is hardly possible to evaluate the quality of decentralization based on the various national texts.

### 16.3.2  Structure of the School System (Primary and Lower Secondary Education)

In the majority of the countries compared, students learn together over a period of at least eight academic years without any considerable differentiation in the educational courses. Canada's and France's school systems, for instance, are strongly aimed at integrating all children in elementary and lower secondary education, regardless of ability. England experienced a historical movement towards an integrative school system from the 1960s onwards. Although most areas of England have adopted this system, some areas have not and still retain the grammar schools. Iran, Lithuania, Macedonia, Romania, and Slovenia also describe a similar school structure, which enables common learning for all children over a period of eight or nine years. The Hungarian report refers to the country's dramatic reform period during the 1990s, which included the re-organization of the education system to introduce an eight-year single-structure school. In Slovakia, we find primary schools comprising primary education and lower secondary education in one organizational unit, which covers nine years. Students also have the option of switching to the *gymnázium* after having passed Grade 4 and an entrance examination. This means that there is, at least to some extent, segregation at an early point in time. Finally, in Germany, *all* German students change to secondary school after just four years of common learning in heterogeneous groups. According to the homogenization logic, secondary schooling is normally tracked into three types of schools.

The debates about school structure and its effects on learning results are intense in Germany, for example. In those countries where the organization of the school system has changed during the past decade, an evaluation of the implemented actions on the basis of PIRLS data is also of interest.

### 16.3.3  Pre-Primary Education, School Enrolment, Afternoon Care, and Language Policy

The texts written by the national experts provide no comparable qualitative information or quantifiable data relating to pre-primary education. It is worth mentioning that in France nearly all children between three and five years of age attend pre-elementary school, although this is not compulsory. The same applies to the age at which students start primary school. The range is clearly between six and seven years.

Some country descriptions include the afternoon care situation. For those parents unable to be with their children in the afternoon, schools provide afternoon care. This is the case in Sweden for children from one to 12 years of age. In Slovenia, all elementary schools provide afternoon care up to Grade 4, and in Macedonia, day care is organized in most schools of elementary education. Lithuania used to be well organized in this respect, but afternoon care is now on the decrease due to financial problems. The German colleague remarks that afternoon care is not compulsory in Germany, but that there are several options open to parents and their children.

In relation to the existing literacy policies described in some of the texts, it needs to be noted that they only sketch selected aspects. In Canada (Ontario), the orientation towards real world issues in concert with promotion of positive attitudes to reading is an established key element of the curriculum. Content and achievement standards exist for four levels. England introduced a National Literacy Strategy some years ago, which included a distinctive teaching methodology. In Romania, the recent introduction of a so-called "communication-functional model", integrating the separate three domains of reading, lecture, and communication, cannot be taken into account when looking at the PIRLS results, because students have not yet been taught according to the new curriculum. The Slovakian experts refer to the fact that literacy education used to emphasize perfect reading skills, so losing sight of students' ability to understand and reflect on the content of a text. The question of how national strategies have been confirmed or changed as a result of PIRLS is dealt with in the following sections.

## 16.4  Experience in Large-scale Assessments

Presumably, the impact of studies such as PIRLS depends largely on a country's familiarity with these kinds of surveys. The results of former studies may have drawn attention to strengths and weaknesses. As noted below and evident in Table 16.3, some countries are well experienced in international and national assessments conducted on a large scale, whereas, for others, taking part in PIRLS has been one of their first contacts with these types of studies.

### 16.4.1 International Surveys

We first look at the states that have participated regularly in international surveys during the last three to four decades. They are England, France, Hungary, and

Sweden. In the last decade, England participated in all the important international studies, except the IEA International Reading Literacy Study (RLS) in 1991. England also took part in early studies like the First International Mathematics Study (FIMS), and the First International Science Study (FISS). This experience has enforced school effectiveness research and the wish to identify key educational processes to increase realization.

The French report outlines the reasons for early and constant participation in large-scale assessment studies: educational expansion, standardization of the education system, and improvement of the information basis for measurement-driven policy actions. However, the French colleague characterizes decisions to participate as somewhat selective. In addition, since the middle of the 1990s, attitudes in France towards international testing have become more critical, questioning the psychometric conception and methodological relevance of the studies. This concern led to the establishment of the European Network of Policy Makers for the Evaluation of Education Systems under the French presidency of the European Union. The Network has conducted several international comparative studies since then.

IEA has conducted reading literacy studies in Hungary since the 1970s. Sweden has also been acquainted with large-scale assessments from their international beginnings collecting comparable student performance data. Since the early 1960s, there has been a close connection in Sweden between the international assessment and reform of the country's education system. Sweden is among those countries that continuously develop methodology, data management, and data analysis.

Germany exemplifies a second type of participation, characterized by interruptions. Germany took part in FIMS and FISS, but then withdrew from international comparisons in favor of concentrating on reforming the education system without testing the impact empirically. Twenty years later, Germany was involved in the International Reading Literacy study (RLS). However, it was the country's participation in the Third International Mathematics and Science Study (TIMSS) in 1995 and the shock created by the unexpectedly poor performance of the country's students in this study that led to Germany becoming a regular participant in large-scale assessments.

The third group of countries comprises those that commenced regular participation in all the important international surveys during the last 10 to 15 years. They include Canada (Ontario) and Hong Kong. Iran, Lithuania, Macedonia, Romania, and Slovakia present a fourth group—recent participants. The Republic of Iran first became involved in TIMSS, followed by TIMSS-Repeat and PIRLS. Iran, like Germany, experienced a "TIMSS-shock". However, its Ministry of Education distrusted the methodology and results of the study due to lack of experience in interpreting these, and consequently did not introduce reforms.

## Table 16.3: Participation in international studies by the Impact of PIRLS countries and their implementation of national surveys

| Country | International studies | | | | National studies | | | |
|---|---|---|---|---|---|---|---|---|
| | Regular | | | Long tradition but irregular | Long tradition | Last decade | Recently | No tradition |
| | Long tradition | Last decade | Recently | | | | | |
| Canada (Ontario) | | ■ | | | | ■ | | |
| England | ■ | | | | ■ | | | |
| Germany | | | | ■ | | no consistent pattern | | |
| France | ■ | | | | ■ | | | |
| Hong Kong, SAR | | ■ | | | | ■ | | |
| Hungary | ■ | | | | ■ | | | |
| Iran, Islamic Rep. of | | | ■ | | | | | ■ |
| Lithuania | | | ■ | | | | | ■ |
| Macedonia, Rep. of | | | ■ | | | | | ■ |
| Romania | | | ■ | | | ■ | | |
| Slovak Republic | | | ■ | | | | ■ | |
| Slovenia | | ■ | | | | ■ | | |
| Sweden | ■ | | | | | | | ■ |

■ = Applicable.

Source: National country reports of the Impact of PIRLS Study.

Lithuania, Macedonia, and Slovakia also commenced international assessments with TIMSS, or rather TIMSS-R, and continued with PIRLS. Faced with weak results for their students, the national experts from Iran, Macedonia, and Romania portray the situation as very disappointing, all the more so as very talented students from these countries had achieved the best results in numerous international competitions. These experiences exemplify the necessity of assessing representative samples of the respective age cohort.

### 16.4.2 National Surveys and Final Examinations

The countries' international experiences in the field of large-scale assessments are also predominantly reflected in their national traditions of assessing and evaluating student performance.

England, France, and Hungary have a long tradition in testing. In the first of these countries, and starting in the 1970s, the Assessment of Performance Unit (APU) conducted representative national surveys of student achievement throughout Great Britain. The APU's task was to promote the development of methods of assessing and monitoring the achievement of children at school, and to seek to identify the incidence of under-achievement as well as trends over time. At the end of the 1980s, this kind of sample testing was replaced by national curriculum testing of complete cohorts of students (that is, ages seven, 11, and 14) to promote schools' accountability. The French system of school evaluation distinguishes between diagnostic and monitoring assessments, which are both widespread. Placing tests at the beginning of Grades 3 and 6 instead of conducting them at the end of a year stresses their diagnostic intention of enabling quick reaction to the assessed deficits. A databank of assessment tools is also offered to teachers. Surveys for monitoring purposes are conducted on a regular basis at the end of primary and secondary education to identify trends over time. In Hungary, the authorities have been monitoring students' reading literacy since 1986 and mathematical literacy since 2001. Since 1991, tests in mathematics, science, and IT have been conducted regularly (every two years of the school career).

In another group of countries, we find an approximate 10-year tradition of national student testing. In Canada, a national system of province-comparing assessments has been developed (the School Achievement Indicators Program (SAIP)), which assesses the main subjects in a three-year cycle. Within Ontario, a showcase for examination, tests for Grades 3, 6, and 9 take place every year. There is also a common graduation literacy test at the end of secondary school. Some German federal states started testing in the middle or at the end of the 1990s. Hamburg, Brandenburg, and Rhineland-Palatinate were the first to start their own state-wide evaluations. Furthermore, it is now usual in Germany to extend the samples provided by international studies so that the country can focus on differences between the states. So-called "comparative tests" have also been introduced within the *Länder*, at key stages, in order to compare achievement state-wide. Finally, half of the *Länder* use a traditional model of external assessment in the form of centrally conducted final examinations, although nearly every other federal state has now decided to establish central examinations.

The education system of Hong Kong, which was a British colony until 1997, follows a British pattern in that it conducts its own large-scale assessments every year, with data fed back to schools and individual teachers. Since the middle of the 1990s, Romania has regularly conducted national assessments at the end of primary schooling, and it initiated a program for the assessment of educational progress in 2000. Macedonia is one of the PIRLS participants that more recently established national assessment (in 2000, as a consequence of its participation in TIMSS and PIRLS), followed by the formulation of national standards. Macedonia conducts national monitoring, repeated every four years, as well as an external assessment at the end of each three-year cycle. The Swedish report describes a lack of regularly collected nationally representative data, and Iran and Lithuania have just started to discuss national assessments.

### 16.4.3 Feedback Systems and Quality Agencies

Germany and Macedonia explicitly specify the problem of teachers lacking statistical knowledge. A second difficulty stressed by the authors relates to data being too general to be of interest to individual teachers. One consequence of this is that countries are striving to present more individualized data, to change the publication strategy, and to train schools in such as way as to make data useful for school development purposes. Iran, for instance, prepares quality report cards, with PIRLS results for individual schools comprising context data. Macedonia offers seminars and workshops for school principals and school developers. In Slovenia, school staff received training, after which a network of counselors was established to work with individual schools to aid the understanding of data sets. Some reports mention quality agencies, which maintain and develop assessments and examinations (Canada (Ontario), Macedonia, Romania, and Slovenia). Other accounts do not mention these, although they do exist (for example, in England, France, and Germany).

There is no doubt that some countries are test-experienced nations, with generally long traditions of evaluation procedures. Nevertheless, the reports also outline the issue of sample participation rates or the issue of acceptance on the part of teachers, who feel, to some extent, that the procedures are time-consuming and challenging. Other countries are now, with some delay, focusing on quality development by introducing a (partly) diversified system of assessment procedures at different levels of the school system. In all countries, linking the rich database to school development remains a challenge.

## 16.5  National PIRLS Results at a Glance

### 16.5.1  Average Reading Performance and Reading Achievement for Different Reading Purposes

Sweden and England were among the nations topping the charts with the most literate Grade 4 children (Table 16.4). Sweden also selected Grade 3 students for participation to enable comparisons with the International Reading Literacy Study of 1991, and it is important to note that Swedish students are significantly older than the average at Grade 4. Sweden accordingly devoted considerable effort to maximizing comparability across the grades and ages tested. The results for the Grade 3 students were close to the international mean, indicating a decline in level of reading performance between 1991 and 2001, which throws—and this is underlined by the authors—a less optimistic light on the Swedish results. The Swedish situation aside, it was difficult to ensure comparability across countries due to different ages at the start of formal schooling. For example, the students in Slovenia had one year less schooling than had the students in the other participating countries, and the English students were in their fifth year of schooling (Mullis, Martin, Gonzalez, & Kennedy, 2003).

Canada (Ontario, Quebec), France, Germany, Hong Kong, Hungary, Lithuania, Romania, and Slovakia (listed in alphabetical order) also performed well, reaching significantly higher levels than the international average. Nevertheless, Lithuania and Romania had particularly old students (Table 16.4). Slovenia achieved the international average, and the remaining countries, Macedonia and Iran, had significantly lower achievement. (For further details, see Chapter 2 in this volume.)

In relation to different reading purposes, Canada (Ontario, Quebec), England, Hungary, Iran, and Lithuania achieved significantly better results in literary reading than in informational reading (country reports and Mullis et al., 2003). Conversely, students from Hong Kong as well as from France, Macedonia, Slovakia, and Slovenia performed better in informational reading.

### 16.5.2  Gender Differences, Achievement of Different Language Groups, and Reading Attitudes

In all countries, girls had significantly higher reading achievement than did boys. France, Germany, Romania, Slovakia, Lithuania, and Canada (Ontario, Quebec) had an 11- to 18-point difference, which is below the international average of 20 points, where we find Hong Kong and Macedonia. The other countries displayed significantly higher average reading achievement differences between girls and boys.

**Table 16.4: Summary of reading achievement on PIRLS 2001 within the 13 Impact of PIRLS countries**

| Country | Reading achievement, Average scale scores (Standard error) | | | | | | Years of formal schooling | Average age |
|---|---|---|---|---|---|---|---|---|
| | Overall | SE | Literary | SE | Informational | SE | | |
| Sweden | 561 | (2.2) | 559 | (2.4) | 559 | (2.2) | 4 | 10.8 |
| England | 553 | (3.4) | 559 | (3.9) | 546 | (3.6) | 5 | 10.2 |
| Canada (O, Q)* | 544 | (2.4) | 545 | (2.6) | 541 | (2.4) | 4 | 10.0 |
| Lithuania | 543 | (2.6) | 546 | (3.1) | 540 | (2.7) | 4 | 10.9 |
| Hungary | 543 | (2.2) | 548 | (2.0) | 537 | (2.2) | 4 | 10.7 |
| Germany | 539 | (1.9) | 537 | (1.9) | 538 | (1.9) | 4 | 10.5 |
| Hong Kong, SAR | 528 | (3.1) | 518 | (3.1) | 537 | (2.9) | 4 | 10.2 |
| France | 525 | (2.4) | 518 | (2.6) | 533 | (2.5) | 4 | 10.1 |
| Slovak Republic | 518 | (2.8) | 512 | (2.6) | 522 | (2.7) | 4 | 10.3 |
| Romania | 512 | (4.6) | 512 | (4.7) | 512 | (4.6) | 4 | 11.1 |
| Slovenia | 502 | (2.0) | 499 | (1.8) | 503 | (1.9) | 3 | 9.8 |
| **Int. Average** | **500** | **(0.6)** | **500** | **(0.6)** | **500** | **(0.7)** | **4** | **10.3** |
| Macedonia, Rep. of | 442 | (4.6) | 441 | (4.5) | 445 | (5.2) | 4 | 10.7 |
| Iran, Islamic Rep. of | 414 | (4.2) | 421 | (4.5) | 408 | (4.6) | 4 | 10.4 |

* Canada is represented by the provinces of Ontario and Quebec only. Note that the national country report in this volume is based on Ontario only.

Source: Mullis et al. (2003, pp. 26, 36, 38).

Two countries compared different language groups. In Canada (Ontario, Quebec), the French-language students scored significantly lower than did the English-language students, and in Macedonia, the Macedonian students outperformed their Albanian peers, which led to national discussions in both cases.

The PIRLS report outlines the generally positive attitudes towards reading in nearly all countries, with about half the students belonging to the high category of the index. In this context, it seems remarkable that the English country report as well as the report from Hong Kong outline students' poor attitudes towards reading. Despite high achievement in the reading tests, children in England were reported as having relatively poor attitudes to reading compared to children in many other countries. This attracted comment in the media.

### 16.5.3 Comparisons to Former Student Assessments and to Other Countries

Germany experienced different overall achievement levels for the younger students in PIRLS and the older students in PISA. The PIRLS results were significantly better than the PISA achievement. Some groups in Germany ascribe the results to the different organizational structure of schooling (comprehensive at primary level, tracked at secondary level); others refer to different pedagogical concepts. The Hong Kong report establishes that the country's Grade 4 students did not achieve top ranking on PIRLS as they had on TIMSS. Lithuania looks for explanations for the differences between the poor TIMSS results and the surprisingly satisfying PIRLS achievement. French researchers and politicians refer to the fact that the French results—when compared to those for PISA—are widely influenced by the study's question format, because French students are more likely to omit open questions and tend not to risk giving a false answer. On the other hand, they outperform their counterparts from other countries when asked to apply technical reading mechanisms.

The assessment results must be viewed in the light of the wider range and complex interplay of factors that are internal and external to school systems. Careful comparisons can be undertaken between countries with socio-culturally comparable contexts. Thus, the England report offers comparisons with the top-ranked Netherlands. The Lithuanian author looks at Latvian results, as Latvia is a neighbor and an important reference country. Romania and Slovakia undertake comparisons with former communist countries with similar cultural, political, and economic situations. Overall, the comparisons in the country reports articulate the need for adequate benchmarks to allow comparison with a particular group of reference countries.

# 16.6  Reporting of PIRLS Results and their National Impacts

## 16.6.1  Publications, Media Interest, and Data Feedback to Schools

Obviously, the publication of the PIRLS results received different levels of national press coverage. However, an evaluation of the level of public interest appears to be rather difficult due to the different yardsticks used in the Impact Study's country reports. Some authors compare the media response to PIRLS to the response to PISA, for example. Others evaluate the public attention in terms of the coverage received by other headlines during the timeframe of the PIRLS release. Also, it is not possible to compare the media interest in different countries. Despite these uncertainties, there seem to be two large groupings: one in which PIRLS has received little attention, and one in which there is a broad public awareness of the national results achieved by primary school students.

The text concerning the situation in Canada (Ontario) merely describes the publication of the rankings and the main results in national and local newspapers without analyzing the intensity of public interest. In the light of the regular national assessments of Ontario's and Canada's participation in international surveys, and given the habitually satisfying results, the apparent restrained interest is not too astonishing. England reports that there was relatively little public attention, although nearly all serious newspapers did carry reports. All French major national and local newspapers reported, as did the midday television news, mostly giving a short presentation of the international rankings. However, according to the French author, the public paid little attention because the results were average. Likewise, Iran, Macedonia, and Romania only reported several articles and presentations based on the national PIRLS releases. In Slovakia, where the national report was still being printed when the international results were published, data were presented in the daily press and in teachers' and educational journals, and were announced on the radio. However, as the achievement seemed satisfying, the results received scant public attention. Finally, a peculiar situation in Sweden, in which only the good Grade 4 results were published, led to little public awareness. The National Agency did not allow release of the negative Grade 3 results, so there were no Swedish reports at the time of the international releases, which meant little media interest.

Two books have been released in Germany: one covering the German PIRLS population, followed by an in depth-analysis of seven federal states with extended examples. PIRLS has been the topic of many press articles, television news items, educational journal articles, and numerous presentations. Nevertheless, the debates have been "less emotional" than the ones concerning PISA. In Hong Kong, newspapers (some providing special features), radio, and television all dealt with PIRLS, with the level of interest seemingly huge due to the perceived weak results. The Hungarian media were mostly interested in the differences between the PISA and PIRLS results. The good news concerning the Lithuanian achievement was widely broadcast by national, local, and educational newspapers as well as by national radio and television. There was a relatively high level of interest in Slovenia, too, where there were articles in the newspapers and news on the radio, although the national television station was not interested.

In some countries, all schools received a national report or booklet containing the key results and selected items (for example, France, Macedonia, and Lithuania) or participating schools received individual feedback and detailed analyses (for example, Hong Kong and Slovakia). In Hong Kong, Iran, and Lithuania, workshops were organized for primary schools to explain new theories and concepts of reading instruction.

### 16.6.2 Data as a Source of Policy Decision-making

In all reference countries, the data generated by large-scale assessments form the basis for political decision-making processes to a greater or a lesser extent. However, the national governments and authorities have different experiences given the length of time they have been participating in these surveys. Hong Kong and France, for example, emphasize the important role of international monitoring studies as an information source. Iran and Macedonia describe policy-makers as starting to become aware of the usefulness of empirical data as a starting point for interventions.

Educational researchers differ in their judgments of the implemented actions. The German report, for example, accuses policy responses of not being systematic and of just dealing with snapshots. After the disastrous PISA achievement, policy-makers were of the opinion that primary education was responsible for the situation and decided on innovations for primary schools prior to the PIRLS release, thereby acting without any empirical evidence. The German federal structure, the long tradition of the tracked school system, and lingering suspicions in relation to such empirical studies seem to be obstructing concerted, target-oriented action.

The following sections analyze the impact of PIRLS and/or the impact of other similar surveys in four higher-level categories already evident in school effectiveness research. Context influences include family and community variables, which are considered to be indirectly related to school achievement. Impact indicators most directly relate to school learning. They include education system structures (input) and processes at the level of the individual school as well as classroom instruction. Finally, how countries deal with the results (outputs) is of special interest. The term "impact" includes discussions initiated as well as steps taken.

### Impact on Schools' Context and Input Qualities

*Context factor parental support*: The Canada (Ontario) and Hong Kong reports both describe efforts to strengthen parental support by encouraging parents to help their children develop reading literacy. Guidebooks are handed out to parents and talks are organized in order to show them how to support their children read with pleasure. Further activities concentrating on context factors are not mentioned in the texts.

*School structure-related input factors*: In Germany, the country's tracked school system has a specific impact on discussion of school structure. Some stakeholders in Germany argue that postponing students' segregation into different educational courses as long as possible would improve quality. In this regard, the decision to track students after Grade 4 is viewed as being too early and that, at the least, mobility between tracks should be ensured. In some countries, debates concern pre-primary education. Compulsory pre-school is discussed in Germany, and a pre-primary program is planned in Iran. In Slovakia, the compulsory school age is to shift from seven to six years in order to start literacy education at an earlier stage, and literacy skills are to be stimulated in kindergarten.

*Additional resources as an input factor*: In Ontario, more time will be given to literacy by dedicating one hour each day to it. The Canadian text also reveals that Ontario's political decision-makers believe strongly in the correlation between smaller class sizes and improved student performance at school. Measures to reduce class size in primary grades are receiving top priority. The same political direction is evident in France, where about 100 first-grade classes are taking part in an experiment relating to a significant reduction of class size. Achievement in these classes is being compared to achievement in another 100 classes working in similar circumstances. The first results of the experiment have not been too optimistic, as the size reduction appears not to have prompted different teaching practices.

*Teacher development and support as an input factor*: In some of the countries compared, governments and municipalities pay increased attention to teacher development, and support reading and writing instruction (Ontario) and empirical research methods (Slovakia). In Germany, this support is also a part of teacher training at universities. Hong Kong, Iran, and Macedonia explicitly report on (planned) activities relating to teacher training programs (pre-service and in-service). The promotion of diagnostic competencies and the capability of dealing with the heterogeneous nature of classroom settings are particularly important.

*Teaching methods and revision of curricula as input factors*: In England, a new steering philosophy emerged after the PIRLS success. Schools are no longer expected to follow a prescriptive and distinctive methodology (as expected by the National Literacy Strategy) but rather to develop their own strategies. France published new reading literacy curricula in 2002 and now emphasizes reading different text documents across all disciplines. Hong Kong, Hungary, Iran, Macedonia, Romania, and Slovakia are examining their curricula and conceptualizing new ones in the light of a changed concept of reading literacy.

### Impact on Process and Output-centered Strategies

*Process factors*: Some countries discuss intensive reading programs for special target groups (Canada (Ontario) and Germany). In Ontario, struggling schools will receive extra support from literacy experts, and all teachers will receive guides covering effective tuition in reading in order to promote knowledge of teaching and learning processes, or they can download web-based learning modules for these purposes. Hong Kong is encouraging schools to create reading environments (for example, reading corners).

*Output-oriented factors*: Ontario decided to re-design its reading comprehension tests, and Hong Kong is promoting additional diagnostic testing. So is France, which plans to introduce new assessment tools for pre-primary education and the first grade of primary school in order to make early diagnoses possible and to enable quick reactions to prevent students from falling behind. Diagnostic and support materials are similarly being made available for older students, to allow adequate reaction to existing difficulties. Macedonia is introducing national tests for Grades 4 and 8 on the basis of representative samples, and Slovenia also wants to put more emphasis on regular assessments in the future. As for schools' accountability, Ontario now lets schools set targets every three years, and Germany, Macedonia, and Slovenia have specified output-related standards covering particular achievement levels. The intention is for the standards to play an increasing role as a control element in educational policy.

### Impact on Further Research Schemes

Most of the countries in question are conducting secondary analyses of PIRLS data sets as well as in-depth comparative analyses in order to identify relevant factors influencing reading results and successful strategies in other countries. Slovenia will have a look at schools with high reading achievement but poor learning environments. The experts from Germany continue to analyze achievement differences between the federal states, and they will conduct a longitudinal study from Grades 3 to 4. Their Swedish colleagues have similar plans and will analyze changes from Grades 3 to 4 within the same school, which means observation of the same factors over a longer time in order to identify trends. Some participating countries also plan to analyze teaching and learning processes (Hong Kong) through, for example, video-classroom studies (Germany). Hong Kong and Iran intend to analyze bilingual reading.

## 16.7  Conclusions

The intention of this volume has been to provide a summary of some of the changes in educational policy and instruction within the 13 countries participating in the Impact of PIRLS Study, as well as follow-up research concerning reading literacy. On the one hand, the impact of large-scale studies in general and of PIRLS in particular is difficult to assess. On the other hand, it still seems too early to identify real consequences. This reason seems to explain why most of the reports appear rather cautious when describing the influences. It is also hard to identify the starting point of discussions and actions. Despite the limited information in the country reports, some general ideas regarding impact are apparent. The main and common factors are summarized in Figure 16.1, although their interplay in the different national contexts is not examined.

**Figure 16.1: Selected factors supposedly influencing the impact of PIRLS in the 13 participating countries**

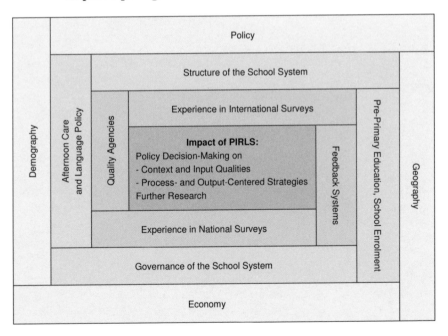

Clarifying the relationship between the PIRLS data and quality development in the schools and determining how to operate obviously remain challenges in all countries. Most of the countries in the comparison are investing in input-related quality factors and, at the same time, strengthening output-oriented actions, such as introducing more assessments for diagnostic and accountability purposes. In most cases, these actions link to a comprehensive national strategy, set up during the past decade(s) or planned for the future. The long-term strategy of PIRLS will help to enrich the national pictures, to monitor progress, and to highlight future directions for policy and schools. The activities and experiences reported hopefully will encourage other countries to undertake initiatives proven worthwhile elsewhere, although there is—unfortunately—no universally valid concept.

## References

Central Intelligence Agency. (2005). *The world factbook 2005.* Washington, DC: Central Intelligence Agency.

Mullis, I. V. S., Martin, M. O., Gonzalez, E. J., & Kennedy, A. M. (2003). *PIRLS 2001 international report: IEA's study of reading literacy achievement in primary schools in 35 countries.* Chestnut Hill, MA: Boston College.

# Chapter 17
# Concluding Remarks

*Knut Schwippert and Martin Goy*

The main goal in putting this volume together was to provide in-depth qualitative information on the impact of the Progress in International Reading Literacy Study (PIRLS) in 13 of the 35 participating countries. Impact was defined as the study's influence on public and published opinion, on education policy, on teaching and curriculum development, and on educational research. As occurred with an earlier publication on the impact of the Third International Mathematics and Science Study (TIMSS) (Robitaille, Beaton, & Plomp, 2000a), we hope that the results documented here will encourage policy-makers, curriculum experts, and researchers to use the information provided as incentives to consider taking initiatives that have proven worthwhile in other countries. Such an exchange of ideas on an international level is one of the great benefits of international studies like PIRLS, as IEA's Executive Director Hans Wagemaker pointed out in his keynote address on the occasion of IEA's 45th anniversary:

> While much of what international studies like those carried out by IEA do is to describe "what is" in terms of how education is practiced in a country (the within-country perspective), the power of such studies is most fully realized when the international context they provide is considered (the between-country perspective). Given the differences in the ways in which education is organized and practiced across cultures and societies, a comparative perspective not only enables an understanding of its many forms but also serves to expand a nation's horizon as to what might be possible. Identifying models or practices of education from countries around the world as a means of reflecting on one's own practice and experience was—and arguably still is—a key function of international comparative studies and the work of IEA. (Wagemaker, 2004)

The country reports in this volume reveal that PIRLS has had a significant impact in terms of its public visibility as well as its influence on policy and practice. As the author of the synthesizing comparative chapter points out, the impact documented in the reports is almost as heterogeneous as the countries themselves because of the complex interplay of factors (national, home, and school) influencing the dissemination, interpretation, and application of the PIRLS data in each. A central challenge documented in many of the reports was to clarify and operationalize the relationship between the data provided by the study and the development of schools. However, a number of general ideas about the impact became apparent: in most of the countries, the results of the PIRLS study were taken as an incentive to invest in input-related quality factors while simultaneously strengthening output-oriented actions, such as an increase in assessments for diagnostic purposes.

In terms of the methodology evident in this volume, we chose to employ an identical framework for all country reports so that we could place the impact of the PIRLS study within the participating countries' respective national socio-cultural and political contexts. This decision offers some explanation for the differences in the national impacts and will help the readers of this volume identify those contexts that suit their own tasks and settings.

We advise readers, however, to keep in mind the limited amount of time that has passed since the publication of the PIRLS results. In Germany, we use the image of a supertanker as a metaphor for the slow maneuverability of an education system: once in motion, it takes a long time to alter the ship's course. This slowness might be partly due to the structure of the German educational administration, but it also points to the fact that it will take longer than only two to three years after the dissemination of the study's results for the impact of such a large-scale assessment to be fully visible. In addition, the different viewpoints of the authors of this volume have to be taken into account when reading the national reports. Impact and (more importantly) educational success lie in the eye of the beholder. Some researchers will judge the results and developments documented by the PIRLS data as indicating a deadlock situation, whereas policy-makers might apply different categories and see the same situation as an indicator of success—or vice versa. Since the interpretation of the results is, to a certain extent, always influenced by the institutional viewpoint from which it is written, this volume offers some insights into these contexts by providing information on the contributing authors and their home institutions.

As Robitaille, Beaton, and Plomp (2000b) point out, there is no "royal road" to education, as each national educational system has its own socio-political context. However,

> [s]ystems can learn from one another. They can learn that different approaches to common concerns—such as the streaming of students by some measure of ability—are taken in different countries. They can study the relative success and efficacy of those different approaches and then make decisions about what might work in their setting. (Robitaille, Beaton, & Plomp, 2000b, p. 169)

The impact of PIRLS already visible at this point certainly reveals the study's capacity to contribute to educational policy reform. In the long run, the impact of PIRLS will increase and become more diverse once the results of the second (2006) cycle of the study are disseminated and we are able to incorporate more observations into an analytical review of changes and developments in education systems. A longitudinal documentation of the study's impact with—hopefully—an extended number of countries contributing national reports would surely be valuable to reveal (and to allow us to exchange commentary on) the progress achieved by the iterative design of PIRLS.

**References**

Robitaille, D. F., Beaton, A. E., & Plomp, T. (Eds.). (2000a). *The Impact of TIMSS on the teaching and learning of mathematics and science*. Vancouver: Pacific Educational Press.

Robitaille, D. F., Beaton, A. E., & Plomp, T. (2000b). Concluding comments. In D. F. Robitaille, A. E. Beaton, & T. Plomp (Eds.), *The impact of TIMSS on the teaching and learning of mathematics and science* (pp. 168–169). Vancouver: Pacific Educational Press.

Wagemaker, H. (2004). IEA: *International studies, impact and transition*. Speech given on the occasion of the 1st IEA International Research Conference, University of Cyprus, Lefkosia, Cyprus, 11–13 May 2004. Retrieved 19 August, 2005, from https://www.iea-dpc.org/download/ieahq/IRC2004/wagemaker.pdf

# Bibliography of International PIRLS Publications

Campbell, J. R., Kelly, D. L., Mullis, I. V. S., Martin, M. O., & Sainsbury, M. (2001). *Framework and specifications for PIRLS assessment 2001* (2nd ed.). Chestnut Hill, MA: Boston College.

Gonzalez, E. J., & Kennedy, A. M. (Eds.). (2003). *PIRLS 2001 user guide for the international database*. Chestnut Hill, MA: Boston College.

Martin, M. O., Mullis, I. V. S., Gonzalez, E. J., & Kennedy, A. M. (Eds.). (2003). *Trends in children's reading literacy achievement 1991–2001: IEA's repeat in nine countries of the 1991 Reading Literacy Study*. Chestnut Hill, MA: Boston College.

Martin, M. O., Mullis, I. V. S., & Kennedy, A. M. (Eds.). (2003). *PIRLS 2001 technical report*. Chestnut Hill, MA: Boston College.

Mullis, I. V. S., Kennedy, A. M., Martin, M. O., & Sainsbury, M. (2006). *PIRLS 2006 assessment framework and specifications* (2nd ed.). Chestnut Hill, MA: Boston College.

Mullis, I. V. S., Martin, M. O., & Gonzalez, E. J. (2004). *International achievement in the processes of reading comprehension: Results from PIRLS 2001 in 35 countries*. Chestnut Hill, MA: Boston College.

Mullis, I. V. S., Martin, M. O., Gonzalez, E. J., & Kennedy, A. M. (2003). *PIRLS 2001 international report: IEA's study of reading literacy achievement in primary schools in 35 countries*. Chestnut Hill, MA: Boston College.

Mullis, I. V. S., Martin, M. O., Kennedy, A. M., & Flaherty, C. L. (Eds.). (2002). *PIRLS encyclopedia: A reference guide to reading education in the countries participating in IEA's Progress in International Reading Literacy Study (PIRLS)*. Chestnut Hill, MA: Boston College.

# Information on the Contributing Authors

## Colmant, Marc

Marc Colmant is in charge of studies in the DEP, the Department for Assessment and Forecasting, of the French Ministry of Education in Paris. Responsible for coordinating France's participation in PIRLS 2001, he is the National Research Coordinator for PIRLS 2006 and a member of the questionnaire development group for this study. Since 1992 he has been involved in several diagnostic and monitoring assessments at the national level (start-of-year tests in Grade 3, bank of assessment tools) and in cooperation with other countries (Scotland, Brazil). He has also been involved in other international large-scale assessments (DIEPE).

*Address for correspondence*: Marc Colmant, Ministère de l'éducation nationale, de l'enseignement supérieur et de la Recherche, DEP C1, 61-65 rue Dutot, 75732 Paris Cedex15 (marc.colmant@education.gouv.fr)


## Daeipour, Parvin

Parvin Daeipour is a clinical psychologist who works mainly with children, adolescents, and their families. She is a member of the PIRLS team in Iran. As the study's data manager, she was responsible for preparing the national database, and for conducting the national analysis of the PIRLS 2001 results.

*Address for correspondence*: Parvin Daeipour, Sobhe Sadegh Counseling Center, No. 7, Kaveh Medical Building, Kolahdouz St., Tehran, Iran (pardaeipour@gmail.com)


## Doupona Horvat, Marjeta

Marjeta Doupona Horvat works as a researcher at the Educational Research Institute in Slovenia. She was the country's National Research Coordinator for PIRLS 2001 and for PIRLS 2006. She has been involved in other national surveys and research on reading as well. She is a member of the National Commission on Reading. Her main areas of research interest are language and its use, written communication, and the relation between society and knowledge. Currently she is finishing her doctoral thesis in the field of linguistics pragmatics.

*Address for correspondence*: Marjeta Doupona Horvat, Educational Research Institute, Gerbiceva 61, SI-1000 Ljubljana, Slovenia (marjeta.doupona@pei.si)

## Elijio, Aistė

Aistė Elijio (previously Mackeviciute) is a Ph.D student at the Department of Econometrical Analysis, Faculty of Mathematics and Informatics, Vilnius University. She also works as a senior specialist at the Research Unit within the National Examinations Center. She was the National Research Coordinator for PIRLS 2001 and is NRC for PIRLS 2006. Her interest in returning to university to conduct doctoral studies in statistics was aroused mainly by her work with the international educational surveys PIRLS and TIMSS. Her main interests include statistical methods in educational surveys, implications of complex sample design for statistical analysis, and the education of gifted students.

*Address for correspondence*: Aistė Elijio, National Examinations Center, Katkaus 44, LT-09217, Vilnius, Lithuania (aiste@nec.lt)

## Goy, Martin

Martin Goy is a student research assistant of Knut Schwippert, the editor of the present volume. From 2001 to 2005, he worked for the National Research Coordinator for PIRLS Germany, Wilfried Bos. He is currently writing his Master's thesis, the subject of which is the relationship between reading self-concept and reading achievement.

*Address for correspondence*: Martin Goy, Lutterothstr. 68, D-20255 Hamburg, Germany (martin.goy@gmx.net)

## Gustafsson, Jan-Eric

Jan-Eric Gustafsson is a professor of education at the Department of Education, Gothenburg University. He was involved in PIRLS 2001, from its start in 1999, as a scientific advisor to the Swedish part of the project, and has worked on issues of design, analysis, and reporting. His main areas of research concern individual differences in educational contexts, educational measurement, quantitative methods with a special focus on structural equation modeling, and comparative educational research. He is currently a member of the Technical Executive Group of IEA.

*Address for correspondence*: Prof. Jan-Eric Gustafsson, Department of Education, Gothenburg University, PO Box 300, SE-405 30 Gothenburg, Sweden (Jan-Eric.Gustafsson@ped.gu.se)

## Jodouin, Hervé

During his 18 years in the classroom as a teacher and departmental head, Hervé Jodouin established an action research program. He encouraged his staff to become familiar with the latest large-scale assessment research and results and to apply findings to their classes. Since July 1996, he has been involved, in his role as education officer at EQAO, and as a member and team leader of various national assessment consortia, with ongoing research into the performance of Canadian students in mathematics, science, reading, and writing. In PIRLS 2006, he is responsible for the national scoring session of the study. His main area of research interest is the delivery and assessment of programs for minority populations. As a member of two minority groups, Francophones outside of Québec and French-speaking Métis, he has a special interest in the development of strategies to improve student learning for these groups in particular and for all students in general. He intends to continue his research by using information from national and international databases to explore how learning is different for minorities and what modifications can be made to education systems to ensure all students reach their full potential. He has been involved with other international large-scale assessments (PISA, TIMSS).

*Address for correspondence*: Hervé Jodouin, 117 Gerrard Street East, apt. PH9, Toronto, Ontario, Canada, M5B 2L4 (hervejodouin@gmail.com)

### Karimi, Abdol'azim

Abdol'azim Karimi is an associate professor of learning psychology and a faculty member of the Institute of Educational Research. He is manager of both PIRLS and TIMSS projects in Iran and is also the country's National Research Coordinator for PIRLS. He has written several books and articles in the field of children's learning and educational issues, with the aim of helping both teachers and parents.

*Address for correspondence*: Dr. Abdol'azim Karimi, Ministry of Education, Research Institute of Education (RIE), 196 Keshavarz Blvd., Tehran 14166, Iran (http://www.karimi.ir, karimi@rie.ir )

### Litoiu, Nicoleta

Nicoleta Litoiu has a Ph.D in learning assessment and is deputy director of the National Assessment and Examination Service, Romania (NAES). Her position there involves the following: elaboration of the assessment standards, procedures, and instruments required for monitoring educational progress; diagnosing students' achievement results; certifying competencies at the end of an educational stage; selecting students for the next stage of education; predicting students' performance; and counseling for school and career.

*Address for correspondence*: Nicoleta Litoiu, National Assessment and Examination Service, Str. G-ral Berthelot, nr. 26, Bucureşti, Romania (llitoiu@yahoo.com)

## Loh, Elizabeth Ka Yee

Elizabeth Ka Yee Loh is the research officer of the PIRLS (2001 and 2006) project for Hong Kong, SAR. Her Ph.D study in the University of Hong Kong is in Chinese writing. Her research interests include new methods in teaching literary writing, assessment of Chinese characters, writing and reading, and new teaching strategies to help children with special educational needs learn Chinese language.

*Address for correspondence*: Elizabeth K. Y. Loh, Faculty of Education, The University of Hong Kong, Pokfulam Road, Hong Kong, SAR, China (ekyloh@ hkucc.hku.hk)

## Lukačková, Zuzana

After completing her Master's degree in the Slovak language and literature and in English at Comenius University, Bratislava, Zuzana Lukačková taught at a secondary grammar school. Since 2000, she has been working as a researcher in the National Institute for Education (ŠPÚ) as the head of the Department of International Evaluation Projects; IEA representative for the Slovak Republic; and the National Research Coordinator for PIRLS 2001. Her PIRLS-related work has included co-authoring the national report and further disseminating tasks concerning reading literacy issues in the national and international context. She has been involved in national testing since 2005. In 2006, she left ŠPÚ.

*Address for correspondence*: Zuzana Lukačková, Povazanova 2, 841 02 Bratislava 4, Slovak Republic (mazulu45@hotmail.com or zuluk@chello.sk)

## Mickovska, Gorica

Gorica Mickovska is a psychometrics expert in the Department for Examinations and External Assessment of Macedonia's Bureau for the Development of Education, where she is jointly responsible for national data analyses. She was jointly responsible for the national analysis presented in the first published report of Macedonia's participation in PIRLS 2001. Her main areas of research interest are national large-scale assessment methodology, standard-setting procedures, and civic education.

*Address for correspondence*: Gorica Mickovska, Bureau for the Development of Education, Department for Examinations and External Assessment, Vasil Gorgov bb., 1000 Skopje, Republic of Macedonia (mgorica@yahoo.com)

## Naceva, Bojana

Bojana Naceva is head of the Department for Examinations and External Assessment of Macedonia's Bureau for the Development of Education, where she is the National Research Coordinator for PIRLS. During PIRLS 2001, she was responsible for administering the project and jointly responsible for the national analysis presented in the first publication on Macedonia's participation in PIRLS 2001. She is also the NRC for PIRLS 2006 and a member of the study's questionnaire development group. Her main areas of research interest include international and national large-scale assessment methodology and organization; standard-setting procedures; and school-based assessment.

*Address for correspondence*: Bojana Naceva, Bureau for the Development of Education, Department for Examinations and External Assessment, Vasil Gorgov bb., 1000 Skopje, Republic of Macedonia (bojananaceva@yahoo.com)

## Noveanu, Dragoş

Dragoş Noveanu has a Ph.D in educational sciences. In his capacity as associate senior researcher at the Institute of Educational Sciences, he was data manager for Romania for PIRLS 2001 and will continue this role during PIRLS 2006. Dragoş has also been, since 1995, data manager for Romania for TIMSS. Dragoş has a special interest in information and communication technology, particularly in relation to educational software design.

*Address for correspondence*: Dragoş Noveanu, Institute of Educational Sciences, Str. Stirbei Voda nr. 37, Bucureşti, Romania (dragosnoveanu@yahoo. com)

## Noveanu, Gabriela

Gabriela Noveanu was the National Research Coordinator for Romania for PIRLS 2001 and is senior researcher at the Institute of Educational Sciences. She will continue her role as Romania's NRC during PIRLS 2006. Gabriela's special interest is science education. She has been involved in TIMSS since 1995 as Romania's NRC, and in developing the country's science curriculum, work that has included preparing programs and textbooks for chemistry and integrated sciences.

*Address for correspondence*: Gabriela Noveanu, Institute of Educational Sciences, Str. Stirbei Voda nr. 37, Bucureşti, Romania (gabrielanoveanu@yahoo. com)

**Rosén, Monica**

Monica Rosén is a senor lecturer at the Department of Education, Gothenburg University. She was the National Research Coordinator for PIRLS 2001 in Sweden, and also a member of the study's international questionnaire development group. Her main areas of research concern individual and group differences in educational contexts, educational measurement, educational evaluation and assessment, comparative educational research, and quantitative research methods.

*Address for correspondence*: Dr. Monica Rosén, Department of Education, Gothenburg University, PO Box 300, SE-405 30 Gothenburg, Sweden (Monica. Rosen@ped.gu.se)

**Schwippert, Knut**

Knut Schwippert is professor for educational science in the Faculty of Education and Social Science at the University of Münster. During PIRLS 2001, he was jointly responsible for coordinating Germany's involvement in PIRLS, and he was responsible for preparing the national database and the national analysis presented in the first publications on Germany's participation in PIRLS. He is a member of the PIRLS 2006 national steering committee for Germany. His main areas of research interest are methods in international large-scale assessments, heterogeneity in schools, and organizational development.

*Address for correspondence*: Prof. Dr. Knut Schwippert, University of Münster, Department of Education, Institute II, Bispinghof 5/6, D-48143 Münster, Germany (knut.schwippert@uni-muenster.de)

**Szabó-Rábai, Annamária**

Annamária Szabó-Rábai joined the Hungarian Center for Evaluation Studies in 2002 as a reading literacy expert. In the PIRLS 2001 study, she was mainly engaged in the national publication documenting the performance of Hungarian students. In PIRLS 2006, she is responsible for the national implementation and coordination of the study. Her main area of research interest is students' reading literacy performance in national and international large-scale assessments.

*Address for correspondence*: Annamária Szabó-Rábai, Hungarian Center for Evaluation Studies, Sulinova Kht.–Agency for Educational Development and In-service Teacher Training, Váci út 37, H–1134 Budapest, Hungary (annamaria.szabo @sulinova.hu)

## Tse, Shek Kam

Shek Kam Tse is professor for Chinese language education in the Faculty of Education, and the director of the Center for the Advancement of Chinese Language Learning and Research, at the University of Hong Kong, Hong Kong, SAR. He is Hong Kong's National Research Coordinator for PIRLS 2001 and 2006. His research interests include the following: students' reading literacy performance in national and international large-scale assessments, the process involved in writing Chinese, development of multimedia computer-learning packages related to Chinese language, child language development, and new methods in teaching Chinese language.

*Address for correspondence*: Prof. Shek Kam Tse, Faculty of Education, The University of Hong Kong, Pokfulam Road, Hong Kong, SAR, China (sktse@hkucc. hku.hk)

## Twist, Liz

Liz Twist is a principal research officer in the Department for Research in Assessment and Measurement at the National Foundation for Educational Research, England. She was the National Research Coordinator for PIRLS 2001 in England, and in PIRLS 2006 is the NRC for England and for Scotland. At NFER, she works on projects related to developing the national assessments in English for primary school students. Before joining NFER in 1997, she was deputy head teacher of a primary school and has taught children from age four to 12. Liz Twist's main research interests include the assessment of reading, attitudes to reading, special educational needs, and standards setting.

*Address for correspondence*: Liz Twist, National Foundation for Educational Research, The Mere, Upton Park, Slough, Berkshire, UK, SL1 2DQ (l.twist@nfer. ac.uk)

## van Ackeren, Isabell

Isabell van Ackeren is university professor for educational research at the Pedagogical Institute of Johannes Gutenberg University, Mainz. Her main areas of research interest are comparative studies, analysis of large-scale assessments, data use in schools, educational indicators, science education, and education–business partnerships.

*Address for correspondence*: Prof. Dr. Isabell van Ackeren, Johannes Gutenberg University Mainz, Department for Social, Media and Sports Sciences, Pedagogical Institute, Colonel-Kleinmann-Weg 2 (SBII), D-55099 Mainz, Germany (isabell.van-ackeren@uni-mainz.de)

## Vári, Péter

Péter Vári was the National Research Coordinator for many studies run by the IEA. His first study was the International Reading Literacy Study from 1991, and he was the NRC for TIMSS, PIRLS, SIALS, SITES, and CivEd. He was also the IEA representative for Hungary. Besides his position as the director of Center for Evaluation Studies from 1991 until his retirement in 2005, he has been involved in several monitoring assessments at national level in the fields of mathematics, reading, and science. His main research interests are national and international large-scale assessment methodology as well as standards-setting procedures. (Information provided by Knut Schwippert and Ildiko Balazsi.)

## Zápotočná, Oľga

Oľga Zápotočná is a senior researcher at the Department of Social and Biological Communication, Slovak Academy of Sciences. She is also a visiting associate professor at the Faculty of Education, Trnava University, where she teaches and supervises several courses on early childhood literacy education. In collaboration with the National Institute for Education, she was involved in PIRLS 2001 as an expert advisor for methodological issues. Her research career has involved work in the field of neuropsychology as it relates to written language; written language communication; and the psychology of reading and the like, mainly with respect to the literacy education of young children.

*Address for correspondence*: Dr. Oľga Zápotočná, Department of Social and Biological Communication SAS, Klemensova 19, 813 64 Bratislava, Slovakia (Zapotocna@savba.sk)

**Waxmann**

MÜNSTER · NEW YORK · MÜNCHEN · BERLIN

Wilfried Bos, Eva-Maria Lankes, Manfred Prenzel,
Knut Schwippert, Renate Valtin, Gerd Walther (Hrsg.)

## Erste Ergebnisse aus IGLU

Schülerleistungen am Ende der vierten Jahrgangsstufe
im internationalen Vergleich

2003, 312 Seiten, br., 19,90 €, ISBN 978-3-8309-1200-2

Mit IGLU werden zum ersten Mal an einer großen, für Deutschland
repräsentativen Stichprobe Leistungen von Grundschülerinnen und
Grundschülern am Ende der vierten Jahrgangsstufe in mehreren Fächern
international vergleichend untersucht.
Die IGLU-Konzeption für die Grundschule beruht auf einer Vorstellung
von Grundbildung und betont die kulturelle Bedeutung von Bildungs-
inhalten. Die Testaufgaben sprechen Grundkompetenzen im Leseverständnis, in Mathematik und in den Naturwissenschaften an, die in der
Lebenswelt von Grundschulkindern bedeutsam sind und zugleich als
wichtige Basis für das weitere Lernen dienen.
Die IGLU-Ergebnisse ermöglichen einen ersten differenzierten Blick
auf Stärken und Schwächen des deutschen Bildungssystems im Primar-
bereich.

Wilfried Bos, Eva-Maria Lankes, Manfred Prenzel,
Knut Schwippert, Renate Valtin, Gerd Walther (Hrsg.)

## IGLU

Einige Länder der Bundesrepublik Deutschland im nationalen
und internationalen Vergleich

2004, 236 Seiten, br., 16,90 €, ISBN 978-3-8309-1360-3

Der Ländervergleich zu IGLU berichtet die Schulleistungen von Grundschülerinnen und Grundschülern am Ende der vierten Jahrgangsstufe in
einigen Länder der Bundesrepublik Deutschland und verortet diese Ergebnisse international. Dargestellt werden die Leistungen im Lesen, in
Mathematik, in den Naturwissenschaften und in der Orthographie. Zur
Einordnung der Ergebnisse werden die unterschiedlichen Ausgangsbe-
dingungen der Schülerinnen und Schüler in den Ländern berücksichtigt.
Ein Kapitel ist der besonderen Situation des Übergangs nach der vierten
Jahrgangsstufe gewidmet. Eine Beschreibung der unterschiedlichen Lehr-
und Lernbedingungen in den vorgestellten Ländern rundet das Bild ab.

Waxmann

Wilfried Bos, Eva-Maria Lankes, Manfred Prenzel,
Knut Schwippert, Renate Valtin, Gerd Walther (Hrsg.)

# IGLU

Vertiefende Analysen zu Leseverständnis, Rahmenbedingungen
und Zusatzstudien

2005, 432 Seiten, br., 29,90 €, ISBN 978-3-8309-1580-5

Nachdem in den ersten beiden IGLU-Bänden die Leseleistung deutscher
Schüler im internationalen und nationalen Vergleich analysiert wurden,
werden hier zum einen weitere Analysen der Ergebnisse vorgelegt und
zum anderen die Rahmenbedingungen schulischer Leistungen be-
schrieben und Zusatzstudien vorgestellt. Im Mittelpunkt stehen unter
anderem der Leseverständnisprozess, die Lesekompetenzen in sehr
leistungsschwachen Ländern, orthographischen Kompetenzen sowie die
Beziehungen zwischen der Leseleistung und dem Textschreiben. Eine
wichtige Rolle spielen außerdem die Faktoren Schulorganisation und
Lernkultur und deren möglicher Einfluss auf die Lernleistungen.

Wilfried Bos, Eva-Maria Lankes, Manfred Prenzel, Knut
Schwippert, Renate Valtin, Gerd Walther (Hrsg.)

Unter Mitarbeit von Irmela Buddeberg, Solveig Gneckow, Uwe
Hügle und Kerstin Kowalski

# IGLU

Skalenhandbuch zur Dokumentation der Erhebungsinstrumente

2005, 456 Seiten, br., 89,00 €, ISBN 978-3-8309-1581-2

Dieses Skalenhandbuch dokumentiert die Erhebungsinstrumente der im
Frühjahr 2001 durchgeführten internationalen Lesestudie „Progress in
International Reading Literacy Study" (PIRLS) auf Basis der deutschen
Datensätze. In Deutschland wurde diese Studie unter der Bezeichnung
„Internationale Grundschul-Lese-Untersuchung" (IGLU) durchgeführt.
In dieser Skalendokumentation werden die von der internationalen Stu-
dienleitung (Boston College, Lynch School of Education) entwickelten
und freigegebenen Instrumente als auch die im Rahmen der nationalen
Ergänzungen entwickelten Erweiterungen (IGLU-E) dokumentiert.

MÜNSTER · NEW YORK · MÜNCHEN · BERLIN